Reclaiming Magdalen

Reclaiming Magdalen

A Memoir of Sexual Healing

Debra Jean Hawley

Shame Shaman Press
Middletown, California

Copyright © 2011 by Debra Jean Hawley

All rights reserved, including the right to reproduce this work in any form whatsoever, without permission in writing from the publisher, except for brief passages in connection with a review.

The author of this book does not dispense medical advice or prescribe the use of any technique as a form of treatment for physical or medical problems without the advice of a physician, either directly or indirectly. The intent of the author is only to offer information of a general nature to help you in your quest for mental, emotional and spiritual well-being. In the event you use any of the information in this book for yourself, which is your constitutional right, the author and the publisher assume no responsibility for your actions.

Some of the names and locations have been changed to protect the individuals' privacy.

Final product editor: Jean Laidig
Editor: Vicki Werkley
Copy editor: Sage Knight
Proofreader: Linda Guebert

2 3 4 5 6 7 8 9 10

Shame Shaman Press
Middletown, CA 95461
http://www.shameshamanpress.com

Library of Congress Control Number: 2011913177

Publisher's Cataloging-in-Publication Data

Hawley, Debra Jean.
  Reclaiming Magdalen : a memoir of sexual healing / Debra Jean Hawley.
    p. cm.
  ISBN: 978-0-9837083-0-8
  1. Adult child sexual abuse victims—Biography. 2. Spiritual life—New Age movement. 3. Life change events.   I. Title.
RC560.S44 .H39 2011
616.85—dc22
                                                  2011913177

Printed in the United States of America

"Do you not know that your body is a temple for the Holy Spirit . . ."
~ 1 Corinthians 6:19

Contents

Foreword xi

Preface xvii

1: Incest 1

2: Looking Back 6

3: Reality Slips In 10

4: The Dads 16

5: The Red Dot Club 22

6: The Split 29

7: The Real First Time 36

8: Heartbreak 43

9: Betrayal 50

10: Big Sisters 55

11: Biker Chick 59

CONTENTS

12: Hollywood 68

13: Poker Face 75

14: The New Girl 79

15: Life at Danni's 84

16: More Lessons 90

17: Getting Out 97

18: A Change of Venue 103

19: A Musician of My Own 108

20: Dysfunctional Bliss 113

21: Party's at My Place 120

22: You Don't Want to Do This 126

23: A New Track 132

24: Here We Go Again 138

25: Pre-marital Bliss, Take Two 145

26: The Next Big Day 151

27: Worlds Collide 156

28: Fresh Start 164

29: Recovery? 170

30: Confrontation 175

31: Fundamentals 182

32: Unseen Help 188

CONTENTS

33: Loving Kindness 192

34: Ecstatic Dance 203

35: Boundaries 210

36: Connecting with Heart 216

37: Is This Love? 223

38: Enough Is Enough 230

39: My Own Best Friend 235

40: Life Patterns 244

41: Happy Fiftieth 253

42: World Traveler 257

43: A Gift of Heart 266

44: Merry Christmas to Me 271

45: A Different Kind of Bath 275

46: Lily and the Rose 280

47: Grandpa's Key 286

48: Flushing Puppies 290

49: A Shaman's Vision 296

50: Setting the Stage 306

51: Soul Retrieval 314

52: A Clean Spring 322

53: Tenderness 326

CONTENTS

54: Moving Into the Light 332

55: First Communion 343

56: Welcome Home 349

Epilogue 351

Acknowledgments 360

Permissions 362

Resources 363

Foreword

Every now and then, a book comes along that is so deeply conceived and profoundly written that it indelibly penetrates the soul of the reader.

Reclaiming Magdalen is such a work. In the making for fifty years and put to paper only in the last five, this memoir tried to not be remembered. Living in psychic darkness for decades, the author buried the painful, cruel, and life-numbing memories of monstrous childhood sexual abuse held in terror-ridden secrecy even from herself.

Now those decades of darkness are brought to light. Prompted by a seemingly small incident that opened the door to her hidden memories, Debra Jean Hawley tells her harrowing story, evoking a vision of vulnerable little girls everywhere, robbed of their innocence by the men mandated to protect them. Women whose abused child is still locked inside are left with unresolved fear, shame, and confusion about their own beings and evolving identity, sometimes for a lifetime.

Writing this introduction has been a gift to me to have an opportunity to sort out my own feelings and ideas about *Reclaiming Magdalen* and its themes. It is such a powerful book that I was afraid I would not find my own voice about the way it evolved as an unfolding puzzle in Debra's life. What courage it had to take for her to endure as a child such an unbelievably brutal experience, and now to inscribe it on our psyches in a way that produces enlightenment. Even though her story is unique in its details, its significance and universal resonance fit almost any metaphor throughout history of male aggression, dominance, and victimization of women.

Shocked senseless in a few places, catching my breath in others, and shedding unexpected tears, my responses were from deep pain and vague memories paired with the shock and agony of Debra's experiences. Looking at the material this closely and yet from a trained therapeutic objectivity has been a valuable exercise in discipline and balance.

What makes the book endurable and even palatable with all its graphic tragedy is Debra's elegant writing style. It reads like a well-constructed novel. I enjoyed the short chapters and clear sentences that allowed me to clip along during quiet times of the day, and still read a little before falling asleep at night, with a tasty bite of the material and a natural stopping place. Also, her one-pointedness embedded in broader themes throughout the book assists the reader to breathe in the material in its universal context, while relating it to his or her own life and psychic experiences.

In addition to my own awakening within the context of Debra's story, I am grateful for the opportunity to ponder more deeply new understandings about domestic violence against the background of the book. Surprisingly, I found that *Reclaiming Magdalen* would be fitting for male perpetrators of intimate partner violence as well as for sexual assault victims of both genders. The dangerous and deep repercussions of breaking boundary issues with intimate partners or with children at any age in any context are little understood, and they create uncivil lives. Betrayal of trust in relationships between intimate partners or between children and their abusing caregivers gashes the heart and crushes the spirit, creating lasting trauma in the psyche as well as in mind and body. Ironically, perpetrators often suffer as much as or more than their victims.

From a depth psychological perspective, such devastating injury from childhood is further magnified through repetition of the trauma, such as through witnessing or experiencing domestic violence. Enacted unconsciously with and by victims of incest and other gross sexual abuse, offender violence can develop beyond its addictive habit as a self-soothing antidote for anxiety to further reduction and hardening of its core, into a frozen neurological state. In a degenerative and somatized process, a syndrome called "normalization through abnormalization" emerges from the twin poisons of trauma and unfulfilled hope plus the numbing prohibition from belonging (due to abuse and betrayal in early childhood, frequently by a trusted caregiver). Normalization through abnormalization offers a theory of behaving increasingly abnormally to evoke normal feelings of worthiness.

The abuse, torture, and cyclic behavioral repetitions contribute to a whole genre of "bad girls," not uncommon in our culture today. Males of all ages use and abuse females for their pleasure and catapulting addictions—many times unconsciously fulfilling their own unresolved grief, shame, depression, and child dependency needs through gross and driven manipulation, victimization, and terrorizing sexual crimes: rape, incest, sadomasochistic behaviors, and bullying. As with alcohol and drug abusers, the drive to normalize through these abnormal ways of being goes unrecognized by perpetrators, or if it is acknowledged, the effect of it is minimized, rationalized, or dismissed.

Women so abused experience a condition similar to the perpetrator's frozen state; they become nullified and numb, devoid of feeling, and move into survival modes of "bad girl" behaviors. Acting largely on false instincts created and developed by betrayal, pain, fear, and shame, their sexual intimacy and affection are founded on need and control rather than delight, trust, or emotional security, further driving abusers into their own narcissistic reactions. Like strange and malicious intoxicants, the distorted needs of both perpetrators and victims entrap and hold them in a pervasive sense of codependent worthlessness and inadequacy, frequently unreversed their whole lives. Women are driven to fill the void through repeated but unrealized hope in yet another relationship that might provide safety, but more likely repeats the trauma.

Male perpetrators—even the most horrific criminals—enact these patterns cyclically, descending into rigid stone-like neurological states that lead to irrationally lurid behaviors; and male victims of child abuse and neglect express buried pain in increasingly driven power and control actions, often with unregulated anger, rage, and violence. Both female victims and male perpetrators spiral downward until some genuinely caring and positive dynamic intervenes and is not dismissed.

Magdalen energy, as experienced by the author, is such an intervention. Also buried by pain and trauma avoidance, Magdalen resides deep in the souls of all individuals of both genders. Awakened, it gently guides the sufferer in the process of recognizing her or his core identity, and provides a mirror of deep self-revelation, along with the hope and guidance for fully growing into one's essential self.

In this way, *Reclaiming Magdalen* may ultimately contribute to the spiritual literature of liberation for all adults, including male criminals in rehabilitation, as men explore their own lives and psychic history. Through depth counseling, education, creative development, and other processes, not the least of which is the mysterious Magdalen spiritual energy, men and women may find new and fulfilling ways to meet their own forgotten childhood needs and develop into their full potential.

It is professionally heartening to recognize that men, too—from young males discovering their own sexuality, to bored house husbands, to combat veterans, to hardened criminals—can claim their own divine feminine or compassion for self and others. Any male exposed to violence and trauma, in war or childhood—even after his will has been distorted by adult violence and trauma—can ask for the tender mothering of his inner Magdalen to link with the fathering of the Earth.

It is a simple process that does not come easily or quickly. With patience—if he asks within and acts from the part of himself that would not harm another—he can become active in the natural collaboration of God/Goddess to nurture him into wholeness.

Until cultural changes are adequate to provide security for all children to be safe and free from gross abuse and neglect, parents, educators, and mental health resources in neurological and psychological institutions, correctional institutions, and criminal courts are morally mandated to continue to bring perpetrators to justice, while developing legal, psychological, and spiritual rehabilitation programs for such violators.

Meanwhile, perpetrators of monstrous crimes, who undoubtedly lived as innocent children somewhere in their development, will continue to be held in airtight prisons where their own lives are endangered by the threat of murder and rape by their peers. The hierarchy of prisoners holds that child sexual abuse is the most horrific crime of all. Justifiably, but nonetheless tragically, perpetrators of such acts are at the bottom of the heap, more likely to be killed by their peers than to be paroled.

Debra Jean Hawley takes steps toward cultural changes through the telling of her story and her unusual brand of radical understanding and forgiveness. It is a story she did not know until the moment an unexpected event sparked her consciousness and cognitive mind with something she knew was real. At last, she was released to formulate the truth of her life and expel the evil abuse that never even let her think about what happened to her as a child. Thus began her path of healing, bringing her into a gradual but miraculous awakening, and the courageous and continued balancing of mind and heart into her true self.

Reclaiming Magdalen provides a key to the inner path of the soul. It celebrates the synchronistic signs that appear to guide us when we least expect them, often at the nadir of disaster when all hope is lost. Men and women everywhere can read this story and find greater understanding of their own unconscious pain and hidden secrets. They, too, can be inspired to open the forbidden and menacing doors to the truth of their own history or her story, by daring to heed their deepest feelings and instincts and follow them into the caverns of their own inner truth.

Debra speaks to the centermost part of ourselves. Her precarious journey led her through the most remote corners of her unconscious into conscious experience, as she searched first on the rocky path, then to a more awakened state, then back again in her ever-evolving cycle toward increasingly refined realms. Step-by-step, Magdalen finds and comforts her true self, opening Debra's eyes, her mind, and her resynthesizing body to her own pure essence. The restoration and resolution of her early childhood are woven into the nucleus of her ongoing individuation, assuring us that this is the beginning of Debra's/Magdalen's story—our story—not the end.

As we witness her true substance revealing itself again and again through strength, hope, courage, risk, and acceptance, we see her will to create her existence on her own terms. We know she is walking a sacred path.

Within another few years, I hope to see Debra's continued memoir in a new volume which reveals her unique perspectives of evolving inner peace with ever-fresh, intuitive, and intelligent steps toward her wholeness. It is fated that she will continue to create and accept the marrow of her own internal maternal love and, with her fiercely independent spirit, maintain the mystery, integrity, and natural healing of Magdalen.

Taira St. John, Ph.D., MFT
September 26, 2011
http://www.tairastjohn.com

Preface

*Our sense of worthiness—that critically important piece
that gives us access to love and belonging—lives inside of our story.*
~ Brené Brown

    I was a teenager when I first put pen to paper, searching for meaning in my life. Back then, the words weren't my own; they belonged to popular songs, my beloved rock 'n' roll. It would be many years before I found the courage to look within, name what I found there, and commit those findings to ink.

    Once started, the process of writing became a comforting routine; a time I offered myself absolute attention, absolute freedom, and absolute honesty. Held safely in volumes that have progressed over the years from spiral-bound notebooks to artist sketch books to hand-made paper works of art in their own right, my admissions remained free from the judgment and ridicule so pervasive in other areas of my life.

    On the rare occasions I reopened a completed journal, curious to relive a time gone by, I was consistently struck by the sense of sadness beneath the words. Like a never-progressing soap opera—or a scratched LP—my life's major themes revolved around heartbreak and a quest for meaning.

As time passed, my silent companions moved in and out of favor. Sometimes months would pass before I'd remember to connect. I knew I couldn't—or wouldn't—lie to my journal, so the "reflection-less" periods often correlate with periods in my life when it was easier to stay busy and distracted, when I told myself, *I'm happy, just don't look too close.*

I felt safe spilling my heart and soul into my journals, because they were private. No one read those pages—except one boyfriend who didn't last long after he confessed his crime. Those sacred texts contain disclosures and investigations I felt certain would never be revealed. Thank God. Even my daughter, who likes to be kept abreast of all things pertaining to family, told me to destroy the ever-growing collection before I died. When I asked why, she told me, "If you don't, I'll read them. And I'm not sure I want to know about the dark side of you." I don't blame her for wishing to remain ignorant of her mother's inner workings, especially since she'd had to deal with the outer effects.

Then I turned fifty, and something about the mid-century mark struck a bold chord within. *It's time, Debra,* inner guidance said. *Tell your story.*

At first, I shared my up-until-then secrets in small groups, workshops with fellow writers, men and women I figured I'd never see again; what did it matter if they knew the worst about me? A few trainings later, I caught writer's fever—it's sort of like the flu—and with it I barfed my life's elated highs and desperate lows onto the page.

For six months the memories poured forth in a sort of chaos-driven, connect-the-threads—if you dare. Even though I had lived the story recounted in that initial draft, the dizzying tale left me gasping for breath. This period also allowed me to deepen my spiritual connection and comfort with calling on Jesus Christ and Mary Magdalen, what I now see as a requisite alignment. It was August 2009 when I first said, "Done."

It had been a rough birth, and for several months I simply let my "baby" settle while I returned my attention to everyday concerns like clients and their accounting software. When I started the project, I didn't realize what a dangerous road I would be traveling as I poked and prodded, uncovering aspects in my psyche who were not the slightest bit interested in the light of loving kindness and forgiveness I offered to my war-torn soul. Sometimes the battle got downright ugly.

By fall, as the trees surrounding my home changed colors, then shed their leaves, exposing their bones to the impending winter cold, I too felt naked, questioning, *What have I done?* Fortunately, I also felt excitement. And when I tuned in to the inner spiritual team I call upon for encouragement and direction, I heard, *You're on the right track. Trust.*

This early process was as much about me finding my way as an author as it was about speaking up about the sexuality I've experienced—the abusive aspects, the sometimes wildly provocative adventures, and the divine union. To continue moving forward, I knew I would need to find external support—editorial, as well as emotional.

Initially, I had shared a few chapters with a dear girlfriend, and while her loving feedback encouraged me to continue, it became obvious she couldn't hold my hand through the whole editing process. Besides, she lives five hundred miles away, and I wanted support in the form of warm, live bodies, not email messages and comments in the margin of a Word doc.

Not just any bodies would do. I needed to share my story, to re-craft my words, with women who could understand. Women who—while they may not have been directly affected by the horrors of sexual abuse—held the ability to open their hearts and listen with compassion. It felt like a huge order, yet I held the vision with clarity, trusting the new-age cliché, "if it's meant to be."

It was.

Thus began the next stage of owning my life's story: sharing it with others.

Once a week we met: four women, all writers, all brave souls who had asked their own core questions, and then reached deep down into the depths of their beings to reveal what they found there—hell and heaven.

After consoling the part of me that held on to being "done," I once again started at the beginning, this time at a slower, gentler pace. As I untangled the knots, additional light slipped in to penetrate areas of myself long held in dark, shame-filled prisons.

I knew about the transformational potential of writing—it had been pouring into my journals for decades—but the amplitude of healing increased dramatically with my sister writers. Reading aloud, being witnessed as I spoke the very things I thought could never be told, let alone put into print, opened the door to healing at a level I had no concept of until it occurred.

We stepped into the fire together, warrior women willing to celebrate our triumphs and grieve our losses while at the same time holding each other accountable to our highest potential: the core truth of our work. After reading, I often heard, "How did you feel about that? I want to hear more about your feelings." And so I would sit with my words yet again, reaching back, reaching in, then ultimately settling into my body to experience the rumblings of emotions I had tried for years to ignore or suppress.

Thankfully, by the grace of God/Goddess/All that Is, I made it through the sometimes twisted house of mirrors also known as memoir. I didn't just make it, I triumphed. I found my voice. After years of questioning my worth as a human being and my right to take up space, through telling my story, I stumbled into a life that allows me to revel, as well as be seen, in all my glory, a concept I never dared to entertain prior to stepping onto the storyteller's path.

It is from this stance of grace, I offer these pages to you.

1: Incest

I lean over the kitchen counter of my tract-style suburban home, glance at the open *TV Guide*, and forever change the direction of my life. I read the upside-down text like I've done hundreds of times. My brain says, *Must be a typo.* The single word, "Incest," is incomprehensible. It is 1984.

Twenty minutes later I sit in my husband Mark's recliner, mine and my baby's for the day, nursing her while I watch women's topics skillfully dissected for us hungry housewives. I love this ritual of holding my precious child close. I've never felt so connected to another human being. Time glides by on these leisurely mornings, and it's hard to say which of us is fed more.

It's funny how memories wrap a veil around the truth. For almost twenty-five years, I had lived with occasional glimpses and tell-tale behaviors that today present themselves as obvious signposts to my abusive foundation. And yet, in my twenty-seven-year-old's world, I'd neatly buried the atrocity of my "special time" with daddy and granddad. Well, almost. As I think back on that winter day, I remember a warning tremor of the coming seismic activity.

I'm enjoying our comfortably worn brown recliner, the one we bought for Mark that goes just right in the corner of the family room, balancing out the meticulously arranged space with the perfectly sewn drapes. I love these nubby, loose weave, earth tone drapes. Working with such massive amounts of fabric on my mother-in-law's huge dining room table was tough, but they came out beautifully. Everyone is impressed when I tell them they're home-made; no one ever guesses.

My favorite white ceramic mug is within easy reach on the oak side table that's designed to look like an old-fashioned ice box. Next to my cup sits the TV's remote. I've already got the set on the required channel, not wanting to miss any of the mystery topic on my morning talk show. I'm holding my daughter close for her morning fill of breast milk, making sure to switch sides—nothing worse than being lop-sided or suddenly oozing warm liquid down the front of my comfy, red chenille robe.

Mark is in the kitchen taking care of himself. I hear a clink, not sure if the item is a bowl or a glass as it's placed on the tile counter. The refrigerator opens and closes. That's the gallon of milk. Milk is a requirement for either of Mark's usual breakfasts, but so far I have no clue which he's chosen, option one or two. Monday through Friday it's always one or the other. I don't care enough to glance over my left shoulder and look. I'm focused on my hot herbal tea; I'd prefer it be black, but have learned caffeine goes straight through me to my baby.

In the four years we've been together, I've also learned Mark likes routine. The topic of our first date was "The Dessert Cart of Life." His position: you get one choice and have to stick with it. Mine? I want to take at least one bite of each beautifully decorated, alluring, sticky, sweet delicacy that might be offered.

I hear the pantry door open and realize Mark's breakfast choice as Honey Nut Cheerios cascade into the bowl. Damn. Although I love my husband, I crave the stillness that settles in when he's gone, and Carnation Instant Breakfast—chocolate, please—goes down faster. I hear the door to the garage open, then close. The silent kitchen says Mark has taken his breakfast out to the workbench—he's always tinkering with something out there. A few minutes later, the door opens and I hear water flowing. Next come the clinking sounds of the rinsed bowl and spoon as he leaves them in the otherwise spotless sink. I've stopped bothering to ask him to please open the dishwasher and put the dirty dishes inside. Some routines just don't change.

Now I hear his work boots, the safety style with iron toe, as his long legs take four or five large steps across the kitchen floor. He makes a hard right around the counter and in two strides leans into the recliner. Warning lights go off around me, but I have no words to say what's happening. Although he's happy and smiling, I've gone into intruder alert. I feel an alarm, like a mild electric shock, wanting to push him out, to push him away.

Mark bends over the recliner. The oat and honey flavor lingers on his breath. With his routine good-bye kiss, his scratchy winter beard tickles my lips. As he moves to kiss our one-year-old daughter, I surprise myself by instinctively gathering her closer to my heart. In that instant I feel like a tigress protecting her offspring.

After I hear the kitchen door once again open and close, the automatic garage door open, the Saab's engine start and fade away, and finally, the garage door clunk shut—signaling Mark's full departure—I realize I've been holding my breath.

I exhale fully, inhale deeply, and wonder, *What the hell frightened me?* If Mark noticed me pull back, he didn't let on, and he would have. So my reaction must have been subtle, though it was obvious to me. Something within said, loud and clear, *Stay away.*

Although Mark and I have had our rocky times, everything has been wonderful since my pregnancy. Our beautiful daughter adds to the ideal picture of my life: I am the perfect wife in the perfect home with the perfect child.

The TV announcer's voice rips my attention from musings on perfection, "And for today's show I'd like to introduce our expert in sexual abuse and incest."

I know that word. I've heard it before, but I've avoided connecting sex and father. . . .

I'd recently turned eighteen and, like many teenage girls, had headed to Hollywood to make it big as an actress or a model.

My father worked there as a boom man, the guy who holds the microphone on a long extension pole. A good boom man strategically places his mic where he will get the best sound while keeping that foam-covered device out of sight of the camera. Because I was hanging around the set, I landed a job as a stand-in for an upcoming out-of-town shoot. I felt great about the job, but it was odd being around my father.

There I was, breaking into the industry, standing in line with him as we checked into a funky little hotel in Sonora, California. The location manager, a petite woman with hot pink sunglasses perched on her short-cropped curly brown hair, was busily handing out room assignments. My father bent over her neatly organized folding table to survey the colorful display of 3x5 index cards.

"Hi, doll," he said in his usual flirtatious tone. "Where do you want me?"

The perky brunette's eyes crinkled as she looked up and smiled, batting back an equally loaded pick-up line. I felt disgusted as I watched this man's all too familiar mode of seduction. All I wanted to do was grab my room key, take a hot bath, and get some sleep.

Once my father was checked in, he stepped aside and said proudly, "This is my daughter, Debbie."

Still glowing from her playful interaction, the manager picked up my index card and stated, "You'll be staying in Room 35 with your dad."

"What?" I whined. "Why can't I have my own room?"

"Incest is best," she replied, with a sassy wink at my father.

Stunned, I clenched my jaw. My stomach churned, any comeback blocked and frozen in my throat. I wanted to spring over the table and rip her head off. Instead, I lowered my eyes and focused on the cheap plastic key holder. Tears screamed for release, as I told myself I had a right to privacy, but I willed them away, along with my rage. Silently I followed my father to our room.

It's only in hindsight that my silent, furious reaction makes sense. At eighteen, I had not yet unearthed the secret between Daddy and me.

"Many victims have no memories," the TV expert continues. "But there are signs. Often they play games with their dolls that involve sex or age-inappropriate behavior."

Oh my God, I think, feeling as though I've been kicked in the gut. . . .

INCEST

I guess I'd known all along it wasn't normal for little girls to play Ken and Barbie games that included sex on the beach. During my solo playtimes, I'd create long involved scenarios that typically began with Ken asking Barbie out for a date. They'd drive their imaginary convertible up the coast, enjoying the view of the Pacific Ocean. Perhaps they would find a quiet cove and have a picnic lunch. They'd laugh and maybe even swim in the salty surf. However, the outing always ended up the same: Ken and Barbie would find a cave and fuck. Barbie knew it was what Ken wanted, and she would willingly spread her legs, enticing him to climb on.

The sexual abuse expert on the TV continues listing symptoms as if looking directly at me. I sit riveted, holding my daughter, tears streaming down my face. To reach for the remote and change the channel simply isn't an option. The talk show has stolen my attention and refuses to give it back.

"And if there is a history of abuse," continues the commentator, "watching a program like this could cause uncontrollable crying."

So there it is. A perfectly clear explanation from a hellish perspective. In a way I'm relieved. The diagnosis, "incest survivor," makes so much sense.

Looking back on that TV show day, I wonder if it would have been simpler to have kept the demon buried, even if it might have cost me my life—like it did Aunt Franny, my father's older sister. She took the family's secret to the grave with her uterine cancer, but I hear her calling me, encouraging me. . . .

Tell the story, Debra. Speak up. Break the chain of silence. I'll support you. We all will, those of us who know hell intimately.

It has nothing to do with bravery, and everything to do with power, power that was taken, power that must be reclaimed.

2: Looking Back

I wish I could say the TV show on incest triggered a bubbling to the surface of all that had happened to me, and that those images sparked an instantaneous, easy path of integration, forgiveness, and recovery. However, incest doesn't allow for a quick, pain-free fix. Incest sinks its roots in deeply, and my mind wasn't ready to give up its closely guarded secrets. However, a series of connect-the-dot memories did begin to trickle in. *If this is true,* I thought, *then perhaps the 'survivor' diagnosis is also true.* Like the Friday night when my step-mother Liesl went out of town.

It's probably a good idea to explain a bit of the family tree at this point. Liesl had been married to my father for as long as I can remember, though I never called her "Mom," or "Mother," or any of those familial terms of endearment. Liesl's daughter is Ingrid. Ingrid's a lot older than I am; I've only known her as an adult. Ingrid's daughter is Anna, so Anna is Liesl's granddaughter. That makes Anna my step-niece, though I'm only a year older.

Anna and I were friends. While it may not seem odd to be friends with a family member, how we met is one of those real life stories that's better than fiction. . . .

I was walking home from second grade at Brockton Elementary, in West Los Angeles. Back in those pre-Amber Alert days, people didn't think twice about letting their children walk alone. My eyes down, I focused on my saddle shoes as they skillfully avoided the cracks in the sidewalk. About half-way up the street's steep incline, a young female voice just off my left shoulder caught my attention.

"Hi."

I glanced up to see a smiling, brown-haired girl who looked as though she was around my age.

"Hi," I said, smiling back.

"I'm Anna."

"I'm Debbie."

"Wanna come over and play?"

"Sure."

As we talked, we walked by my apartment. I doubted my mom would worry; she never had before. We continued past four more boxy, stucco buildings, and right before the gas station at the end of the block, we turned in, then raced up the concrete steps to the second floor landing. We were laughing as Anna opened the front door and we spilled into the small front room.

"I'm home, Mom," Anna called out. "And I brought a friend."

"That's nice," Ingrid said. Her tone changed to puzzled surprise when she saw me. "Debbie! What are you doing here?"

And so I came to grow up around my step-mother's daughter and granddaughter. Ironically, I spent more time with Ingrid and Anna than I did with my father.

Now, let's get back to that first, emerging-from-the-fog, recall of his impropriety in 1971. I was fourteen. . . .

It was a Friday night, and my father had me all to himself. In the past there had always been someone else around, like Liesl, her family, or my younger brother. Other people helped deflect the underlying and ever present discomfort I felt being near this man.

I had a fun weekend planned with Anna, but unfortunately I couldn't convince my father to chauffeur me down to her place in Torrance until Saturday morning.

Looking back, it's probably best he stayed off those L.A. freeways, since the bar had opened at straight up three o'clock—like it always did.

Our big time Friday night consisted of watching TV. Nothing exciting; monotonous programs to pass the time until sleep. At nine o'clock I excused myself to brush my teeth and put on my nightgown, robe, and slippers. When I returned to the living room, I was surprised to see he hadn't made up the sofa. Shrugging it off as something Liesl had always done, I went to get the sheets.

"There's room in my bed," my father said, standing in the doorway, pointing to his king-sized mattress. "Wouldn't you be more comfortable with me?"

I froze on the spot, but my mind raced ahead. What is he saying? He wants me to sleep with him? Am I hearing this right? *I was only fourteen, but I wasn't stupid. I knew this invitation was just plain wrong, and nothing good could come from a compliant response.*

"No, I'm fine here on the sofa." My cool, nonchalant tone didn't relay the screams of injustice and alarm running though my head. Oh my God! He wants me to sleep with him? This can't be happening.

"Oh, come on," his slurred invitation continued, "we can pretend you're my girlfriend."

I chose to ignore the outrageous request coming from my obviously drunk father and quickly prepared my spot with noticeably shaking hands. He laughed a thick, throaty rumble, amused with his game of cat and mouse.

"Okay. I promise I'll stay on my side of the bed."

I continued to ignore his plea and climbed under the covers, still wearing my robe and slippers. With one hand I pulled the blanket up tight to my chin. With the other I reached back and twisted off the lamp sitting on the side table.

"Good night," I said in my sweetest, nonchalant voice, doing my best to act as though nothing was amiss.

Although my father was clearly disappointed, he wasn't a forceful man, and he wasn't a violent man, and for that I was grateful.

"Good night," he replied in a sullen tone. "I'll leave the door open, just in case you change your mind."

As I lay there in the room filled with sideways shadows, I felt anything but fine. I was scared, on high alert. I listened to his every breath and snore. It was an all-night vigil.

The next morning brought not only blessed sunlight, but a father who apparently didn't remember anything of the previous night's offer. Or if he did, he didn't make any move to apologize, or claim too much to drink as an explanation for his audacious request. Being the good girl—and terrified of reminding him and perhaps starting the game up again—I too kept my silence.

The bedtime game of father-request/daughter-deny dove deep into the do-not-touch, do-not-talk-about zone of my psyche. At least until that TV show yanked back the covers and said, "Hum, what do we have hiding in here?"

In that forbidden zone, I also found a memory from the following year. I was fifteen. . . .

It was a cold November afternoon, rapidly approaching evening. I was with Ingrid and Anna. We stopped by my father's latest place, so that Ingrid could get something from her mom. The three of us climbed the weather-beaten stairs that ran along the side of the garages and entered the unlocked apartment. The overly taut screen door slammed to announce our arrival.

"Hi, Mom," Ingrid yelled as we piled into the fading light of the living room and began removing our coats.

My father stepped into the room, directly across from us. In his hand was an ice-filled, though otherwise empty, glass. By the time of day and his big, dopey grin I guessed he had belted back drink number three or four. Striding his tall, thin frame across the room, he reached out to greet us. First I, then Anna, then Ingrid, received the standard wet kiss, which reeked of Scotch.

"Stop trying to stick your tongue in my mouth," Ingrid protested, pushing him away.

I was stunned. Up until that moment, I'd thought it normal and acceptable for him to send a probing tongue through my wary lips. Along with my shock, I felt a sense of relief. Finally, I had a reflection outside of myself to confirm things weren't quite right with the man I reluctantly called Dad.

I wish I could say I took the opportunity to talk with Ingrid about the discomfort I felt around my father, or that I used her example of boundary setting to define my own perimeter. Unfortunately, those concepts were still far ahead on my journey of self discovery. At fourteen or fifteen, like most teenagers, I was simply a young adult doing my best to stay afloat in a rapidly changing world.

3: Reality Slips In

Funny thing about going back over my life . . . the longer I look, the more the memories unravel. They're like compact fluorescent bulbs. At first their glow is soft, almost dim. Then slowly, imperceptibly, they brighten, taking on their full luster. Some of this brilliance is appreciated—it feels good to reclaim these cobweb-covered recollections—but some of the details are hard to witness, hard to hear, and hard to admit. Even to myself. This is exactly what happened with that first reclaimed incident, when I was fourteen and spending a Friday night with my father.

First I began to question how I got there—literally. How did I arrive at my father's apartment that afternoon? If he had picked me up from school, why didn't he simply take me straight to Anna's? Initially I brushed the question aside, telling myself it's not important to the story. That was naïve thinking. Now, it's obvious my initial response came from the protective ego, an inner aspect who keeps saying, *You can't tell this story. How dare you tell this story?*

As much as I'd like to ignore, diminish, or dismiss these latest baubles, it's become clear I must include the memories which now, nearly forty years later, have popped up from the depths to say, "Surprise, there's a bigger picture here. . . ."

REALITY SLIPS IN

Wednesday, April 21, 1971. Ironically, it's my father's birthday. I show up at school like any other day and meet up with my friends Sue and Sue. Like me, they are new students at University High in West Los Angeles. I'm there because my mom and step-dad, Greg, are in the process of building our new house in Newport Beach. To save money, we're living with Greg's parents in Bel Air, a nearby upscale community. Brunette Sue's mom and blond Sue's dad have recently married and moved to the same swanky neighborhood.

Sue and Sue were quite different from the friends I had at Van Nuys High, where I was a member of drill-team and an honor student. Mom would call the Sues wild girls, but she never met them. Ours was a short lived friendship, partly due to the events of that one fateful day....

"Come on, let's get out of here," blond Sue beckoned as I stepped off the standard yellow school bus.

"Get out of here?" I questioned. *"Where are we going?"*

"It's a surprise," answered brunette Sue. *"Think of it as a field trip."*

Thus I came to explore the magical world of truancy. We walked the short distance to Wilshire Boulevard and stuck out our thumbs; three miniskirt-clad girls ranging in age from 14 to 17. We were immediately picked up.

"Where to, ladies?" asked the young man behind the wheel.

"UCLA."

Ah, the destination was well known: UCLA, the University of California, Los Angeles. I'd explored the campus a few times before—mostly with baby-sitters who dragged me along for study time, though I do recall a nice neighbor who simply took me and my brother for a fun day of exploring the massive campus. Our current visit was more focused; Sue rattled off the destination's exact coordinates to our driver.

A few minutes later we pulled up to a row of campus housing—three-story, wood-sided apartments—and climbed out of the car. As though controlled by some teen-age girl beacon, we tossed back our long hair and laughed at the same time, donning an air of mock sophistication and maturity. We were on hallowed ground. A college campus was a big deal and we didn't want to appear young or out of place.

"Up here," blond Sue called. She was the older of the two girls, the one who arranged our outing for the day.

To make a long story somewhat short, the door at the top of the stairs not only introduced me to the world of college-aged boys, but also to smoking marijuana and to sex. In a way it was convenient, having all those big-time firsts rolled up into one grand day. However, this day-in-a-life wasn't cut and dried. I did smoke my first-ever joint, and I did end up in the bedroom with one of those hormone-rich young men, but that's where the memory takes a strange twist and comes back to consciousness with a matching wrench of embarrassment....

I was having my first-ever menstrual cycle. It's not that I hadn't prepared for my official entrance into womanhood. I had even practiced inserting tampons with samples I'd ordered from one of those teen magazines I regularly read from cover to cover—desperately looking for clues on how to grow up.

That day, I had a two-fold problem. On the one hand, I felt mortified at the prospect of telling the more than anxious boy that my private parts were already occupied by a small piece of absorbent cotton. On the other hand, I really didn't want to have intercourse with him.

I didn't know how to say no, so instead of speaking up, I simply shoved the tampon and its telltale string deep inside—and clenched. It seemed the only plausible solution—that and to pray my vaginal muscles held out.

They did, much to my wannabe lover's disappointment. After what seemed like hours of trying to coax me to relax, he finally admitted defeat, and we returned to the living room, where we once again met up with my partners in truancy, glowing from their own hot times with their respective partners.

All of this occurred on Wednesday morning. Wednesday evening, the story took another odd turn—in the form of who I chose to share the day's events with....

It was 5:30 p.m. when Mom yelled downstairs, "Debbie, Mr. Stewart is here."

Mr. Stewart was my regular Wednesday employer. He and his wife lived back in our old neighborhood, Sherman Oaks, but since Mr. Stewart worked on the southern side of the hills separating Los Angeles from the San Fernando Valley, he picked me up on his way home. Mrs. Stewart always drove the return route, after I spent several hours baby-sitting for them. It had been a good arrangement, keeping me in ongoing money and providing them with a trusted individual. We had a real win-win, until that night.

"See ya later," I called back to Mom as I slid out the kitchen door, and into Mr. Stewart's shiny red Mustang.

"Hi, Debbie. What's new with you?"

Here's where everything took a wrong turn. In retrospect I wish I had simply said, "Ah, you know, the usual, school and homework." Instead, a pressure cooker of energy that had built up over the afternoon burst forth.

"I had my first sex today."

It's hard to say which of us my admission shocked more, but there it was, sitting in the air between us, a hook of what I realize now is many a man's fantasy. Of course, I knew I was lying, or at least bending the truth, since sex hadn't really happened, but that didn't matter. Suddenly I found myself testing the waters as an alluring seductress. I felt both exhilarated and terrified by my new-found power.

"Is that so?"

I kept my eyes forward but could feel Mr. Stewart's hungry gaze poring over my suddenly clammy skin.

"Yeah," I continued, spewing out the morning's tale of ditching school, hitch-hiking, and meeting up with the college boys. The only thing missing from my string of nervous chatter was smoking pot—and the fact that sex hadn't really occurred. I left out the part about my first period too. Basically, I spun a temptation-laden tale.

Thankfully, Mr. Stewart didn't respond, so we spent the rest of the drive through those hillside neighborhoods in blessed silence, but I knew I had gone too far. Part of me wished for a stern reaction, a lecture, the "nice girls don't …" speech similar to the one running through my head. Another part hoped for guidance and understanding from the kind, loving father I'd gotten to know over the past year, the one I've seen be so tender and gentle with his own beautiful baby girl. But Mr. Stewart wasn't offering any sound, nurturing advice. Later that evening, it became clear just how far I'd overstepped my youthful ignorance.

"I'll drive Debbie home tonight," Mr. Stewart announced to his wife.

"Are you sure?" Mrs. Stewart asked, apparently not picking up the hint of lust coming through his statement of fact. "You're not too tired?"

I knew he wasn't too tired. I guessed he'd been thinking about me the whole evening. I knew I'd been thinking about him, about how the hell I was going to back myself out of the corner I'd created with my brazen comments.

Once back in the car, I began to silently pray.

Please, God. Help me get home safe and sound. Please keep Mr. Stewart from pulling over to the side of the road. Please help me to find a way to talk my way out of this mess.

We were halfway home, driving along Mulholland Drive, the local and well known lovers lane, when Mr. Stewart made his move. "So, Debbie, how would you like to explore sex with a real man, someone who can teach you what it means to be a woman?"

"Well, you know, Mr. Stewart, that's going to take some time. And Mrs. Stewart will worry if you aren't back right away. How about instead of doing anything tonight, you pick me up after school on Friday and drive me to my father's apartment? Then we can have some time together."

Phew. My ploy worked—at least for the time being. I made it home unscathed physically, although mentally I was a wreck. I knew Friday would require another trick of verbal dexterity, but I'd worry about that later.

I was so embarrassed by the events of the day, both the reality of the tampon and the non-sex, and the embellishment to Mr. Stewart, that I didn't have the nerve to tell anyone, not even my new classmates Sue and Sue. That meant I also didn't have anyone I could confide in about the upcoming date. To make things worse, I didn't have Mr. Stewart's office number and certainly didn't see any way I could get that information from Mrs. Stewart, so come Friday afternoon, I simply paced the school's front walk, waiting for my ride across town. . . .

When the pristine convertible pulled up to the curb, I took a deep breath and climbed in. I'd purposefully worn jeans, but I piled my books in my lap to add another layer of protection. On top of that went my small overnight bag, packed with necessities for the weekend.

"How about you put all that down and get comfortable?" *Mr. Stewart smiled, reaching across to remove the barrier between us.*

"Ah, no thanks. Let's just get out of here."

"Fine with me."

Although the drive across West L.A. seemed excruciatingly long, in reality it only took about ten minutes—ten minutes of hell. I kept Mr. Stewart at bay, using idle chitchat, while my insides screamed for freedom. With a sweaty palm, I clutched the leather arm rest, ready to grab the door's handle and leap from the vehicle at a moment's notice. When Mr. Stewart placed his hand on my knee and gave it a little squeeze, I could feel his body heat radiating through the denim. Even now the tactile memory makes my stomach turn.

Fortunately, there was something different about that ride—something about being in the daylight, instead of the dark of the preceding Wednesday night. I had a bit of strength, a bit of courage, and I wasn't about to let myself get pulled into sex, especially my first sex, with that lusting, wife-cheating man.

Once we were safely at the curb of my father's apartment, I sprang the reality of the situation on my hot and horny companion.

"Thanks for the ride, Mr. Stewart, but there's no way you can come in with me."

"What!" His dashed hopes switched his mood from passion to rage. "Why, you little slut! You prick tease! How dare you. . . ?"

At first I feared Mr. Stewart was going to lash out and hit me, but the reprimand turned out to be purely verbal—though his statements regarding my promiscuity struck me deeply. Despite an internal voice pleading with me to get out of the parked car, I sat quietly. With my head low, I allowed Mr. Stewart to cover me with a heavy blanket of shame, his words directed to the perfect resting place in my psyche craving punishment.

Yes, I am to blame. Yes, it is all my fault.

After several humiliating minutes, Mr. Stewart's tirade wound down, ending with, "Out. Get out of this car now!" He didn't have to tell me twice.

That's how I came to be at my father's apartment on a Friday afternoon in April 1971, emotionally crushed, hopelessly bewildered, and decidedly wary of my awakening sexuality.

4: The Dads

Thinking about Mr. Stewart reminds me of life on Longview Valley Road. We moved there in the summer of '66, just before I turned ten. By we, I mean Mom, my brother and Mom's new husband, Greg, who Jimmy and I were instructed to call Dad.

The first month of our new life in the San Fernando Valley was wonderful. Post-honeymoon bliss filled our cookie-cutter three-bedroom, two-bath, fifties ranch-style home. Mom became unusually sweet, smiling and laughing a lot. She told Jimmy and me that soon we'd all have the same last name because "Dad" was going to adopt us. Mom's choice of hubby number two also brought another set of grandparents, an aunt and uncle, and two girl cousins close to my age, who all shared the same last name.

I was so excited to send in not only a change of address but a name change for my monthly subscription to *Barbie Magazine*. Little did I know that fan-based periodical would become an agonizing reminder of what could have been. The change from idyllic family life came abruptly, one sweltering August afternoon....

Mom was sitting in one of the four lemon-yellow cast iron chairs surrounding the kitchen table when I came in to escape the summer heat. She held the mustard-yellow phone receiver in one hand, while nervously wrapping the spiral cord around the fingers of the other. She glanced up as I entered, and I saw tears in her eyes, but she quickly bowed her head and turned away.

I had rarely seen her cry, and it scared me. A moment later she ended the call stating, "I've got to go."

"What's wrong?" I asked, uncertain I really wanted to know.

Her reply was cold and detached. "You and your brother aren't being adopted." Shocked by her words, I asked why as tears streamed down my cheeks, but Mom had nothing more to say. I knew that tone, and once she used it, the conversation was over. All I could figure was that Jimmy and I had somehow screwed up and ruined the plan.

Years later, in my young adulthood, Mom shared her cut-and-dried thought process from that pivotal afternoon.

She felt she had to make a decision—him or us. And she didn't want to go back to being a single mom, so she chose him. From that bright, sunny day forward, despite the fact that we shared the same roof, Mom treated Jimmy and me with the same efficiency she dedicated to those annoying piles of dust that liked to gather in the corners. The light and joy that momentarily blessed our happy family got sucked away by a vacuum of "don't upset your step-father."

It's only now, reflecting back on that flip-the-switch day, I see another possibility. Dad may simply have stated he talked to an attorney and it wasn't legally possible to adopt us because our father was still alive. It's completely feasible Mom's misguided reaction—which I absorbed in the form of thinking I wasn't good enough—became the tap root for the tension which filled our home, not Dad's actual words.

Because new-Dad decided it was about time real-Dad paid his dues—also known as child support—my father came back into my life with every-other-weekend visitations.

That first Friday night, when I was ten years old, is every bit as disturbing a memory as the one that took place four years later, when Liesl was gone. For years I couldn't understand what caused the crying binge which lasted—literally—all night long. I told myself I missed my Mom, and my new house in the San Fernando Valley. In those hours of darkness, nothing more ominous came to the surface of my pre-teen mind. . . .

My little brother and I had been put to bed at a normal, kid-friendly hour. We shared the guest room, each getting a twin bed that made up the corner unit. I slept in the bed on the right, Jimmy had the one on the left, so our heads formed a ninety degree angle, meeting next to the dark wood center table.

It was a quiet evening, I didn't fill up on sugary or caffeinated drinks, but something about being in my father's house tipped the scale of my tender young emotions.

Crying loud, I held onto the hope I'd wake up someone—preferably my father, since Liesl didn't drive—and convince him to take me home. I had the whole thing worked out. All I needed was the ride. I didn't care I'd be locked out of Mom and step-Dad's house—even in my fragile state I knew better than to wake them—I would simply sleep on the front porch. Curling up there, like a neighborhood cat, I'd be safe. It was a much better prospect than continuing the night here.

As the darkness wore on I became more and more desperate. At one point I even broke the sobs with choked statements such as, "Please take me home," or, "I want to go home," but my pleas were unanswered. Cry and wail as I might, no one woke up, or if they did, they didn't make any move to alleviate my pain. Even my brother, whose ears were less than two feet away, seemed deaf.

The thought of going into my father's bedroom and physically shaking him awake did cross my mind, but opening his closed bedroom door was a scarier path then weeping, so instead I simply carried on, hour after miserable hour. By dawn I had settled down to a wounded animal whimper.

At breakfast my father sat across from me and flatly stated, "You sure were upset last night."

I couldn't believe my ears. He'd heard my appeal, my outright begging to go home, and had chosen to simply ignore me. How could this man, who supposedly loved me, be so cool and detached? Didn't he care about me? And what about Liesl? As a mom, didn't she know how to handle hysterical children?

I kept my red, puffy eyes lowered, focused on the bowl of puffed rice my stepmother silently placed before me. I felt too drained to shed another tear. If my father or his wife weren't offering care and compassion, I certainly wasn't going to let them see my vulnerability. And besides, in the morning light, I felt foolish about my nighttime collapse. It was pretty clear I wasn't going to get nurturing from this set of parents any more than the set at home.

Thus I settled into a typical divorced parent's routine, spending every other weekend with the opposite side.

When Anna and her mom came over, I at least had someone to play with—and no, my brother wasn't a viable option for companionship—shifting the weekend visits into a more tolerable mode. But even those good times bring up a memory that lands with a thud. . . .

It was a Saturday afternoon. I was ten, which meant Anna was nine. We were fooling around in the second bedroom, the one Jimmy and I shared for our weekend stays. Everyone else was out back in the detached garage they'd converted into a game room, complete with beer on tap and a pool table.

"Look at this," Anna said as she pulled a small plastic utensil out of the dresser drawer and plopped down to the floor, pulling me down next to her.

"What is it?" I asked. To me it looked like a mini electric mixer. Except instead of having beaters, it had a small suction cup on the end.

Anna crawled over to the wall and plugged the mystery device into the socket.

"It's my grandma's massager. See?"

She flipped the switch and I jumped, startled by the loud buzz.

"Here, you use it like this." Anna leaned over and placed the appliance on my surprised crotch. "See. It feels good."

After a couple of seconds, I pushed her hand away.

"No, it doesn't. It stings. And now I have to pee."

"Well, I like it," she said as she lay back on the floor, placing the vibrator between her own legs.

I played dumb to Anna, but I understood the point of the noisy tool and was horribly embarrassed to be there in the room while she played with herself. I was not the slightest bit curious. In fact, I was more afraid of getting caught by my brother, or worse, by one of our parents, so I was glad I could disappear to the bathroom. By the time I came back, Anna had returned the massager to its storage place, and we dropped the topic.

My fear of detection wasn't merely idle paranoia. A few months earlier I'd been caught in an explorative act, and I didn't want a repeat performance.

Perhaps I simply tapped into healthy pre-teen curiosity. Perhaps my newlywed parents had filled the house with sexual hormones that oozed through the plain white walls. Perhaps I felt bold because I finally had a bedroom to myself. Whatever the cause, the result remains the same; another memory that lands with a thud....

A neighbor girl and I were in my room playing an innocent game of Clue on the gold shag carpet.

"Miss Scarlet, with the rope, in the ballroom," I said, completing the game.

Looking for another way to pass the time, I hit on a regrettable plan. "Let's take a nap."

My new friend agreed, so I quietly closed the bedroom door and pulled back the pink polka dot chenille bedspread covering my single mattress. "Come on," I said, as I slid between the cool white cotton sheets. "Let's get in."

As she snuggled in next to me, I pulled the covers up to our chins. I knew the game wasn't really about sleeping, and was excited she'd followed my lead. "Now let's take off our shirts."

We both fumbled around, trying to keep the covers intact while disrobing under them. Nervous giggles released the mounting tension. As our clothing came off, I became braver, but also sensed I needed to move slowly. "Okay, now let's take off our pants."

A moment later, while we were both squirming under the tangle of fabric, my friend's mother opened the door.

"What's going on in here?"

"Nothing," I blurted, though it was obvious that something was indeed going on.

By some miracle I was spared any lecture or punishment. In fact, the neighbor mom didn't say a word to me or my mother about her findings as she gathered her daughter and left, but reprimand or not, I felt mortified. Shame and humiliation sent my budding curiosity about the naked form and sexuality deep into hiding, where it remained for several years.

I never discussed these few minutes of curiosity with either Anna or the neighbor girl. Those events—and any potential subsequent encounters—moved into the realm of do-not-touch. But two things from that long-ago day with Anna locked into my gut, each with their own twist of queasy trepidation.

First, Anna knew of the sex toy's location and enjoyed pulling it out for a quick buzz. I suspected that topic would lead down a path I wasn't prepared to explore, so I simply told myself I wasn't interested. But I was, and to this day I wonder if any sinister events led to Anna's preteen desire.

Second were questions regarding my step-mother and her use of the noisy device. I did my best to push aside these questions, convincing myself Liesl only used the "massager" for medicinal purposes. I didn't want to listen to the nagging little voice saying, *Sure, right . . . it's for sore muscles*. It was only a quick leap from questions regarding my step-mother's sexuality to those regarding my father, and I certainly didn't want to ponder him and his sexual activities—not at ten and not today, as a post-fifty-year-old.

5: The Red Dot Club

My pitted path of self-exploration continued with boys in our Sherman Oaks community. In fact, the plentiful oak trees and rustic lay of the land are major contributors to the story.

All of the backyards in our neighborhood were rugged and overgrown—probably because they were so damned steep you couldn't do much except let them grow wild. Our dead-end street fell at the bottom of the rough canyons, and the houses on the hill above us stood on stilts. In a way it was fun living in such a precarious setting, but nature's layout was also a bit alarming.

I'd often lie in bed and ponder the outcome of a major earthquake. Sometimes I'd escape safely from my back-of-the-house bedroom, but often my imaginings left me dying in a pile of rubble.

Because our street didn't have sidewalks, I traded my city form of entertainment, roller skates, for a bicycle. After one nasty run-in with the same bumpy asphalt that prevented me from skating, I became comfortable on my new two-wheeled friend. I loved the thrill of a downhill run, but dreaded the return trip up the mile-long, steady incline. Our third summer in that oven-hot, breezeless gully, when I was "almost" twelve, I settled on the perfect solution. I could pump hard past the six houses between us and the end of the street and then simply relax, gently cruising around the cul-de-sac, known as "the circle."

The circle was the place to be. You were neat—or groovy—if you lived in the circle, and although I wasn't into boys in the least, I did want respect from the few that lived there. These boys teased Jimmy mercilessly, so better to be on their good side.

Then there was Janet. She lived in the best spot of all. Her driveway went off the circle and continued uphill. No one lived higher than Janet, and being her friend gave me permission to hang out in the cool kid zone.

Kenny was the ringleader of the adolescent clan. Big Kenny, to be precise. He lived on the west side of the circle with his dad and older brother, Robert. Little Kenny lived across from him, and Doug, the final boy in the group, lived next door to Little Kenny.

Of course, I wanted to fit in, and I wanted to be liked, despite having the weakling brother and the not-with-it house. So when Big Kenny offered me membership in their exclusive club, I couldn't refuse....

"You'll have to pull your pants down," Kenny informed me. "We'll all go up on my hill, you'll pull your pants down, and I'll give you the red dot."

Kenny probably expected me to say, "No way." Or giggle and blush. Any sane girl would have done exactly that, but belonging was more important than modesty that summer. And besides, Janet agreed it was a necessary step.

"Come on. Do it. I'm a member."

Thinking back, I wonder about the validity of Janet's statement. This same group of kids had my brother believing in the ivy monster, a malicious green beast that would leap out of the vine-covered yards and eat him alive. However, as I said, belonging was important, and I hadn't yet developed a capacity for discernment.

"Okay. I'll do it."

Kenny set the date. "This Friday, three o'clock. We'll meet here, in front of my house."

I felt nervous, but I wasn't going to chicken out. At "almost twelve," acceptance was worth a little embarrassment, but only a little. Because my teenage hormones had recently kicked in, I'd sprouted my first pubic hair. No way I was gonna leave that coarse black oddity for public viewing, so come the big day, I snuck into my mother's bathroom and used her tweezers to pluck it out.

The still, dry afternoon gradually ticked by. I passed the time riding my bike in a large loop, slowly and steadily pushing away the adrenaline flowing through my veins.

At the appointed hour, the boys, ranging in age from ten to thirteen, emerged from their respective houses. I rode over to Big Kenny's driveway and climbed off my three-speed, solemnly pushing the kick-stand into place. We were all restless and for a moment paced around like a pack of hyenas waiting for the kill.

"You ready?" Kenny asked in his best commanding, though still little-boy, voice.

"Yes," I replied in a rough croak.

One by one we filed down the concrete walkway to the left of the garage. First Big Kenny, then me, then Doug, and finally Little Kenny, weaving through garbage cans and assorted junk strewn along the way. After crossing the equally cluttered back patio, we started up the brick stairs covered with lichen.

I kept my gaze down, not only to focus on the faulty and neglected steps, but to avoid any eye contact with the boys. After about thirty feet of upward climb, our path changed to dirt and headed off into the dense brush.

At this point the boys were careful to avoid coming into contact with the red leaves of poison oak. Immune to the rash-inducing oils of the plant, I showed my bravado by holding back vines that leaned into the narrow trail.

Despite my outward display of calm, my heart was pounding. A couple of minutes later I heard another set of footsteps crunching dried leaves as Janet ran to catch up with us.

"Sorry I'm late," she said as her Keds fell into place behind mine. Leaning in close to my ear she whispered, "You don't have to go through with this."

"Too late now," I grumbled.

When we got to the appointed gathering spot, a small clearing surrounded by Valley Oaks and scrubby brush, each of my witnesses took a seat, forming a circle around me.

Big Kenny's solemn words began the ritual, "We come together to make Debbie a member of the Red Dot club. Now take off your clothes."

I stood up, took a deep breath, and pulled my blue and white striped tee-shirt over my head, passing it to Janet. The hot air felt chilly against my perspiration-covered and now bare chest. Next I unzipped and slid down my orange capri shorts. Unfortunately, the legs were too tight to slide easily over my shoes, so I stumbled and wobbled around, then lost my balance, landing with a plop on the sharp oak leaves.

Laughter broke out among my audience, but I was determined to keep what little resolve I had left. I wiped the dried foliage away from my butt and continued disrobing, first removing my navy blue sneakers, then stripping off my previously clean white socks. Once again I stood up, this time wiggling my tight shorts down and off. All eyes were riveted on my nearly naked white torso.

I took another deep breath and slid my thumbs into the sides of my plain white cotton underwear. They were mid-thigh when the hushed silence was broken by a booming male voice.

"What are you kids doing up there?"

"Oh, shit," Kenny hissed. "It's Robert."

Panic broke out. The boys scattered first, though amazingly Kenny had the presence of mind to touch my butt and say "Red Dot" before disappearing into the bushes with the others. Janet tossed me my shirt, muttering "Sorry," as she followed their lead.

Again big brother Robert called out, anger rippling up the hill, "Hey! What's going on up there?"

"Nothing," Big Kenny yelled. "Nothing's going on."

I was terrified Robert would head up the hill and see me nude. It was one thing stripping in front of a group of kids my age, but Robert was older, practically an adult. I would die of embarrassment if he found me, but fear had me frozen.

"Get down here now!"

Kenny's subdued response was barely audible. "Yeah. Coming."

With a jolt, I snapped out of my suspended animation and began dressing as quickly as my trembling hands would allow.

"Shit," I whispered, squirming into the tight shorts and pulling the damp tee-shirt over my head. "I've really done it this time." My head throbbed as I sat down and pulled on the dirty socks. I yanked hard on the lace of my well-worn shoes and began to cry when it broke off in my hand.

Down on the patio, I could hear snippets of conversation between Robert and Kenny, where Kenny did his best to convince his not-so-easily-fooled brother of his innocence.

I dried my tears and began to wonder if my fear was unfounded. Maybe Robert didn't know I had stayed up the hill. Maybe I could lie low and sneak down after they went back inside to escape the summer's heat.

I had convinced myself I was safe, when Robert called out, "Debbie, I know you're still up there."

Damn. Busted. As I worked my way back down the wooded trail, I tried to come up with viable reasons for being up there, but guilt had grabbed my brain and wouldn't let go.

I'm in so much trouble. I'm sure he knows I got naked. He's probably going to tell his dad. Then his dad will tell my parents and, hell, his dad will probably tell all the parents. Instead of being one of the likable, nice kids, I'm going to be the bad girl no one should be seen with.

Yikes, you really did spiral into fear, one of my current day inner voices comments. *You could have simply called down, "We're just playing." What's the big deal?* I recognize the bold, self-assured voice of the Brazen One.

Where are you when I need you? questions the Regretful One. *Your big idea for what I could have said doesn't help much after the fact!*

Oh, it wasn't that bad. You survived, replies another aspect, this one with a critical edge to it. *You're the only one who made such a big deal out of it. Sure you were embarrassed, but let it go. It was a long time ago.*

The inner debate is familiar. It's habit. Even now, more than forty years later, I beat myself up for what I did or didn't do. Fortunately, another voice speaks up as I relive these events of the past.

Hey, are you forgetting the jewel in all this? asks a practical aspect. *Robert broke up the ritual. God only knows where it could have gone. Chances are it was innocent childhood exploration, but on the off chance there was a more sinister agenda, let's try being grateful to him for stepping in.*

Well, there you go—an "aha" moment.

It's true. Robert did break the momentum. It's only from my adult vantage point that I recognize the darker tale that could have spun that day. Red dot. Broken virginity. Group ritual. As a child I simply glommed onto the regret and tucked it into my "reasons I'm a bad person" bag.

I'd like to go back and talk to my pre-teen self, that shy young girl who simply wanted to fit in. Now, I could speak with her as a wise and caring adult, but as a child I didn't particularly trust the grownups in my life. So instead, I think I'll travel into the world of the shaman, a land where anything is possible. In that land I can shape shift, taking on the form of a trusted four-legged ally, a squirrel. . . .

"Hi, Debbie," I'd say from a nearby branch.

"What? Who said that?" The guilt-ridden me would look around, trying to find the source of the greeting.

"I did," the squirrel would respond. "Up here, in the tree."

"Squirrels can't talk."

"Sure we can—when we want to."

"Well, I can't talk right now. I'm in a lot of trouble. Robert is down there, and he knows I'm up here, and well, I've got to go."

"I know, I've been watching. It's okay, you know. Robert isn't going to tell anybody about today, and the other kids won't say anything either. You're not in trouble. Robert is worried about you."

"Huh? Worried about what?"

"Well, it's not really a good idea to take your clothes off. I know it was just a game, but sometimes games get out of control. What you did isn't bad, and you aren't bad; you're trying to fit in. You can fit in without taking your clothes off. Robert just wants to know you're okay."

"I'm okay. But what should I tell him if he asks what we were doing?"

"Well, you could tell him the truth."

"The truth! I can't tell him the truth. He'll yell at me. He'll think I'm an idiot."

"I don't think so. I think he'd be surprised. I think he'd be angry with Kenny, and he might even be angry with you, but he'd get over it. People get angry, and then they get over it. You don't have to be afraid of people when they're mad."

"Yeah, that's what you think. My step-dad gets mad a lot, and I'm scared of him."

"That's true. I'm sorry you are living with someone who is so hard to get along with. I know it sounds like a long way off, but you'll be free of him when you're older. He's an angry, confused man. You're going to know several angry, confused men in your life. Someday that will change. You're learning hard lessons now. Do your best to treat yourself kindly. When things get scary or you get lonely, look around for me. I'll be as close as a nearby tree."

"Thanks, Mr. Squirrel."

Running lightly down the hill, I'd call out, "Hey, Robert! You'll never believe who I've been talking to up here."

In real life, Robert was waiting for me when I sheepishly appeared at the base of the hill. He didn't say anything, but he glared at me in a way that bored disgust deep into my tender young spirit.

Janet and I never talked about that day on the hill, though we remained good friends. And the cool guys, well, I kept my distance after that bungled attempt at camaraderie. I saw them around, but I never felt comfortable hanging out, and we certainly never spoke of the Red Dot ritual. It remained a secret.

Until now.

6: The Split

Looking back over these pivotal life events, I see a gap had developed in my malleable, young psyche.

My good girl appears innocent, pure, almost fragile; the image of a buttercup comes to mind. On the other hand, my bad girl is bold, adventurous. According to the good girl, this polar opposite persona throws tradition, and its accompanying morals, to the wind. The wild one's flower is more along the lines of a daylily—bright orange, please—that stands up and stands out in the garden. She dismisses the buttercup; it could easily be stepped on or missed in its diminutive state.

My witness self of today wonders if the polarities were more related to age and immaturity than to good versus bad. Regardless, the black-and-white thinking and resulting inner strife have been a constant throughout my life. Ironically, a popular TV game show named *Truth or Consequences* rewarded this fragmented personality. . . .

In the late summer of 1970, I'd tagged along to a filming with the Twins Club, not as a twin myself, but as their baby-sitter. My enthusiastic hand-waving, shouting, and bouncing up and down on the auditorium seat got the attention of the show's producer.

"You, the blonde in the back. What's your name?"

A few questions and apparently correct answers later, I found myself backstage preparing for my television debut. When I stepped out from behind the curtain, Bob Barker—before his Price Is Right *days—began the first of a two-part interview.*

"My name is Debbie Hawley. I'm fourteen and attend Van Nuys High where I'm in the tenth grade. I spend my time hanging out with friends or watching TV. I'm not dating anyone. My goal in life is to be an actress or a model."

For the second interview, a three-member panel appeared on stage with me. These women would have to guess if my answers were fact or fiction. Of course, the show's producer asked me to lie, so I fabricated a great life.

"My name is Christy Brown. I'm sixteen and a junior at Van Nuys High. I'm a cheerleader and my boyfriend is on the football team. We spend our time studying or going to movies. After college I'd like to get a job as a stewardess."

It's amazing how easily, and without hesitation, the lies flowed from my lips. In a way I longed to be that likable girl, Christy, with her high school sweetheart and her gateway-to-the-world life plan.

I walked away from that skit seventy-five dollars richer, twenty-five for each of the grandmotherly types who guessed I had been telling the truth. While winning the money felt like a worthy accomplishment, I also felt diminished. For the first time, I questioned the depth of my life goal of fame and fortune. Assuming since none of the elderly women had seen any truth—which I equated with value—in my true dream, it must not be a worthy path.

The polarizing schism continued with my high school activities. Technically speaking, I could be labeled a good girl; I did well in classes, teachers liked me, and I was a member of the drill team. However, I teetered at the edge of bad girl status, testing the dangerous waters. The school's weekly football games provided a chance for both aspects to come out and play.

After our precision halftime performance, I'd sneak off from the bleachers and cheering on the team to cavort with the seedy kids hanging out under those very seats. The rough kids were too cool to watch the jocks in action. Instead, they would smoke cigarettes and feign indifference to who won or lost.

I wasn't bold enough to enter this underbelly world alone; I used my friend Gay as a key. Gay got in anywhere she wanted, which I attributed to her fully developed, voluptuous breasts. Dressed in my uniform—a crimson wool skirt and matching sweater, complete with the school's emblem blazing on my sadly undeveloped front side—I knew I stood out. Thankfully, Gay would vouch for my presence, and I'd puff away to prove my worthiness.

A few weeks after I began exploring the boundaries of high school rebellion, my family packed up the house in Sherman Oaks and moved south, across the foothills, to Bel Air—and I ended up at University High.

Looking back, it's easy to see the daring aspect of my younger and not-so-wise self that enjoyed hanging out with Sue and Sue. But like any teenager trying on multiple personalities, being friends with the sisters was only part of the story. My better side preferred hanging out with another group of kids, the good kids, the non-smoking, pre-hormone-crazy kids.

There were eight of us total, four guys and four girls. Hanging out with them was fun and refreshing. For one of the few times in my life I felt as though I belonged. And I felt accepted, even during the inevitable shy and awkward moments.

Up to that point, and pretty much since then, I've been a one- or two-friend kind of girl, except for that wonderful year plus at Uni High. I actually looked forward to lunch when we'd meet on the large grass terrace between the main hall on the hill and the athletic fields spread across the lower acreage.

Natural springs flowed across the campus, and on hot days we'd have water fights, dipping our cupped hands into the cold water. I'm not quite sure why this group befriended me, but I loved the ease and comfort I felt being with them.

That first semester, none of us dated. It's not like we were asexual; heck, we were teenagers. But we had other things to fill our time, like music. Several days a week, we wound up in one home or another, listening to rock and roll and trying to figure out the deeper meanings behind the songs.

I remember one of the boys, Carl, being totally impressed when I sang along to all the words of "Stairway to Heaven." I should have kept my mouth shut when he asked how I did it, but I gave away my trick by showing him the album liner, complete with lyrics. He was the cutest of the bunch, and my favorite guy, but not in a boyfriend kind of way.

Like all things in life, the school year ended, bringing with it a change in my daily routine. I spent a good part of the summer vacation between tenth and eleventh grade in my familiar solitary mode, working on my tan and perfecting the art of baking cookies.

I know it sounds odd, but I looked forward to September. Not only is it my birthday month, but I welcomed the return of my social group. Unfortunately, when the eight of us reconvened on that Indian summer day, things had changed. Some of the differences were obvious, like the facial hair on the guys and the larger chests on the girls—though, unfortunately, I was still left out of the latter category. The other changes came into play as the school year progressed.

First up, there was a new member to the group, Mandy. Her family had just moved from England, so now we were nine. Then Paul got a girlfriend, and suddenly we were ten. Ten is one of my favorite numbers, but it didn't work for us as a close-knit band of teens. Damn those hormones. My treasured group of easy friends had discovered pairing. This kicking in of testosterone affected me directly when, one afternoon, my good buddy Carl tried to kiss me.

There I was, minding my own business, hanging out with Carl in his bedroom like we'd done dozens of times before. I sat on his bed, legs crossed beneath me, leaning back on the wall. The late afternoon sun fell through the wooden shutters, illuminating the words as I happily sang along. In the momentary quiet between songs, Carl leaned in for his attempt at a peck.

Instead of a warm wash of pleasure, or perhaps a blush and a giggle, I reacted with fear. I quickly backed away and shut down; I couldn't even look at him. My throat tightened as if stifling a scream, and my heart pounded wildly. I gathered my things as quickly as I could and left, stumbling over some lame excuse.

I felt bad about running away—then and now—but simply didn't have the ability to explain my reaction. Hell, I didn't understand my reaction. I only knew I was terrified and had to get away.

It's not as if I hadn't kissed a boy. I'd kissed the college guy at UCLA. And before that, I'd even experienced a pleasurable kiss. In fact, my first kiss is one of the few good memories from being fourteen. I have Gay to thank for it. Not only had Gay been fun to hang out with at school functions, she fixed me up on my first blind date. . . .

Mom would never have allowed such a thing, especially a date doubling with Gay, so I didn't ask for permission. My mom knew Gay's mom and dad worked in the industry (L.A. shorthand for "the entertainment industry"), so that branded them as irresponsible parents. I think it's an odd assumption for her, since Mother also grew up in an entertainment-supported home. Apparently, those who worked behind the camera possessed morals and scruples, while those in front of the camera did not.

Anyway, Gay dated a young actor, and they matched me up with a friend of his, another young leading man. Although I didn't watch his show, I remember being quite impressed, and somewhat star-struck, by his television history. The date itself has faded from memory, but oh, not that kiss.

We'd returned to Gay's house up on the hill overlooking the San Fernando Valley and had gathered in her bedroom to listen to music. The Doors. L.A. Woman. Still one of my all-time favorite albums. Maybe it's because David and I were tangled up in arms and legs and tongues in the oversized bean-bag chair through pretty much the whole LP. To this day, hearing "Riders on the Storm" makes my heart beat faster. Ah, yes, that was a wonderful first smooch. Turned out to be the only one, at least with David. That's okay. What it lacked in repeat performances, it made up for in duration.

Carl, on the other hand, was a friend, and somehow going from friend to boyfriend simply didn't add up. In fact, now that I think about it, I've never been friends with someone before getting sexual. I realize a lot of people get to know each other first, and it does sound like a healthy way to start a relationship; I've simply never explored that path.

First attraction, then sex, followed by getting to know each other, and finally falling apart is more my style. So even though I didn't explore kissing with Carl, I did find the act itself quite enjoyable. That's where Anna, and the weekends I spent with her, came into play. . . .

Time with Anna brought out the reckless, assertive girl in me, and we were wild young things on the weekends when we got together. We'd play spin the bottle in the back driveway, next to the splintery wooden fence that separated the concrete-edged pool from the parking lot.

Later we graduated to someone's garage where the older kids hung out, a full-on den of iniquity. Thoughts of that near dark, mattress-lined wooden structure still appear like a scene from a bad movie.

I went there because that's what the gang in Anna's neighborhood did, but the low sounds of sucking and moaning that filled the air, and the smell of musty sweat, were never appealing to me. I guess the pure and innocent girl did have a bit of say; I never let a guy past first base. And I definitely kept my eyes shielded from what was going on all around me. I didn't want to know.

However, one of those weekend visits with my step-niece and nameless boys takes the prize for longest kiss—even longer than the Doors-accompanied smooch with David.

My marathon lasted all the way from Torrance to Bel Air, a sixty-minute drive door-to-door. Anna and I and my sucking-face companion were in the back of Ingrid's little truck, right there in the open. During that late Sunday afternoon drive up the 405 freeway, I distinctly remember feeling split into two people: the participant and the observer.

One part of me focused on the physical sensations of the twirling and swirling tongues while another part looked outward, focusing on the drivers in the general vicinity. I had to wonder, "Is this public display of teenage lust entertaining, enticing, or perhaps embarrassing to the passing audience?"

I'm curious if my penchant for public kisses relates to the school play during my sophomore year at Uni.

I loved being in that production, *Don't Drink the Water*, by Woody Allen. Cast in the role of the teen-age daughter, I felt tentative with the onstage kiss at first, but by the night of the show I locked lips and frenched like nobody's business. I remember overhearing an audience member comment under her breath about the duration of the scene. I'd like to say I didn't care, that I easily brushed off the comment, but I didn't. I heard it and subsequently used it as ammo from the good girl, in cahoots with the inner judge.

"Nice girls don't kiss like that, especially not on stage."

The other comment that sticks in my collection of wrongdoings relates to the length of my skirt. My mother and I engaged in a long-term battle over the current fashion of dresses barely covering the derrière, but for that night, thanks to a wardrobe change, I got away with wearing two of my favorite outfits.

I'd learned the trick to shortening those cap-sleeved knit dresses; add a belt after leaving the house—and mom's watchful eye. Depending on how much I ballooned out the fabric above the waist, I could be downright indecent. At least that's what the anonymous female voice from the audience said.

"Her skirt is so short. It's downright indecent."

I blame these overheard comments from spectators on the layout of the theater; the school's cafeteria. Thanks to the 1971 Sylmar earthquake, that's where we staged our production "in-the-round." The quake's damage to the school was a devastating blow. I had so looked forward to strutting my teenage stuff on the grand stage of our beautiful and stately old auditorium, the same stage that had housed school plays for nearly fifty years. Damn those California quakes. If the shaking earth hadn't forced us into that stark, chrome and white, wooden-bench-filled dining hall, I would have been safely buffered from the biting remarks.

My mother never saw the show, but my father did. He was proud. His shy and quiet little princess was up there on stage acting like a mature seductress, a role I refined as the years passed. I shudder to think he may have also been turned on. The thought makes my stomach crawl, but knowing what I know today, it's horrifyingly possible.

7: The Real First Time

One good thing came out of the high school play's two-night run: I met Drew. Drew attended a nearby prep school with Brian, and Evie, a girl from my comfortable group of friends, invited the two of them to the show.

As excited as I was to meet Drew, it would be months before I got to see him again at our school's next presentation, a Christmas play, just weeks before we moved to Newport Beach. More on the night of that holiday extravaganza soon, but first, more about Evie.

Evie was probably my closest friend from the cozy group during my time at Uni High; at least we spent the most time together. She'd turned sixteen during the summer before our junior year, and her parents trusted her with the family car, so she could get me home after school and the all-important hanging-out time. Having access to transportation became a major bonus, especially since my mother refused to run me anywhere.

In addition, Evie's vehicular freedom opened the door to relative privacy for investigation of her exploding teen hormones. She loved to tell me stories of adventures that took place in either the front or back seat of her mom's dark green Buick Riviera. Evie also liked to keep count. Standard "base" statistics included how long and how many times. From Evie, I learned my future practice of drawing little stars in my calendar, one for each time I did "it".

Concerned about my inexperience with sex, Evie decided to match me up. So one fall weekend we dated a pair of cousins who lived in Northridge, a suburb over the hill in the San Fernando Valley. I don't recall how Evie met her date, Alan, but she swore his cousin would be perfect for me.

"They have their own place and go to junior college."

Yikes, college boys. Evie didn't know about my foray into the world of older boys the previous spring, but I decided to trust her taste in men and join her for the blind date. Since Evie's driving privileges didn't extend beyond our local neighborhood, her mom drove us over the hill for our day of adventure. Alan would make the return trek.

It seemed like a good plan until I met my companion, Lewis. If we'd met at Evie's house, I could have easily made up some excuse and walked home. But thirty miles was a long way to walk, so I didn't see an out. We were spending the day together. The sweltering heat and our destination—Magic Mountain, a local amusement park—made me one less than happy-faced first date.

I hate to be callous, but his pimply complexion combined with his gangly frame and overly anxious-to-please, puppy-dog attitude definitely stacked the deck against him. The harder he tried to be fun and interesting, the more aloof and withdrawn I became.

Then there was the park itself. I'm not a fan of whipping wildly around a rickety-framed track suspended in mid-air. In fact, doing so would have added a sour stomach to my already sour demeanor, so I spent most of the day simply waiting around for the others to complete their adrenaline rush. I would then stand in line for the next thrill ride, only to duck out again come boarding time.

Midway through our day of fun Lewis surprised me with a stuffed animal, probably a gift to make me feel better. Unfortunately, that simply added to my irritation, as I then felt compelled to be nicer and more engaging. Finally, our time to head home came around, and we piled into Alan's unimpressive four-door sedan. Evie, of course, had shotgun, which left Lewis and me in the back.

The minutes ticked by in agonizing slowness. And despite feeling tired from a long, hot day, I sat bolt upright, keeping a good, safe distance between me and my escort. If I'd been into him, the dark skies and bench seat would have been the perfect atmosphere for some fondling, like what had occurred between Evie and Alan in that same space. Adding to my torment, Evie kept pestering me from the front seat, urging me to follow her lead.

"Debbie. It's late. We've had a long day. Lay your head down in Lewis's lap."

"No, thanks. I'm not tired."

"But really, it's comfortable. Try it."

"No, thanks. I'm fine, really."

"But you'll like it, it's like a pillow."

Yeah, right. Maybe a lumpy pillow. I wasn't about to put my head and face anywhere near the guy's crotch, despite the fact that I felt somewhat obligated, since I'd accepted the cute and cuddly bear. I tried to leave the gift behind when they dropped me off, but they noticed, and Lewis bounded out of the car to return the abandoned plush toy to me.

As we stood there in my driveway with the lights of Los Angeles flickering in the distance, I had the perfect opportunity for a romantic good-night kiss. I could feel Lewis wishing it so, a hopeful, maybe-the-day-didn't-go-as-badly-as-it-seemed, moment. But bottom line, fear had once again shown up.

I didn't want to go any further with this boy, and a kiss would have opened a door I didn't want to go through. So instead of even a peck on the cheek—what the nice girl says I should have done—I grabbed the teddy bear and ran down the driveway, yelling, "Good night," over my shoulder.

I felt bad about my abrupt departure from Lewis, but not bad enough to say yes to a request, via Evie, for a second date. Instead, I asked my friend to focus her attention on my interest from the previous spring.

"Find me a way to see Drew again."

Evie put the wheels in motion, making a call to her friend Brian. "Hey, let's fix up Debbie and Drew." Nothing like putting both boys on the spot.

I wish I could report that Brian said, "Hey, great idea. I know Drew has been talking about seeing Debbie again; it would be great to fix them up." The reality was more like, "Ugh, I hate putting my friend in an awkward position like that. How about I pass along her number to him, and we just stay out of it?"

After that conversation, my attraction intensified. Despite Drew not calling, I convinced Evie that driving by his house, just to get a glimpse, was a good thing. Fortunately, I didn't allow my adoration to bleed over into obsession, and I didn't stake out the neighborhood, hiding behind the neighbor's philodendron.

However, I did fantasize: I'd happen to be in the area and run into him. How surprised and pleased he would be to see me. We'd strike up an easy conversation that would lead to a first date. Heck, I could dream, couldn't I?

I'd had similar fantasies about boys, but those boys were of the pinup variety, like Bobby Sherman, until Evie told me I was too grown up for my pre-teen crush, prompting me to remove the magazine posters from my bedroom wall. So my rich interior life, and rampant fantasies, revolved around Drew.

The chance to see him in person came in December with the annual holiday play; it provided the ideal excuse for an invitation. To add to the perfection of the moment, I wasn't in the performance, so I'd have time to flirt and hang out, not only before and during the show, but also at the all-important after party.

I had big plans. We'd meet at the venue, the Veteran's Administration Auditorium, in nearby Westwood. I'd wear something cute and just a little bit sexy. We'd sit together during the play, maybe even hold hands. Then we'd attend the celebration, where we would laugh and dance, enjoying each other's company. Of course, he would find me so charming he would ask me out, and I'd not only have my first real date, but my first real boyfriend. Ah, what a divine plan.

Unfortunately, reality didn't quite play out as I had hoped.

We did meet at the auditorium, backstage, before the program started, and I did look hot, wearing one of my favorite winter outfits, a pair of skintight corduroy pants and a soft, fuzzy, pearl-white sweater.

But instead of joining the audience as the house lights came down, we instead headed out the stage door, into the crisp night air.

I was so excited to be in Drew's actual presence, and not in my imagination, I didn't question being led out to the far reaches of the vast parking lot toward our destination: a beige Ford Fairlane station wagon.

I would like to say Drew opened the front door of the obvious mom-mobile, but instead, he headed straight to the tailgate. My body shook from the combination of no coat and adrenaline racing through my veins.

Turn around. Now. Before it's too late.
No! I want to be with him. I've waited a long time for this.

The sexually curious me won the brief debate, and while it wasn't the "Cinderella being welcomed into the coach" moment I had hoped for, I wasn't going to miss the opportunity to be with my heartthrob.

Eyeing the cargo hold, where an old blanket was already spread out to protect us from the cold metal, I realized this wasn't a last-minute spark of desire. Bending over, I crawled in, followed by Drew. The small space prevented me from sitting upright, so I slouched over, unzipping and removing my knee-high boots before placing them neatly by the closed hatch.

The smell of motor oil mixed with my patchouli oil caused me to sneeze. I got a Kleenex out of my purse and wiped my nose before setting the shoulder bag down by my shoes. Drew, reclining back on one elbow, reached over and cracked the window, allowing some fresh air into our love nest.

"You want to lie down?" he asked gently.

Stretching out next to Drew was heavenly. And oh, that first kiss. It was even better than I had imagined, as our tentative tongues searched for one another, then met, causing a pleasurable zing in my gut.

I grew nervous as his hand slid up the front of my sweater, wondering if my small chest would disappoint him. Rolling onto my side, I allowed Drew access to my bra clasp. Taking the hint, he released the elastic band. While his fingers explored my boobs, our kisses became deeper, more enthusiastic.

Enjoying second base, my body warmed and relaxed into the chilly night air. But only a few moments later I tensed, as Drew's hand slid down my belly, stopping momentarily to unbutton and unzip my pants. Once again internal dialog pulled my attention away from the physical sensations.

Stop. Tell him to stop.

No, he's just going to third base.

I cringed when Drew thrust his shaky hand between my uncertain-they-were-ready-for-the-intrusion legs, but didn't tell him to stop. I held my breath as he clumsily yanked and tugged my pants down and quickly undid his own zipper.

Despite the interior babble, I allowed romance, or what I called romance, to sweep me away—the reality of finally being with Drew pushing past my lingering hesitation.

Some of the interior gang cheered on the process. I felt as though I was sitting at the top of one of those huge roller coaster hills. Only this time, part of me enjoyed the ride and the anticipation of diving into the unknown. Refusing to acknowledge the resistant part of me, I kept silent as Drew climbed on.

A few pumps later, he fell away with a heavy, contented sigh. I, on the other hand, wasn't so satisfied. I felt confused with the stinging, throbbing aftermath.

Is that what I've been waiting for? That's what the fuss was all about?

We lay in silence for a few minutes, our heavy breath matching the steady rise and fall of traffic out on Wilshire Boulevard. Then, continuing the lack of dialogue, we redressed and walked back to the theater's stage door to find the first act still going on.

Feeling awkward and unsteady on my rubbery legs, I went straight to the ladies room, anxious to wipe the wetness away from my aching crotch—Evie had never talked about dealing with the side effects of sticky goo.

Although I knew virgins were supposed to bleed, I'd also heard somewhere that a small percentage of girls would lose their hymen without blood loss. Since I didn't see anything red in my underwear, I pushed away the concern, telling myself I simply fell into the rare minority.

Returning to the backstage area to find my friends, Evie spotted me and ran over. "You did it!" she said, grabbing my arm and pulling me aside. She beamed, like I'd scaled a mountain after years of preparation.

"How can you tell?" I whispered, somewhat horrified I was a marked woman.

"You're walking different."

Yikes. I wondered if everyone could tell.

Even though my master plan didn't include going all the way the first time Drew and I were alone together, I still hoped the dream fantasy would hold out: the dating, the going steady, and eventually the white picket fence with dog and kids. Apparently he didn't see the same picture.

Drew did at least grace me with his presence during the after party, but the end of the evening also marked the end of us. He blamed my impending move to Orange County, telling me he didn't want to be in a long-distance relationship—an explanation that was both logical and convenient.

A few weeks later my mom, step-dad, brother, new baby sister, and I headed south, leaving behind the group of easy friends—and my virginity.

8: Heartbreak

My sexual explorations gathered steam in our new conservative, coastal neighborhood. I won't go into a blow-by-blow of my adventures with their awkward bumps and grinds, and longing, and searching, and finding a way to fit—that didn't. Instead, I will offer the highs and lows of my time at Corona del Mar High.

I had four love interests total; well, four boys actually scored. Two of them have almost faded from memory, but I managed to pull together a poem for each. It feels right to acknowledge their presence, even if it is simply a stanza for each week we called the other friend.

>BOB
>VW Bug
>Crammed full of students
>daily lunch time run
>
>One hand bra un-snapper
>Deep blush
>There in the school parking lot
>
>Chicago
>Damn you loved them

> The horns hurt my ears
> But I didn't let on

CHUCK
> Even less to remember
>
> Therapist aunt
> Looking for guinea pigs
>
> A study on people
> Those who heard voices
>
> I didn't speak up
> (and neither did they)
> Best to keep silent
> about words in the head

The other two lovers left indelible stains on my young and impressionable psyche. First up: Ben.

Ben was a cool guy, a surfer. He had the right combination of wavy, long, sandy-blond hair and aloof attitude. His baby face, with a touch of scruffy ruggedness, made girls swoon, plus he had a perfectly tanned and toned body. He knew he held power. I was simply another girl in a sea of potential lovers.

When I finally did get his attention, we made plans to get together after school at my house. I have no idea where my mom, four-year-old sister, and new baby brother were that afternoon, but it was no big deal to have Ben alone in my bedroom. In fact, Mom preferred my invisibility. It allowed her to focus on her new family in that upscale, look-just-right neighborhood.

Ben, direct in his intent for a sexual conquest, didn't waste time with formalities like foreplay. It's not like he said, "All I want is a quick fuck," but once I had my back on the carpet with him hovering above me, it was obvious. What makes that afternoon memorable isn't the lack of contrived romance, but the lack of even a single shared kiss. To be sure the omission wasn't a fluke, I went back for a second go round, meeting Ben in his bedroom for the repeat performance. That's the first time I felt like an orifice. My role had been clear. Part of me began to suspect I was becoming the whore my mother had warned me about.

The other never-to-be-forgotten crush from my high school days was Peter. Ah, Peter. Peter was a god; tall and slender, with straight dark-brown hair that brushed his shoulders. He wore it parted on the side and tucked behind his ears, where it framed his clear, white skin, turned-up nose, and green eyes.

Peter attended Corona like me, but he'd graduated by the time I spotted him working in the local market. Not only did I become a regular shopper—the dutiful daughter helping Mom out with the semi-weekly grocery runs—I even became friends with the manager's daughter, Melanie.

My new after-school companion and I would sit in the offices over the meat department, peering out the one-way glass, surveying the shoppers below. I never told Melanie the reason I wanted to hang out with her, and was careful not to appear too obsessed with my love interest. It's most embarrassing to admit the ease with which I became a stalker.

It was easy to spot Peter's whereabouts. He drove a dark gray, 1968 Chevy van and lived around the corner from us, so his house was right there on the route we traveled several times daily. As time went on, Mom and my little sister got in on the act, routinely announcing, "Peter's home." He even came into my dreams, and some mornings I felt unclear if we were still strangers.

My tracking routine continued for a good five months before I got up the nerve to speak to him. Christmas Eve, 1972. Mom discovered we were missing cream cheese, a necessary ingredient for her special occasion clam dip. I jumped at a chance to remedy the situation and within seconds had grabbed money and hopped on my bike.

After finding the silver Philly box in the dairy case, I scouted the remaining aisles—Peter's van had once again given up his whereabouts. I spotted him stocking mayonnaise and moved in for a nonchalant glance. It's hard to say what prompted me to finally speak, but after a moment of reviewing the perfectly aligned white jars, I made my move.

"Which brand do you like best?"

I could barely hear his response over the sound of blood pounding in my ears. I did my best to remain calm and cool, while inside, joyful fireworks blazed a magnificent show, celebrating the mighty accomplishment. Even better, he actually took the bait and continued the conversation. Before long, we stepped outside to share a cigarette.

I played dumb, asking questions to which I already knew the answer, like, "Where do you go to school?" I kept up my ruse with the perfect tone of surprise when he told me he'd graduated from Corona.

"Oh, that's where I go. I'm a senior. Did you ever have any run-ins with Mrs. Townsend?"

This was an easy way to see if he had been a troublemaker. Mrs. Townsend, the dreaded on-campus police woman (counselor, actually) made life hell for many of the students. Fortunately, my interactions were limited to getting busted for smoking in the girls' room.

Peter laughed and said he'd avoided any confrontations with the dreaded Betty.

It wasn't long before Peter had to get back inside, so I made my purchase and virtually floated home, blissfully happy; of course, I had given him my number.

When I opened the door, Mom said, "What took you so long?"

I gleefully stated, "I talked to Peter!"

"Well, it's about time," she remarked simply.

Mom liked Peter too, and his daily after-school visits quickly became routine. She even invited him to stay for dinner—the kid's dinner, that is. She and Dad ate late, after Peter had left. Never before had I been allowed to have a friend over for a meal. Mom ran a tight ship and only bought food for the four children and two adults, but Peter brought out a nice aspect in her. Sometimes I'd even find the two of them laughing together. If I'd been more savvy, I might have suspected her of flirting, but I was so enamored with my prize, I simply enjoyed the excitement of having him around.

A couple of weeks after we started dating, Peter stunned me by announcing he had talked to my mother about getting me on the pill. Shit. I didn't even talk to Mom about things like that. Our mother-daughter conversations regarding the birds and bees had been limited: at eleven, she told me someday I'd start bleeding every month. I reacted with horror and ran from the room crying. She never brought up the messy subject again. The only other time she mentioned sex, she simply stated the facts regarding its effects.

"If you get pregnant, you'll be kicked out."

So much for lessons on life's most sacred form of connecting.

Although I felt mortified at the thought of Peter confiding in my mother regarding our intimacy, she agreed with his request and took me to the gynecologist. Soon thereafter—prompted by a need for privacy that didn't revolve around parental schedules—Peter and a friend decided to get their own place. I felt so grown up as I joined them in a search that ended with a two-bedroom apartment in a nearby complex.

Oh, life was grand. I'd go to school in the mornings, then my best friend Keri and I would hang out at Peter's place. (I'm embarrassed to admit it, but Melanie, being a momentary means to an end, had dropped off my rotation when I hooked up with Peter.)

Playing house in the bachelor pad was easy for me and I enjoyed doing Peter's laundry and cooking dinner. I also took full advantage of the freedom to drink, smoke, and do drugs.

Drugs weren't a major player in my life—yet. Keri and I primarily drank; beer or vodka and grapefruit juice. However, one afternoon she got us some LSD, and for a few quirky hours, we laughed and explored the fringes of silliness. That afternoon holds one of my favorite songs in a psychedelic memory. . . .

I was in the standard white-walled apartment with David Bowie blasting from the stereo's speakers. Keri and I were dancing and singing along to all the songs, each and every lyric skillfully memorized. When the song "Changes" came on, I leapt up on the white Melamine dining table, mic in hand, where my performance thrilled the cheering crowd. I was right in the middle of taking my bows when Peter came home and killed the buzz. He said we were being too loud and turned off the stereo.

That's when the real life changes started.

Maybe Peter grew tired of having a younger girlfriend. Maybe he didn't appreciate us using his home as a party place when he was hard at work. Maybe he didn't like me playing mom, doing his domestic chores.

Or, maybe I wasn't sexy enough—though we certainly had lots of sex, with some adventures even spilling over into the bathroom or kitchen. Whatever the reason, one gray, foggy afternoon in April 1973, Peter broke my heart....

We pulled up to the curb across the street from my house, which was odd. Peter usually parked in front. I wondered why he hadn't turned off the engine, but something told me not to ask. Sitting in the cold metal box on wheels, I focused on the motor's rumbling idle. Peter finally broke the silence in a tone as chilled as the surrounding air.

"I don't want to see you anymore."

Devastated, I couldn't believe my ears. "What? Why?"

Peter kept his eyes forward, refusing to offer a reason. "Give me back my key. Don't call me. And don't come over again."

Staring at his profile, I prayed he would turn and smile, say it was a joke, that he was only teasing. But he didn't.

"Please," I begged, choking on sobs. "Tell me what I did wrong."

Silently Peter held out his hand. Reaching into my purse, I pulled out my lanyard key ring, the one I made special for his key; the only house key I'd ever owned. Crushed, I removed the prized possession and dropped it in his open palm.

Accepting the finality, I opened the door and stepped out of the van. My gut felt as though it had been kicked, and I had to force my legs to move. Standing in the middle of the street, I watched as Peter drove away. In disbelief, I walked up to the house and through the garage, before stepping into the laundry room where Mom was matching socks.

"What's wrong?"

"Peter broke up with me."

"Why? What did you do to him?"

Struck by Mom's assumption of my guilt, my grief flipped to fury, which I vented by slamming my bedroom door in the face of that cold-hearted bitch.

Regardless of fault, the reality was clear. I cried for days. Despite Peter telling me not to, I made countless phone calls, begging and pleading for him to take me back. I even hung out at the market, hoping to catch him when he got off work, but nothing could persuade my first true love to come back to me.

If a broken heart wasn't bad enough, I also let go of my dream of attending senior prom. Perhaps every girl imagines going to that big dance, but I thought I'd be particularly special attending with an older boy, a graduate, instead of just another senior, or worse yet, an underclassman. And while some girls might have bounced back and worked the student body for a suitable escort, I retreated into depression and self-pity, allowing my victim status to deeply erode what little self-esteem I possessed. Outwardly, I played tough and acted as if I didn't care about attending such a stupid event. Keri tried to convince me to go on my own, but that would be worse than death itself. I already felt like a social misfit; I certainly wasn't going to flaunt my flawed and unlovable self.

At that point, I pretty much gave up on dating and having a boyfriend. It simply wasn't worth getting excited about a new Mr. Right, offering my phone number, and hoping he would call.

Instead, during the summer after graduation, I perfected a sport Keri and I had started our junior year—cruising the Island for parties. Balboa Island, that is. Most nights we found one or more large events hosted by drunken, fun-loving, and best of all, non-local college students. These gatherings were generally well attended and boisterous enough to allow anonymous flirting, as well as forays into a back bedroom or bath. Basically, that season, I learned the fine art of casual sex. At sweet sixteen, I had rarely been missed.

9: Betrayal

Some parents dread their children's move out of the nest; mine couldn't wait to get rid of me. I don't remember when they first announced that any higher education wouldn't be funded and I'd have to move out when I turned eighteen, but I remember convincing myself I didn't care.

"Who needs college?" I told Keri. "It's bullshit."

So I got a job—entry level, filing countless pieces of pastel paper into hundreds of thousands of folders at Pacific Mutual Insurance. It was a never-ending routine, but the perfectionist in me enjoyed the long, quiet days and color-coded order of those floor-to-as-high-as-my-arm-could-reach cabinets. I did such a stellar job that at my sixty-day review I got promoted. Well, almost. I had to complete ninety days in my current position before heading up in salary grade and over to the key punch department.

Thrilled, I couldn't wait to share the good news with my best friend. Problem was, Keri also worked in that filing department overlooking Newport Beach. She'd started working there the month before me, which meant her review had come and gone in our mundane, repetitive world when I got news of my impending departure. Boy, was she pissed. And she made no attempt to hide her belief that I'd gotten what she deserved.

Keri and I had been a good match when we were both new students at Corona del Mar High, my third school in as many years. I'd even changed the spelling of my name to Debi to match her simple four-letter display. She was gutsy and carefree, had access to her mom's Skylark, and could easily offer transportation, something my parents were still not willing to provide. My step-father wouldn't even allow me to take driver's training, spouting some crap about his insurance going up, so having a friend with a car was an absolute necessity.

When gas prices went up and Keri's mom put an end to my friend running me back and forth across the bay, I managed to stay attached by hitchhiking. I'd heard the warnings, but figured Newport Beach's conservative inhabitants were safe, convenient rides to our usual meeting place on the Island. Plus, I struck a compromise with Keri's mom; if I got to our nighttime party spot, Keri could drive me home. Her mom also presented the option of me paying for gas, but back in high school, before I had a job, I had precious little money. Besides, it was easier—and more daring—to stick out my thumb.

For high school graduation, Keri's parents helped manifest her dream car, an MGB GT, in which I proudly claimed shotgun—the only seat that didn't involve driving. I even contributed to getting around town in that dark green fun-mobile by setting and releasing the emergency brake—what we jokingly called the dildo—thus preventing us from rolling into vehicles on the steepest hills in town. Keri and I were a good team. But try as I might to be Keri's one and only party companion, by the time we advanced into the corporate world, another girl squeezed her way in.

I acted like the shift from twosome to threesome didn't bother me, but it did. I never really liked Judy. She seemed a bit rough and untrustworthy. Besides, she was a brunette. Keri and I were both blondes—same boxed shade—and as the saying went, we had more fun. Judy even crowded into Keri's car for two, but I took it in stride, playfully announcing "Dildo!" before sliding in closest to Keri. Fortunately, by then, she had learned the skill of working a clutch.

I'd begun to worry about losing my best friend before the promotion when I found out "the girls" had gone somewhere without me, but after that review day, Keri turned obviously cooler. I even think the two of them conspired to get back at me for what Keri considered to be my premature advancement. . . .

It was three weeks after my glowing review when a co-worker found me deep in the bowels of the file corridors.

"Debi, you've got a phone call. It's your mom."

I wove my way through the symmetrical rows, puzzled and alarmed, thinking, Mom never calls me at work; Mom never calls anyone. *When I reached the reception area of our fourth floor department, my superior held out her phone. She too seemed both concerned and confused as she walked a discreet distance from her sun-drenched desk.*

"Hello?"

"Debi, did you lend your bike to someone?"

"No." At first I couldn't make sense of Mom's question. It had to be there: the shiny new one along the wall of the garage, next to hers and dad's.

My bike was my pride and joy. I'd saved up for it religiously. After each paycheck, I had gone to visit that cherry-red beauty, paying another fifty dollars towards its purchase price of $300.00. I had never owned something so expensive, but I knew it would be a good investment.

When I finally rode my two-wheeler home, Mom went with me to the fire department to get it licensed. She only went along to drool over the firemen, but I still enjoyed going on an outing with her.

"Well, it's gone," she said abruptly. "The others are there, but yours is gone."

Stunned, my throat closed and tear ducts opened, as I gasped for breath.

I managed to whisper, "It has to be there."

"I'm sorry," she offered in a rare display of sympathy. "I'll call the police."

"Okay." Willing my tears to pause, I placed the phone back on its base.

All I could think about was holding it together until I got away from the eyes I felt boring into my back. I lowered my head, turned, and charged towards the ladies room, no longer able to detain the tears spilling down my cheeks. Just after I passed through our department's glass doors into the open hallway, I heard my manager.

"I wonder if somebody died."

Keri's reply, and vengeful tone, felt like a knife thrust into my back. "Nah. Someone probably just stole her bike."

BETRAYAL

As I relive this act of betrayal, I want to go back to my seventeen-year-old self and give her permission to get pissed. Right there, in the moment. . . .

Spinning around, I'd lock eyes with my friend-turned-foe.
"What did you say?" I'd demand of her. "How the fuck did you know my bike was stolen? Did you arrange it?"

In reality I didn't speak up. As much as I liked to think of Keri as my dear, sweet friend, I knew she had a mean streak, and I knew she had a knack for getting others to do her dirty work. I knew because I fell into the trap of being the "someone" in her "someone should" vendettas during our senior year. . . .

We were walking through the senior parking lot, and there it was: Kevin's shiny new hot rod. Keri didn't like Kevin. I don't remember what he'd done to make her mad, but she wanted revenge.
"Someone should key his car."
"I will," I offered excitedly. "Give me your keys."
Remembering the sound of metal on metal as the key scratched a long deep groove down the previously pristine paint job makes me sick to my stomach. I'd like to say I knew better than to do something like that, but Keri—or her approval—had an odd hold on me.

In my seventeen-year-old working girl's world, my rage stayed internal, like it always did, but the Keri spell had broken. From that moment on, I didn't play nice or pretend nothing was wrong between us. I simply stopped talking to the ex-friend, cutting her off. She became the invisible bitch.

Unspoken tension filled the few days remaining in our side-by-side working relationship. No doubt everyone in the file department anticipated my departure to the opposite side of the building. A couple of weeks later, Keri dealt the final, devastating blow. . . .

I was in the cafeteria, the only neutral zone in our working space, when Keri walked in with a co-worker. She caught my eye because her hair was no longer the same shade of Summer Blonde as mine, but instead displayed an unnatural, ashen-brown tone. I turned my eyes down, remembering to play cool and aloof as I focused on selecting items for my lunch. Keri and her companion approached the end of the line, talking loud enough for me to hear every word.

"Did I tell you?" she asked excitedly. "I'm dating a new guy. Yeah, I met him last year with Debi. His name is Peter."

10: Big Sisters

Losing Keri as my best and only friend had two drawbacks. First, the obvious lack of a troublemaking pal. Second, the loss of transportation to get to that trouble. Being stubborn and resourceful, I decided to walk to the only place I felt safely uncomfortable going alone, Pier 11. Keri and I had discovered the local wine and beer joint a few months earlier, and thanks to mail order fake IDs, had easily gained access to this rock 'n' roll-blasting gift from heaven.

At first, the dance floor intimidated me with its shaking and shimmying, so instead I hung out at the air hockey tables. In no time, I became quite the champ at slamming a plastic puck into my unsuspecting opponent's goal. I guess you could have called me an air hockey shark. For me, it was simply a way to flirt, get comfortable around boys, and stay supplied with cheap beer.

Eventually, I gave in to an invitation to venture into the bump and grind zone. Memory of the guy who offered up the proposal has disappeared into oblivion, but the song remains firmly imprinted—"Brown Sugar" by the Rolling Stones.

"Brown sugar, how come you dance so good? Brown sugar, just like a young girl should." (If you're a lyrics freak, I apologize, but that's what I thought Mick said.)

My heart pounded during those three minutes, as much from wiggling my butt with the other couples as from the sheer terror of conquering my first dance.

It's hard to say if my high was alcohol- or endorphin-induced, but I fell in love. So I said good-bye to the boys on the game side of the club and hello to those who hung around the perimeter of the wooden floor. That's how I met Jack.

An older guy, easily forty or maybe even fifty, Jack was cool and mixed effortlessly with the younger crowd. One night I whined to him about how my life at home sucked and how I had to climb out my bedroom window and then walk across residential streets to get to the club. He offered the perfect solution—move out—and he happened to have a room I could rent for only one hundred dollars a month. I couldn't pack my things fast enough. Although I was only seventeen, my parents made no attempt to stop me. The following Saturday afternoon, I loaded everything I had been given so far in life, including my black-and-white TV, into a friend of Jack's beat-up Toyota truck.

My first post-parents' home was conveniently located just off 17th Street in Costa Mesa. A quick walk led to the bus that took me to work and the paycheck I used to support my freedom-loving self. The combination of easy access to guys—thanks to swaying my hips on the dance floor—and a place to take them led to a string of free-and-easy sexual conquests. (And more hot pink stars in my datebook calendar!) Jack didn't care. He was totally cool about getting laid and said the sounds coming from my room were a turn on. Besides, he always had a girl in his bed, generally more than one.

A couple of weeks after moving into Jack's House of Sin, the balance between responsible employee and party-happy teen tipped in the direction of nightlife. I even started nodding off at my keypunch-card typewriter, so one day I simply decided not to get up and catch the bus.

I adapted easily to the new routine: drink and dance until two a.m., find someone to fool around with until dawn, then sleep all day. Thanks to the State of California and unemployment, I made enough money to pay the rent. Pier 11 offered additional financial assistance: an under-the-table job.

By that time I'd gotten to know the manager, and though he wasn't the slightest bit fooled by my five-dollar Texas driver's license, he was cool with me being there, as long as I stayed focused on the pizza bar and didn't touch the booze. One night, while serving slices, I met Margie.

Older than me—then again, everyone in the club was older than me—Margie possessed the perfect blend of tall, thin, and wild. With waist-length blond hair, perfect Iowa corn-fed skin and big, brown eyes, she spelled "fox" and used her combination of innocence and temptress to attract the guys. Margie didn't go after just any guy; she focused on the musicians who came to perform in our funky little club, preferably the lead singer.

Margie and I quickly became friends. However, it wasn't my charming personality that convinced her to befriend an under-aged, equally attractive potential competitor. It was drugs.

Ordinarily I didn't offer my hard-earned party gifts to girls, but Margie had such a way with the band, I knew it would be advantageous to hang out with her.

It's amazing how often the long-haired hippy drummers, or guitarists, or bassists, who'd scarcely glanced my shy and tongue-tied way, would come around once they knew I had a small, folded-paper envelope filled with cocaine. My inner good girl would sometimes comment on how pathetic it was to be filling noses just so I could mingle with the band, but a toot easily squelched that voice.

Before long, Margie and I developed a strong bond. I think she liked the idea of having a little sister, as we often told our prospective partners. I know I liked the idea of having a cool sibling.

Within three months of moving into one of the four bedrooms in Jack's no-rules house, it became obvious the time had come to move on. It's not that I didn't like Jack; he was an easygoing guy—a bit too easygoing—as once summer and its wave of beach bums hit our coastal town, my previously quiet, though quirky, home became an outright flop house.

Although I had the privacy of my own room, complete with a keyed lock on the door, I still had to venture into the public zones to use the bathroom and kitchen. When I started stepping over bodies strewn across the living room floor, and conversations in the kitchen routinely began with, "Do you live here?" I said, "So long."

Margie came to my rescue. She and another girl, Suzanne, shared a two-bedroom apartment on the other, grittier side of town. At first the landlady didn't like the idea of me moving in—she, like the Pier 11 manager, didn't buy my line about being of legal age—but this time Suzanne claimed me as a younger sister, so the move got sanctioned. Although I had to give up a space of my own in exchange for squeezing my bed and a box of clothes into the dining room, at least I knew my roommates—or thought I did. After I settled in, I learned about the ladies' love of bikers, and I don't mean the peddle-it-yourself kind.

11: Biker Chick

Both Margie and Suzanne enjoyed puttin', so in addition to hanging out at Pier 11, with its middle-class surfer types, we would walk the few short blocks from our home to a biker bar called Finnegan's Rainbow. I even gave up my job at Pier 11 in exchange for one as a waitress in the leather-clad beer-drinkers' dive. In fact, I celebrated my eighteenth birthday with a tray in hand, though I had to tell everyone I was turning twenty-two. In many respects, I felt a lot older than that, in large part due to an innocence-crushing event that occurred a few weeks before my coming of age.

Friday night. I walked in the door and flopped down on the baby-blue sofa, exhausted from my first night on the job. Five hours of weaving through hordes of thirsty customers—laden with pitchers of Coors or Budweiser—had taken its toll. Not to mention the pinches, slaps on the butt, and outright rude comments that were meant to be seductive in a scene I tried to brush off. So when Margie told me to get up, we had dates on the way, I was less than enthusiastic.

"Dates? I'm tired. It's late. I just want to go to sleep."

"Too bad. The guys are headed over, and they're bringing along someone for you."

So off we went, each straddling the back of a Harley Davidson. Margie and Suzanne had cute guys, guys they wanted to wrap their arms around as we sped off into the dark night. I had the leftover. No way my arms could wrap around Grumpy. No way I wanted to wrap my arms around that two-ton, aptly named, scary guy. But I did feel boldly rebellious, in defiance of my step-dad, who'd taught us to be cautious of bikers.

"Keep your eyes forward," he'd warn when we'd come near them on the freeway. I could feel the fear in his voice. I often wondered what would happen if I did glance over from our Ford station wagon.

Now I wasn't only making eye contact, I was right there in the middle of a small, but intimidating, pack. Before long, we attracted the local heat.

Margie hissed, "You stay here," as she joined the guys and Suzanne by the policeman's car.

"IDs, please."

Oh, shit, I thought, *I'm in trouble now.* A fake ID is one thing for a bar that wants cute girls to serve beer; it's a whole other thing with the law.

"What about hers?" the cop questioned while he frisked me with his eyes.

"Oh, that's my little sister," Suzanne responded. "We're on our way home now."

And while home would have been the best place on earth, instead we ended up back on the hogs, rumbling into the unknown. Within thirty minutes or so we arrived at the cute bikers' house. A two-bedroom, "guys" place, complete with filthy bathroom and a garage full of motorcycle parts.

Between shots and beers I learned about Panheads, Knuckleheads, Shovelheads, and other Harley information that might come in handy the next time I was on a ride and needed to sound less like a naïve young chick.

As alcohol continued flowing into the pre-dawn hours, the discussion turned to pompous, tough-guy rhetoric unlike anything I had heard before and thankfully since. It sickened me, listening to those drunk animals one-upping each other with stories of violence and sexual abuse. Were they trying to impress or intimidate? And were the stories for us girls or their own vile pride?

Eventually, talk gave way to kisses and grinding to the rock 'n' roll rhythms on the well worn, black leather sofa. Well, at least for the other girls it did. I tried my best to stay a safe distance from Grumpy, choosing a thread-bare recliner and *Easyrider* magazine for my entertainment.

Suzanne disappeared from the living room first, weaving down the brown shag carpet hallway with her pony-tailed companion. Fear gripped my belly as I realized where things were headed. I pulled Margie into the bathroom and pleaded with her to get me home.

"You'll be fine," she assured me, adjusting her makeup. "Just close your eyes. Grumpy will bring you back in the morning."

"The morning, no fucking way!" I stated boldly. "One way or the other, I'm going home now!"

Margie looked away from her image and focused on mine. "These aren't the kind of guys you tell what to do. If you're smart, you'll keep quiet and go with him."

Holy shit! I didn't want to spend the night with the guy, but I also saw a tinge of fear in Margie's bloodshot eyes. My momentary defiance changed to alarm, as the reality of the situation hit me; I didn't have a choice. I became a prisoner, with no reprieve.

"Come on," Grumpy commanded, announcing our departure.

Memories of the quick ride to my abductor's place have faded from memory, but his simple, studio apartment is stubbornly visible.

Standing motionless just inside the front door, I could see a double bed lengthwise along the standard white wall, its slotted wood headboard like bars on a jail cell. A small, sparse kitchen with white Formica counters opened to my left. From there, a pass-through opened into the main room, where I could see two large airbrushed paintings of choppers and their riders. The only redeeming thing about the place was its cleanliness, but that didn't stop the bubbling up of sheer terror. I was trapped. Trapped in a fat, revolting man's apartment. And I knew sex wasn't far off. No way out of that either.

The image still haunts me. Me lying on my back. Him hoisting his gigantic bulk over my chest. My arms pinned at my side. Nowhere to turn. His butt momentarily suffocating, before he lifts his hips. Then his dick down my throat. Totally helpless, completely unable to say what's screaming in my head.

No! Stop! Get off me! Take me home!

In reality, I complied. I sucked his cock, gagging as he thrust it down my unwilling throat. And then I let him fuck me. Kissing him was the hardest part. If I could've simply been an orifice, it might have been easier. There certainly wasn't any fantasy of romance. I was a robot, a machine, doing the deed.

Reliving that horrifying nightmare prompts me to once again step into the shaman's world of shape shifting, this time into a tigress. She lives within, where she paces back and forth—until now. As I step back in time, she's free, I'm free. . . .

I bite down on his erection and spit it across the room. Powerful claws rip across his stunned face, then throw him up against his white-trash paintings. He slides down the wall, landing on the multi-tone beige carpet in a whimpering, bloody, defenseless pile.

Oh yes, a part of me likes retaliation. The tigress finds satisfaction in the gore. Perhaps I even walk over and pee on the motionless form before turning and strolling across the room, where one push of my powerful feline body breaks through the door.

When I step into the brisk night air, I transform back into Debi, the seventeen-year-old who got herself into a bad situation, but knew how to get out of it.

The truth is I spent the night in a living hell, passing the early morning hours staring at the details of his eerie paintings with their wild-eyed bikers. To this day, that artist's style brings a clenched jaw and knotted gut. Eventually the phone rang, awakening Grumpy and signaling time to reconvene with the girls. *Finally,* I thought, *freedom,* as we climbed back onto his Shovelhead—or was it Flathead—chopper.

The hangout house appeared even more disturbing by daylight, but the girls didn't seem to mind. They looked refreshed and quite happy after nights of great sex with their dudes. My focus remained the same: how to get home, a topic I brought up to Margie as soon as we were alone.

"Are you ready to go yet?"

"Ah, come on. We're just getting started. It's Saturday. Relax."

Relax? Was she crazy? Had she looked at my date? Had she listened to my date? Did she honestly think I was enjoying myself?

"Come on. I have to work tonight. I want to get home and take a nap."

"Nap? You don't need a nap," she said lightly. "Take this," as she handed over a little white pill.

I popped the speed into my mouth, washing it down with the first beer of the day. *Here we go again*, I thought, letting the drugs and alcohol alter my brain.

Before long, the big, fun plans for the day revealed themselves: more alcohol and pool at a local bar. Looking back, I'm grateful the plans didn't include a "run," taking the motorcycles off for a day-or-longer adventure. As we once again rode into the bright, sunny day, I looked for landmarks, trying my best to figure out where we were. Although the streets were a blur of unfamiliar names, I knew we were still relatively close to my coastal community.

Once in their hangout, we sat around, smoked cigarettes, played pool, and of course, drank beer. A jukebox blasted out the only music it could, rock 'n' roll. As the afternoon in that smoke-filled, windowless structure lumbered on, I started up my hushed nagging and moaning.

"I want to go home. Why can't you talk the guys into taking me home?"

My pleas went unacknowledged. Margie and Suzanne couldn't care less about my plight. As time passed, my frustration built. I had to be at work by nine p.m., and as crazy as it sounds, I felt a sense of obligation that outweighed the fear of my captors. I thought for sure my responsibility to the bikers at home would be a viable reason for release, but when I voiced my logic to everyone, it only brought laughter.

Grumpy looped his hefty arm around my waist and pulled me in for a kiss before stating, "You're not going anywhere, little lady."

I truly began to fear I would never again know freedom. To make matters worse—if that were possible—the combined lack of sleep and lack of food brought on the most excruciating headache I had ever experienced. I felt as though someone had locked my jaw in a vise and placed a red hot poker in my right ear.

As the sun sank low in the sky, I knew I had to take action. It wasn't an impulse move; it probably took me half an hour of inner debate to muster up the courage.

Just do it, the voice of reason urged. *Walk out the door.*

But what if they see me, the scared little girl responded. *That would be bad.*

No worse than sitting here all night, reason responded. *You have to get out. You have to get to work.*

Oh, but my head hurts so bad. How can I possibly go to work? the weak one whined.

While the inner debate continued, I made physical progress toward the propped-open exit. First a seat further down the bar. *Good, they didn't notice me shifting.* After another slow motion stretch of time, I got up and casually wandered over to the cigarette machine, just to the left of the slice of sunlight and its promise of freedom. *Good, still no reaction.* My heart pounded, sending stabs of agony through my head, but inner guidance felt encouraged.

"See, they aren't paying attention."

Finally, like taking a plunge into a cold, dark lake, I slipped out.

I'd never run so fast. Being drunk and in pain was no distraction. I ran for my life. I knew west from the glowing orange sky and figured if I ran long enough I'd run into a major road. Fortunately, I came to Harbor Boulevard, a familiar name and route home. I brazenly stuck out my thumb and pleaded with God, *"Please make someone stop before they come looking for me."*

Thankfully, my prayers were answered right away. As I climbed into the vehicle from heaven, I risked a glance back, once again praying my escape remained a secret. The street was empty. I could finally relax—as much as my throbbing head would allow.

I got home at about eight thirty, just enough time to pop some pain killers Suzanne had lying around, shower, and change clothes before walking the quarter mile to work. Once there, I forced my overly adrenalized brain to stay focused on drink orders, well, beer brands. I knew I had risked big trouble, but I refused to let my mind play with any repercussions from the day's events. Besides, I'd gotten a taste of stubborn tenacity and I liked the power it gave me; I simply refused to let fear get a stranglehold.

"Do you realize how close you came to being turned out?" Margie demanded when I saw her at home later that night. Thankfully, she and Suzanne were free of their hard-core companions. As much as I wanted to release the fury once again pounding at my skull, the compliant, down-trodden aspect simply bowed her head in remorse.

"What's that?" I asked meekly.

"That's where they bring the whole club together and do whatever they want for as long as they want."

I knew whatever they wanted included many forms of rape, and a wave of shaky relief flowed through me.

"Oh."

"We begged for you," Margie yelled. "We had to convince three pissed off and insulted guys that you weren't worth their trouble. No one has ever walked out on them. They wanted to call the gang. It was a miracle we could convince them you were a waste of time. It took us hours to calm them down."

"Thank you," was all I could muster, as hot tears of humiliation filled my eyes and fell silently to the floor.

At the time, I figured Margie and Suzanne's recap of how they had talked the enraged men out of retaliation had been exaggerated. And while I was grateful to the girls for their skillful negotiations, I blamed them for getting me into the mess in the first place, though I never pleaded my case. The bold, courageous young woman, who earlier that day had taken matters into her own hands, had once again retreated. Decades later, I accepted what a truly close call I'd had with a pack of notorious outlaw bikers.

As I recall the gravity of my abduction and the terror my body still holds, the inner voices are once again prompted.

I really am blessed, says a wise, gracious woman. *It's clear I was being watched over by angels.*

You should never have been in a situation like that in the first place, counters a critical aspect. *And what about that fantasy of turning into a tigress? It was powerful, yes, but gruesomely violent.*

Ah yes, the fantasy. The power of the tigress. The rage of the tigress. The ease with which she struck, then walked away, apparently unaffected. Yet in the midst of that vision was something else, someone else.

I caught a glimpse of him as I threw the bloodied body across the room. Over there by the bar, next to the kitchen—a little boy. An innocent, pudgy-faced boy. He doesn't want to be there either. The look on his face tells me he's also afraid of this tough guy, that he too is horrified by the abuse. Yet I sense he's tied to the wild lifestyle and can't walk away as I can.

You need to forgive, speaks inner wisdom.

No, is my first response. *I'm still way too angry. I want the power of my rage.*

Can you see you have stepped into a trap? wisdom questions softly.

Yes, I reluctantly admit. *I see I'm responding in a heartless way. I see I'm matching fear with violence. This is the same energy I sensed underlying the bikers' stories of aggression. But power through intimidation is a tricky thing to neutralize.*

As I sit with the suggestion to forgive, the image evolves. I focus on the little boy, my assailant turned victim, at ten years old, before he turned grumpy. As I watch, another child enters the scene. This time it's me. Me at about the same age. These children don't hold any resentment or grudge for each other. They are simply saddened and confused by the whole situation.

Continuing to gaze inward, these innocent yet powerful aspects become the focus of a bright golden light. I recognize it as the healing presence of Christ and the angels.

The sensation in my body—my adult, present day, witnessing the inner drama, physical body—is palpable. My solar plexus radiates heat, heat that I know is powerfully transformative. I sit with the warming sensation as it gently melts long-held anguish and fear. After a few moments, I shift my attention back to the inner vision and step into the scene just vacated by the vengeful feline. In this magical world, I am able to wave my hand and transport myself and the ten-year-olds to a beautiful, sun-drenched meadow.

Here we sit, surrounded by acres of brilliant, green grass dotted with wildflowers dancing in all colors of spring. For a time, we quietly watch the butterflies and bees flit amongst the magnificent array.

I don't know what to say to these children who will endure such hardships as they grow older. In some odd, otherworldly way, they hold more wisdom than I do, and they certainly embrace a purity I thought was long gone.

It's okay, Debra, says the younger me, reaching out her small hand to mine. *We're okay,* she continues, nodding in the direction of our young friend who has gone off to explore the field.

You think your behavior drove me away, split me off, but I've been here waiting all along. I'm still very much a part of you. Sometimes you get so dark, so depressed. It's not good. Come on, lighten up. Just because you don't play as much as you used to, doesn't mean you don't know how. Stop fighting the fun. Let's skip with the butterflies. You'll see; it's easy to be free.

And with that, I rose and followed my innocence into a delightful dance of grace.

12: Hollywood

Shortly after celebrating my eighteenth birthday, it became obvious I needed a change. So, like many teenage girls who've dreamt of a star-studded future, I decided to head to Hollywood.

The glamour-filled city was familiar to me; my father worked in the land of wonder. He even offered to help me move. Unfortunately, his idea of help included borrowing a friend's plane and flying the fifty miles to Orange County, limiting my cargo to what would fit in the back of a twin engine Cessna: two boxes.

Carefully organizing the same parcels I had transported to Margie and Suzanne's, I reviewed my necessities: low-slung jeans, cut-off shorts, an assortment of midriff-baring tops, a few sundresses, and of course, more than enough pairs of shoes. The rest of my worldly belongings remained at Jack's, sadly never to be seen again.

Once in the land of endless possibility, my father set me up in a basement studio on Cahuenga Boulevard, paying my first month's rent. He even gave me the same twin-bed corner unit my brother and I had slept in as children. My mom's mother helped too, passing on the plates, bowls, cups, and saucers that had previously lived in the back of the cabinet next to the Frigidaire. For as long as I could remember, those teal-blue favorites had been in safekeeping, waiting for me to take ownership.

"Everyone needs a nice, matching set of dishes," Grandma proclaimed as she included an assortment of silverware, glasses, and cookware.

So there I was with a bed to sleep in and dishes to eat off of; what more could a girl want? Well, some way to occupy my time would have been nice. As fate would have it, my father supplied that as well, in the form of the out-of-town movie shoot with that smart-ass logistics manager and her "Incest is best" comment.

It turned out being a stand-in was the most boring job I'd had to date. I so wanted to explore the dense pine forest and unharnessed power of the Stanislaus River, but after one very loud scolding by the director, I kept my ass firmly planted in the thick of the slow-speed action. Every hour or two I'd be called in to sit for a few minutes of lighting measurements the stars couldn't be expected to do, then I'd go back to daydreaming.

Often my fantasies circled around one of the movies stars—let's call him Victor. I knew him as a doctor from a popular TV show, and though he didn't play that character in the movie, my cheeks flushed and my heart beat a bit faster when he was on set.

With so many idle minutes, I ran a lot of imaginings through my horny young mind. I even asked my father for assistance in attracting the star's attention, and he came up with a simple, direct plan—he would invite Victor out to dinner with us.

Excited about dining with a real, live, television star, I dressed in my favorite skintight bell-bottoms and a cute little peasant top. Unlike the presenter of my first kiss, David, this actor appeared on a show I actually watched, so I knew others would recognize my "date" as well. I felt special as we walked into the small-town, upscale restaurant, noticing some of the guests turn their heads and whisper between themselves.

After taking charge of the wine list, my father put on his own best act, making quite a performance out of selecting, sniffing, swirling, sipping, spitting, and finally settling on the first bottle for our enjoyment. I wanted to crawl under the table and hide, but did my best to gently support him by feigning interest in each and every word.

Once past my father's dissertation on vintages and varietals, I enjoyed listening to Victor talk about himself and his work in

Hollywood. I made sure to throw in just the right amount of focused eye contact, smiles, and the clincher: head-tossed-back, light-hearted laughter.

By eighteen, I had the innocent, yet alluring, flirtatious act down. Add in a few glasses of wine—not to mention a father who didn't care about my fake ID—and I became an undeniable seductress. Victor didn't have any choice but to fall prey to my charm, not that he wanted an alternative. Our evening flowed smoothly—much like the multiple bottles of burgundy—until the waiter delivered the check.

I fully expected my father to pick up the tab since he'd offered the invitation, but the discreet black leather case lay ignored for an unbearable amount of time. Eventually, the conversation grew awkward, laboring to fill the gap. My father even had the audacity to order another bottle, upping the ante in the men's who's-got-the-power game. If I'd had the ability, I would have taken care of the bill myself.

Our actor friend finally broke the stalemate, briefly glancing at the ticket before dramatically counting out four crisp one-hundred-dollar bills.

I was mortified. Even though I had decidedly plotted the outcome of the meal to include an invitation back to his room, at that point I felt obligated. So, along with dinner, the TV doctor bought the daughter's services. Basically, my father pimped me out, though at the time I didn't have a label for what had happened.

The me of today is once again prompted to stand up and have her say. I imagine going back to the candle-lit restaurant to confront the man who had just caused me such embarrassment. . . .

"What the hell! Don't you have any manners? You invited Victor out to dinner. That means you pay. And the way you chose the most expensive bottles of wine. What a pompous asshole. I'm ashamed of you."

By then, in my imaginary world, Victor has discreetly excused himself, while I continue to vent.

"I wanted Victor to see us as classy. Instead I feel cheap, like you expected him to buy me along with the meal. Was that your intention? Do you have any idea how that makes me feel?"

The reality is, he didn't. Although I don't have any medical proof, I believe my father is a sociopath, incapable of understanding the effect of his actions. His world has always revolved around himself and what he can get from others. So his behavior in the restaurant wasn't new to me, but it was the first time I felt directly entangled.

The wisdom of hindsight also allows me to have compassion for my eighteen-year-old self. Oddly, it's not the lack of sexual boundaries between my father and me causing the tension around this memory, but the feeling of being devalued. I was a commodity, a pawn in his game. Or maybe he thought we were playing together, my prize being the captured prey. Today, the error of enlisting this man into my scheme is obvious; back then I simply didn't know any better. My world, and my self-esteem, revolved around sexual conquests.

I'd like to say being with Victor was magnificent, that he was a skilled lover, living up to and exceeding my fantasies, worth the time and effort that went into the hunt. But in reality, the post-meal event left me hollow. My first actor score was a big letdown, not at all the sparkly star with exclamation points I'd hoped to draw in my calendar.

After completing my role as a stand-in, I returned to my one-room apartment and achieved a whole new level of boredom. That is, until Margie and her 1967 Ford Thunderbird Annabelle decided to join me in Hollywood for the next phase of my life's adventure. Not only did I once again have a friend, I had transportation. It was a fabulous change.

I loved having my wannabe sister back by my side, and this time I didn't have to share her with Suzanne. On her first night in town, we curled our hair, put on makeup, and headed out in Annabelle, searching for fun. It didn't take long for us to discover what soon became our "after dark" home.

The Starwood was the hottest place in town. It had two huge rooms with vast dance floors and a collection of great pinball machines, which I enjoyed when not dancing. There were also multiple bars, including one that served amazingly delicious eggplant parmesan sandwiches. But the best part of that West Hollywood haven were the live bands—good ones like Journey and Bob Seger, and yet to be discovered local ones, too. Of course, Margie and I both got jobs there immediately.

The club provided the essentials: free-flowing alcohol, drugs, sex, and rock 'n' roll—complete with a paycheck—until New Year's Eve. That's when I chose a solo spin on the dance floor over distributing my full tray of drink orders. It wasn't my fault. The band took a break, and all those partiers, who'd been standing around enjoying the amplified tunes, had scattered like drunks at two a.m. No way was I going to search the club, chasing them all down. Besides, my favorite song came on.

Losing my job also meant losing my insider status. While the bouncers all knew me and let me wander the private upstairs dressing room area, without my cocktail waitress position I was just another lustful groupie hoping for access to the band—a most humiliating situation. But I still had my charm and drug-induced confidence, so job or no job, I seduced many a band member after they left the stage.

Then there were the everyday guys, the ones Margie and I sometimes brought home to our twin beds. We'd gotten used to the lack of privacy in our hundred-square-foot room, and it wasn't unusual for either of us to be lulled to sleep by soft moans of pleasure, like the sounds I drifted off to that pivotal night.

"No, stop!" Margie said, breaking both the mood and my drunken slumber.

"Ah, come on, baby. Let me go down on you."

"No. I don't like it."

Don't like it, I thought. *How strange. How is it Margie doesn't like the sensation of a warm, explorative tongue?* My pondering thoughts were interrupted by his next request.

"Well, how about your roommate? How about I slip into bed with her?"

It's not like he was requesting a threesome; he simply wanted to shift ninety degrees and repay the pleasure he'd received from her. To me, his question made sense.

"Fine," Margie snapped. "Do whatever you want."

Oral-sex guy turned out to be very good at his craft. In retrospect, it probably would have been a good idea to keep my findings to myself, but quiet pleasure wasn't my strong point. After our guest took me to repeated heights of ecstasy, he disappeared into the night, leaving me alone with Margie and her fury.

"How could you?" she demanded, flipping on the lamp to glare at me.

"What? All he did was go down on me."

"He was mine!"

"Yeah, but you didn't want him."

"That doesn't matter," she snapped, turning off the light. "He came home with me."

Perplexed by Margie's anger, I clung to my inner defense—*it's just sex, what's the big deal?*

The following day, stubbornly refusing to admit I'd done anything wrong, I went mute, allowing silent tension to fill our small home. Margie's retaliation hit deep; she found a new girl to not only hang out with, but invite over. A couple of nights later, fed up with their banter and chilling attitude towards me, I took a taxi to the club. At two a.m.—with the man *du jour* by my side—I came home to find Margie and my replacement firmly planted in each of the two beds. Ignoring my presence, they stared intently at the television, and I once again found myself lacking the guts to speak up.

Internally I yelled, *Hey, this is <u>my</u> place. Get the fuck out.* But instead of facing the woman scorned, I let my fear of confrontation push me out and into a cheap motel down the street.

The next day, after saying so long to another now nameless one-night stand, I pondered the situation. I'd created the perfect "poor me" scenario—alone, streets of Hollywood, what's a good girl to do?

I felt scared not having a place to call home. The guy who worked the light booth at the Starwood told me I could sleep up there, but that meant I'd have to sleep with him, so I kept his offer as a last resort.

I spent my first homeless night sitting in a local coffee house, sipping endless refills. The next night, I found a guy who wanted to take me home. And while it was nice to once again sleep in a bed, I had no intention of making him a habit.

The third night, I stayed with a nice young girl I knew from the club, but that was really awkward. She still lived with her parents, and I felt like an alien in that happy, well-adjusted home, though I was able to run my not-so-fresh, bright yellow, paisley-print dress and matching yellow underwear through the washer and dryer.

The fourth night, still afraid to go home and deal with the squatters situation, the hand of fate once again touched my life.

13: Poker Face

    My next advancement in the world of sin came from a twenty-something criminal in training. His name was Frankie, of course. With impeccable pinstripe suit, crisp white collar, and enough open buttons to expose his spattering of wavy chest hair, he had the mid-seventies gangster style down. I knew Frankie from the Starwood, though I'd never before been attracted to his small, slender frame, slicked-back hair and New Jersey accent. But he needed a date for an all-night poker party, and I needed something to occupy those moonlit hours.

    It was after midnight as my companion skillfully navigated his black Lincoln Continental through the narrow, twisting roads of the Hollywood Hills. One meticulously manicured hand palmed the steering wheel, while the other slid a polished-steel revolver across the car's bench seat.

    "We've got a system," he said, nodding to his equally cool partner in the back seat, "but just in case, stick this in your purse. And be careful, it's loaded."

    Surprised by the heaviness of the handgun, I nervously slipped it into my purse, wondering what the hell the night had in store.

    The ornately carved entry door opened into a grand, two-story, polished-marble foyer. In the room to our left, the floor to ten-foot-high ceiling windows showcased the lights of the city below. It was the kind of house I felt the need to whisper in. On the wall to the right of the twinkling lights, two ladies, dressed in backless evening gowns, stood warming their hands in front of an equally grand fireplace. I glanced down at my own floor-length, empire-waist sundress, and wished for something more elegant, but the setting refused to let me shift into feeling "less than." With a wave of gratitude, I thought, *At least I got to wash it today.*

Frankie interrupted my silent appreciation of the generous surroundings, saying, "I'll get you a drink," before he and his game-rigging buddy disappeared down the hall.

I stepped onto the white shag carpet of the living room, catching the attention of the two perfectly made-up, bored faces, but neither offered a hello. Fighting off my you-don't-belong-here voice, I quietly surveyed the diversity of world art lining the shelves closest to me. Within a few minutes, Frankie returned, handing me a beautiful crystal flute of champagne.

"Feel free to wander," he said, waving his arm toward the gently curving staircase. "There are more girls upstairs. I'll be in the dining room, but don't interrupt me." Frankie was several steps away when he spun on the heel of his shiny black loafer and returned to whisper in my ear, "And hold onto your purse."

Bored with the lack of conversation in the living room, I decided to explore the upper floor and its promise of more guests. The laughter of the other required, but cast off, dates met my ears when I reached the top of the stairs.

Double doors opened into the softly lit room where a group of beautiful, model-worthy women gathered. Some stood in small clusters, while a few others lounged on a pair of low-slung, cream sofas. Hoping it would release the tightness in my chest, I took a deep breath, straightened my shoulders, and told myself, *You can fit in,* as I stepped into the space.

This room also had a spectacular view of the city lights, but the image on the right side wall is what caught my attention. There, on a screen large enough for a mini movie theater, appeared an enormous erection being thrust in and out of an equally oversized pussy. The sound was muted, but that didn't stop me from being simultaneously embarrassed and fascinated by my first viewing of a clearly X-rated movie.

I certainly knew about skin flicks, and on several occasions had even been invited to join my father for an evening's viewing. Those offers from dear old dad had been easy to dodge with a "no, thank you," but there was no denying this larger-than-life display. From the heat rushing across my face, I knew I'd gone beet red. And my jaw dropped, too.

"Hi," said a voice with an English-sounding accent.

Grateful for an excuse to divert my eyes from the wall of sex, I turned to see a woman with long red hair and an easy smile. "Come on and have a seat. It's going to be a long night."

I made myself comfortable opposite the friendly woman, a placement that allowed me to keep the corner of my eye on the action—I mean, heck, I was curious. Thinking I came off as hip and nonchalant, I chatted casually, though that screen held a magnetic draw for my attention.

There I found amazingly impossible images, like a woman sucking a massive cock and miraculously fitting the whole thing down her throat. If I'd been alone, I would have studied the display, or if I were bold, I would have asked the ladies for pointers on performing tricks like that. But I didn't want to appear naïve, so despite the combination of arousal and discomfort churning in my belly, I acted cool, with a drink in one hand and a cigarette in the other. Only now does it seem odd that porn played for us girls, while the guys lost money in the other room.

The game finally came to an end as the sky over those infamous Hollywood Hills began to blaze with a shifting palette of peach and pink. Since my guys were successful in their plan to leave with more cash than they'd brought, we celebrated with breakfast. Sharing a meal with crooked gamblers didn't really interest me, but it was better than nothing. Besides, I was hungry. While enjoying our hot coffee and early morning eggs, I told Frankie of my homeless plight.

"I know someone who can help you out," he offered. "Her name is Danni. I'll give her a call when we're finished eating."

That's how I came to meet a real-life madam.

14: The New Girl

Danni's apartment was simple: two bedrooms and two baths separated by a living room, dining room, and kitchen. The standard-issue rental furniture was functional and relatively comfortable—nothing ornate. Any home-based business could have been housed in that unassuming second-story unit overlooking North Sweetzer Avenue.

The morning of our first meeting, the atmosphere seemed harmless enough, normal even, as we enjoyed a cup of coffee around the small, wood-tone breakfast table. Frankie had explained the situation: I needed both a job and a place to live. Danni offered both.

After saying good-bye to our hoodlum friend, the busty brunette leaned against the closed front door, barking her first order. "Stand up. Let me get a better look at you." I felt myself blush, but followed her instruction, doing my best impression of a runway model's walk and spin.

"Okay," she said, "that'll do." Noticing a smile as she returned to her chair, I guessed I had passed the first test. Once again seated next to this woman who I guessed was only a few years my senior, I remained quiet, nervously matching her actions by taking another sip of the by then lukewarm coffee.

"My motto is simple," she continued, raising her dark brown eyes to focus directly on my overtired and bloodshot version, "Get 'em in, get 'em off, get 'em out." Suppressing a giggle—and trying not to choke—I forced my brain to focus.

"And cash only, unless I've told you otherwise. You want to move them into the bedroom as quickly as you can, don't let them pull you into long conversations. Get the money up-front, before they get undressed. Once you've got regulars, you can lighten up on that rule, but for now, cash up-front.

"It's sixty if all they're getting is head. If you go all the way, it's a hundred. Sometimes it'll be more, if they've asked for something special, but I'll let you know ahead of time. The split is 60/40. You get the sixty."

"Okay," I tentatively nodded in agreement.

"Alright," she continued, simultaneously standing up and pushing her short brown hair behind her ears. "Let's get on with your first lesson."

We walked to the linen closet outside the room I would soon call home, and Danni opened the cabinet to display its contents: white towels organized by size and a neat stack of small, clear, glass bowls.

"Get a clean washcloth and a bowl, and fill it with hot water—not too hot, it needs to feel good—and put them on the nightstand."

I picked up the items as instructed and stepped into the bath directly off the small hallway. Like the living room and kitchen, it was clean, but lacked any personal touches. Turning on the faucet, I tested the water's temperature while Danni leaned against the doorframe and continued talking.

"Most guys will strip immediately, though occasionally you'll help them along as part of the service. Don't get stuck in the details, just keep things moving."

Seeing that I had completed the first part of the task successfully, Danni turned and walked to the bedroom. I followed her into another efficient space, drying the outside of the bowl before setting it on the nightstand to the right of the full-sized bed.

"Once he's naked, have him sit down and lie back, or let him stand. The key is to have him think he's in charge; and to a degree, he is."

Taking the cloth from me, Danni dipped it into the bowl before once again speaking.

"Wring out the extra water and then give his penis a gentle cleaning. Be sure you fold back the skin, if he's got it, and don't forget under his balls. He should think it's a sensual experience as you freshen him up, but really, you're checking for disease."

I don't recall any instructions for what to do if I did find anything out of the ordinary, and honestly, while I'd had a lot of sexual partners already, I'd certainly never inspected "it" that closely before. Just the thought of performing the initial examination made me skittish.

While I hate to admit it, part of me was excited about the prospect of being a prostitute—the perfect calling for the bad girl. I also guessed my father—though I never told him of the career move—would be proud. Several times he had suggested I consider a job as a masseuse, hinting I'd be good with the "special" services they offered. I had ignored his recommendations, not wanting to admit I knew what he was talking about.

Later that afternoon—following my basic training and a refreshing nap—Danni announced, "Your first trick is on the way over. It's actually two men; you'll take one, I'll take the other."

"How will I know which one is mine?" I asked hesitantly, noticing my stomach cringe with anxious flutters.

"Oh, don't worry," Danni replied with a savvy calm. "One of them will pick you, or pick me; it's easy enough."

The security buzzer rang and Danni pushed the call button, allowing my first customer and his buddy access to our building. A couple of minutes later I met our clients, two middle-aged, average looking men, dressed in slacks and sport shirts.

"This is Debi," Danni said brightly. "She's my newest."

We exchanged some small talk, standing by the now closed door, but it was clear why they were there. A service had been offered and a service would be performed, without the foolishness of flirting, or dinner and a movie. In a way it was refreshing, except for the fact the men were my father's age.

Danni cut our aimless chatting short, asking, "Which one of you is interested in this fresh young blonde?"

With the older of the two in tow, I walked to my side of the apartment and closed the door separating it from the front room, motioning for my customer to head into the bedroom.

"I'll be right in," I said, stepping into the bathroom to prepare his cock bath. I stood at the sink for an extra minute, watching the warm water flow over my shaky hands, hoping it would soothe my anxiety. Knowing I couldn't keep the john waiting too long, I looked at myself in the mirror and smiled my best "you can do this" encouragement, before heading out.

"It's a hundred," I said, noticing the lack of confidence in my voice.

"You're under arrest," my trick replied.

The words struck me—a cold, hard, reality slap in the face. I immediately began to cry and wondered, *How could this be happening?* Danni's instructions hadn't included anything about police.

"I've never done this before," I managed to choke. "I just met Danni. I didn't have anyplace else to go. I lost my job."

The list of excuses poured out of me to the gray-haired, portly cop. "I don't want to be a prostitute. I just didn't know what else to do."

And it was true; I didn't want to be your standard, run-of-the-mill, street-walking whore, but call girl was a whole different ball game. Danni's teachings, earlier that day, had made it very clear—call girls were upper class.

I must have possessed the perfect blend of innocence and remorse, because the cop told me if I promised to leave and never again consider prostitution, he would let me go with a warning. But I knew, even as I heard the words, "I promise," come out of my mouth, that I had already gone too far into the world of taboo and sin to step back out.

The whole bust turned out to be in error, a case of mistaken identity. Danni wasn't the notorious madam they'd hoped for with their sting operation. Still, she didn't get off as easily as I did. Before being escorted out, she pulled me aside to whisper, "I'm leaving the door unlocked so you can keep an eye on the place for me. I'll be back as soon as I post bail."

Bewildered, I stood in the hallway, watching as my new roommate got carted off to jail. With wobbly steps, I moved in the opposite direction, faking my own exit, before returning to the scene of the "almost" crime.

In my fragile state—and needing to talk to someone who could help defuse my overflowing emotions—I called my mother. Given our lack of a nurturing connection, she was an odd choice, but nonetheless, I turned to her for support.

"Mom, yeah, it's me, Debi," my voice cracked into the phone. "Well, yes, I'm okay, but Mom, I was almost arrested. Yes . . . no . . . I'm okay. . . . no, I'm not going to jail.

"Well, you see, I met this new girl and was hanging out at her place.

"She had some friends stop by, well, honestly, Mom, I didn't know much about her, but it turns out she's a drug dealer and the police came to arrest her. Fortunately, they could see I wouldn't do that and they left me alone."

It's amazing how easily the story twisted into a form of defending my innocence. Most likely my mother didn't buy a word of my ruse, but she didn't challenge me; instead she came up with a reason for getting off the phone.

"Oh . . . okay, well I guess I'll talk to you later. Hug the kids for me. Okay . . . bye."

Although I didn't feel comforted by my mother, speaking to her did help dissipate the flood of adrenaline coursing through me.

15: Life at Danni's

Life at Danni's soon took on a routine flow—sex for money by day, give it away by night. An easy walk up Santa Monica Boulevard, the Starwood remained my favorite spot. Someone once asked me if I felt scared walking home alone at two a.m. I didn't. I figured there were enough girls interested in drive-by dates. I kept my eyes focused and my stride direct. I was a call girl, not a streetwalker. I could easily snap, "No, thanks," to any offers that presented themselves. Danni remained completely in charge of the johns, stating who, when, and how much.

On one hand, my new life revolved around an idyllic flow of my favorite things—sex, drugs, and rock 'n' roll, with ample money to boot—but part of me didn't endorse the new form of employment. This puritanical aspect started a crusade, looking for others who agreed with her beliefs.

"I'm a call girl."

"Yeah? What's that like?"

My respondents, random men from the Starwood, always sounded intrigued. No one reacted with the disapproving scowl or desired lecture to match my internal voices:

Stop this behavior immediately! Go home, little girl. You don't belong in the world of sex and sin. Go to college, get a degree, meet some nice boy, get married, and have babies.

That's what the good girls were doing, or so I thought. Perhaps if I had taken my poll elsewhere, I would have received the advice I craved. But with time, and the little yellow pills Danni offered to help me relax, the sermon became an occasional easily dismissed whisper.

Although she supplied my happy pills, Danni didn't approve of being high for work. She ran a clean house, so for the most part, drugs and alcohol were limited to off hours.

I became quite adept at getting my own supply of mood-altering substances. It was the seventies and cocaine was plentiful. It seemed like everyone—or at least the crowd I hung out with—had a little paper envelope or small glass vial filled with white powder. I even wore a demitasse spoon around my neck, a calling card that clearly announced my love of the confidence-building drug. Its size, triple that of a standard coke spoon, was an obvious testament to my do-it-big lifestyle. To balance out the high of cocaine, I got ambitious in hunting out prescriptions for downers.

I'd consume massive amounts of coffee, then head to the free clinics around town, where I'd complain about not being able to relax. The doctors always came through with a scrip for my favorite hard core sedative, Rorer 714s. I even sold the popular Quaalude at the Starwood, five bucks per large white tablet. Quite often a "lude" customer—if he was cute—got a free bonus, in my special space.

One bare lightbulb dangled from the cobweb-covered ceiling of the Starwood's attic storage. Cases of scotch, bourbon, vodka, and everything else you need to stock a popular nightspot lined the open-beam, wooden walls—but I wasn't after the booze. I led my guests to an old, tired mattress that lay in a vacant area, behind a wall of beer. It's hard to say how many men I mounted on that naked bed.

Some nights I visited the dusty storeroom more than once. Although I didn't use the term, several of the guys I took there were mercy fucks, ones I figured didn't get any on a regular basis. With them, I felt more in control and less likely to be turned away, a fear I held with the self-assured, popular guys.

Those charity romps were always quickies, so I could get back to flirting with, and dancing for, the musicians. Often, the no-name patrons didn't know what hit them. They'd look bewildered as I'd yank them back to reality with an, "Okay, let's get back downstairs." I guess Danni's motto—get 'em in, get 'em off, get 'em out—followed me into free time.

Looking back, I see the telltale signs of addiction. But I actually thought having lots of sex was a good thing, that exposing the wild, free spirit within made me more likable and popular. There was nothing sacred about my free-flowing unions; they were definitely the hit-and-run variety.

At the time, I veered away from analyzing my behavior. Like a spinning top, I kept myself busy, constantly pulling my string to prevent the world from toppling over.

When lucky, I'd catch more than the eye of those rockers who hijacked my attention from the hip-height stage. They stayed in hotels like The Hyatt House up on Sunset Strip. That establishment—infamous in the rocker world, and aptly nicknamed the Riot House—was a definite step up from the storeroom. It's not that Danni didn't allow me to bring guys home. That was my rule: no mixing of work and pleasure.

The nights the soon-to-be-famous band members took me "home" were the best. I would captivate my lover of the moment with an easy charm and voracious sexual appetite, but I always felt uncomfortable and out of place the next morning. Without the drugs to boost my confidence, I was just a tongue-tied, shy young girl, afraid she had overstayed her welcome. Fortunately, most one- or two-night stands had their own ample supply of drugs and, like me, were anxious to start the day with a toot or a pill.

Unlike my one-hit-wonders of nightclub sex, I developed a core group of regulars at Danni's. Each had a distinctive preference. Being a good professional, I quickly learned not to confuse who liked what.

There were ass-men and tit-men, though the latter generally chose Danni over me. Some clients preferred lying back, while others liked to stand. There were also the doggy-style varieties, as well as penchants for top or bottom, and the sub-categories of facing forward or back, and legs up or down.

Of the guys who limited their pleasure to oral sex, some held my head, directing its bobbing up and down on their stiffness, while others worked my breasts or fingered me as supplemental fun. Some customers liked a bit of teeth on the balls, and a few enjoyed a finger probing up the rear—best not to confuse the tricks who liked these unconventional turn-ons with those wanting standard stimulation. Of course, through it all, I emitted finely honed sounds of passion that kept pace with their own escalating delight.

Occasionally, we'd get someone who simply wanted a non-judgmental audience, like the guy who folded himself in half and sucked himself off—I guessed he was into yoga. Sometimes we'd get actors or other famous customers. Danni tried to convince me that actors were good; but they weren't musicians. We never had musicians. Too bad.

Then there were the trades. I actually looked forward to their visits. We had one guy who bartered with evening gowns and another with shoes; whole afternoons were set aside for their calls. I liked the designer-gown john best.

He'd show up at the door with a large suitcase that Danni and I dove into like presents on Christmas morning. We had wonderful fun dressing up and modeling each of the slinky, high-priced gowns, but ultimately we'd only get to keep one. Ironically, I never wore my fancy gowns for their intended glamorous purpose. For me, they were work clothes, rarely worn out of the apartment. For out-on-the-town time, I typically switched into skintight hip-hugger jeans and my favorite white cotton tee-shirt—the one that was several sizes too small.

We rarely did house calls, but an afternoon spent at the Beverly Wilshire Hotel comes to mind. I'd been purchased as a birthday present for the client's girlfriend. New to the world of threesomes, I turned to Danni, who offered additional coaching before the big event.

We were in her bedroom, another space with precise, uncluttered order. Slipping easily out of her long summer dress, Danni stretched her naked form onto the flowers of the king-sized polyester bedspread.

"This is the labia," she said, gently separating the folds of skin. "And here, at the tip, is the clitoris. This is what you want to stimulate."

I felt uncomfortable looking at the thick, black, though evenly shorn mass surrounding the exposed pink skin. Danni's clinical presentation didn't help to relieve my embarrassment. I wondered, *Couldn't we have a drink first?* And the room was much too bright, with afternoon sunshine pouring through the open curtains. *Isn't she worried about a neighbor peering through?* Oh, wait, that was my fantasy. I'm the one who wanted to peek through the balcony window to see what went on in Madam Danni's bedroom.

"Doesn't it look good? Come on, get down here and kiss it," she coaxed.

Actually it didn't look good; it looked foreign. I'd never even looked at myself in a mirror. But not wanting to be a failure at cunnilingus, I knelt at the side of the bed, took a deep breath, closed my eyes, and dove in. However, try as I might, I couldn't get into slipping and sliding my tongue around Danni's well-used orifice. After a few minutes of decidedly unskillful slobbering, she granted me a welcome reprieve.

"Okay, enough. You've got the idea. Just act like you're enjoying yourself and you'll be fine."

Before walking out the door for my ménage-à-trois debut, Danni handed me the familiar little yellow pill. "Just to take the edge off," she said.

During the twenty-minute taxi ride, I welcomed the Valium's familiar slide into a more relaxed state. By the time the bellman assisted me out of the Yellow Cab, I felt calm and self-assured. Walking through the hotel's impressive marble lobby, I did my best to hold that sense of composure, ignoring the loud and clear voice in my head declaring, *You're way out of your league.*

Stepping off the elevator into the plush carpet, I cradled my left arm, hoping my bandage-wrapped thumb and inability to use that hand wouldn't be a detriment to the upcoming job. The digit, smashed in a taxi cab door earlier that week, still throbbed in protest to the slightest movement.

I hadn't meant to close the cab's door on my perfectly manicured thumb; I was in a hurry, running up to the apartment for a quick change of clothes before heading back out, ironically, to a hand modeling interview. Talk about the proverbial shooting oneself in the foot.

Entering the Beverly Wilshire's luxuriously appointed suite, I got somewhat comfortable before explaining my slightly handicapped situation. While the three of us sipped flutes of champagne, I shared my woeful story, soaking up the attention I received as a result. Usually the one to make sure my customers were happy and comfortable in bed, I enjoyed being catered to, as the john tenderly stacked pillows under my arm before we got down to business.

Although I didn't find the couple sexually attractive and wouldn't have looked twice at them under ordinary circumstances, the compassion they showed lulled me into a place of gratitude. From that place, I performed the art of making love—to both the man and woman—like a seasoned pro.

A few hours later, with a large grin and a bounce to my step, I once again crossed the ornate lobby and slipped a five to the bellman as he assisted me back into a waiting cab. The combination of setting, champagne, and caring participants had left a delightful buzz of happiness that wrapped around me as I settled into the rear seat. *Sometimes working for Danni isn't so bad*, I thought, enjoying the richness of the setting sun's rays as they slow-danced along the horizon.

16: More Lessons

Danni's tutelage didn't simply focus on pleasuring others; personal gratification held equal importance.

"You need a lesson in self-pleasure," she said one gray, rainy afternoon.

Ah, self-pleasure. Now, there's a place where I had a rudimentary skill level, typically involving a deodorant bottle, though once I used a piece of fruit. . . .

Sixteen and desperate for something more substantial than my Ban roll-on, I borrowed a banana from the kitchen. Yes, borrowed. Mom kept a strict inventory of food, just enough for each meal—no extras. If an item came up missing, it would bring questions.

"Who ate a banana? There's a banana missing."

"Oh, that would be me. But I didn't eat it. I used it to probe around my vagina. Here, you can have it back."

So, I felt it best to return the erotic fruit without Mom knowing where it spent the night. Hard to say which caused the bigger guilt, sliding the yellow dildo into my wondering dark spaces or sneaking it back to the kitchen afterwards—unwashed, for fear the running water would awaken Mom or Dad.

Fortunately, Danni's lesson induced more pleasure than shame.

"Go to the bathtub and turn on the water, but don't put in the plug. Make sure the temperature is warm, comfortable. Then slide down. Put your legs up the wall, and spread your lips the way I showed you before. You'll know when the angle is right."

I took a lot of baths after that.

Another quiet, trick-free day, my lessons on solo pleasure continued.

"I have a present for you." Danni smiled a sly, enticing grin as she pulled an eight-inch-long plastic cylinder from behind her back.

"Go pee first," she directed.

While doing so, I flashed on the vibrator incident of my youth. Relieved the gift bore no resemblance to Liesl's massager, I wondered how life would've been different if I'd peed first back then.

When I returned to my room, Danni sat at the edge of the bed, holding the humming stick.

"Let's get on with it. Panties off," she continued in her typical, direct manner. "Now lie back, get comfortable, and open your legs."

I had mixed reactions about following Danni's directions. However, curiosity overcame my lingering threads of modesty, and I did as told.

"Now lick your fingers and get yourself wet."

Despite being a paid sex worker, I found Danni's gaze intrusive. I felt a flush of heat rise on my face but followed the instructions without question.

"That's it," Danni encouraged, as she handed me the tapered device.

The vibration felt odd as I opened and closed my hand around the cool plastic.

"Now slide it in."

A flood of new sensations filled my awareness—love at first contact. Once again Danni had opened a world of orgasmic delights.

She concluded the lesson, saying, "Twist the knob at the end to control the speed," then left me alone to enjoy my new best friend.

I'd been living at Danni's for a few weeks when she upgraded the original boring, scratchy, beige and brown furniture to a wonderfully soft, pale blue, velveteen sofa and loveseat set. I'd dangle my long legs over the edge of the two-seater, my favorite spot, while staring at the TV. Many an evening I shared the space with my humming friend, who serenaded me into a blissful glow. That very loveseat brought the counterbalance of humiliation.

A tall, burly guy, a friend of Danni's, stopped by for a mid-afternoon visit with her. He lowered himself onto the pastel softness, then shifted his weight to one side, sliding his hand between the cushions.

"What's this?" he asked with a mischievous grin. And there, proudly displayed like the big fish of the day, was my secret friend. The shock of seeing its creamy whiteness in his large black hand was bad enough, but Danni cinched my remorse.

Pointing her finger, she gleefully announced, "That's Debi's."

Her betrayal stunned me. The very person who had introduced me to the heavenly realm of self-pleasure had turned so quickly.

"You don't need things like this," he said, tossing the sex toy aside as he stood up. "Come on," he continued. "I'll give you the real thing."

Great. Shamed and then fucked. Egotistical male.

I faked a good one, letting him believe he possessed more skill than a plastic dick. But after he left, I went back to my battery operated companion; it was too good to leave, despite the embarrassment. I simply became more diligent about putting it away.

I'd been living the privileged life of a West Hollywood call girl for about four months when Danni decided I needed more serious training.

"You're going to Las Vegas."

"What?" I said, both startled and confused. We'd never traveled for tricks, so I saw no reason to head to Nevada. "Why?" I asked.

"I have a friend with a house, a brothel. You're going to live there and work with her for a few weeks."

A few weeks, I thought, *I'm not going anywhere, certainly not to a brothel.*

Danni continued, "It'll be great experience for you. You'll learn a lot and come back polished."

I didn't want to be polished, and the idea of working in a "house" terrified me; no way would I consider going off to a foreign land to live with a bunch of strangers. Even though my current world revolved around being a sex machine, at least I had the freedom to choose partners for my romps at the Starwood. And while there weren't many, I didn't want to leave the few friends I had.

"No," I stated simply. "I won't go. And you can't make me." I felt like a defiant child and remembered another time I had said no to my boss....

"Wake up!" The male voice roused me from a deep sleep. "Come on, you've got to get up."

I'd only been asleep for a few hours when the rude awakening occurred. The voice belonged to a friend of Danni's, a guy she called when she needed a ride and didn't want to take a taxi. She was due at L.A. County Jail by 8 a.m. for her first of six consecutive three-day weekends, her sentence following the bust on my first day there.

Since that afternoon, I'd not been allowed to stay alone in the apartment and had been told ahead of time that I would have to leave for these weekends, but I played dead when Danni's driver nudged me.

"Come on, Debi, you can't stay here alone."

The statement wasn't new to me. I'd been told I couldn't stay home alone ever since Mom married my step-dad. Back then, I served my required lock-out sentence either sitting in the backyard, or if it was cold, the garage. Only once did I make the mistake of passing time in the front yard. That day, when my parents returned from running errands, my step-father made it painfully clear I wasn't allowed to sit where the neighbors could see me and perhaps query as to how I came to be locked out.

But I refused to comply on that cold, spring morning at Danni's. Keeping my eyes closed, I held my ground and tightened my grip on the blankets, ignoring him. When my evictor grabbed the covers and tugged, I held on for dear life.

"She's not moving," he called out to Danni.

"Get some cold water," she replied from the other side of the apartment.

Even with the jarring splash and soggy bedding, I held my post. This was my bed. I'd been paying dearly for the space and damn it, I wasn't going to leave.

"She's still not moving. Now what?"

Danni accepted defeat, announcing, "Okay, forget it. I can't be late."

Fearing this might be a trick, I remained motionless, still clutching the sodden linens.

"Okay, Debi, you can stay," Danni called out a moment later. "I'm leaving the keys here on the table. Just be home Sunday at 5:00 so I can get back in."

After hearing the door close behind Danni and her friend, I took a deep breath and sighed. Smiling, I dried my face and wiggled across the bed to a dry spot. Anticipating a quiet, hooker-free weekend, I easily returned to sleep.

Danni didn't listen to my "no" regarding Las Vegas. Paranoia told me she wanted to offer my room to someone else, that Vegas was just a way to get rid of me. Danni rejected my fear and offered a compelling list of benefits from the extended training. Blocking each pro with a con, I welcomed the unusual feeling of power that came from standing up for myself, but Danni was unrelenting. After several sessions of fatiguing debate, I slipped from confident adult to tearful child.

"Please don't make me go. I'll do anything you want; just please don't make me go."

I'd like to think my emotional outcry reached Danni's heart, and out of compassion, she dropped the topic of brothel training, but more likely she backed off upon realizing I'd be useless to the Nevada madam in my tenuous state.

Even though life in the spring of 1975 revolved around paid sex, compensation didn't always come from johns.

I double-checked the address of the three-story brick building on Sunset Boulevard, to be sure we were at the right place. Relieved it didn't look like a seedy, underbelly establishment, we stepped inside. Danni was hesitant about our daytime adventure, but I had convinced her the outing would be cool, something out of the ordinary.

"Here it is: Suite 341," I announced, wandering ahead of Danni down the long quiet hallway. "Ready?"

Without waiting for her to answer, I opened the door to find Bruce, my producer friend, sitting alone in a quiet, sparsely furnished office. I'd met Bruce a few nights earlier, at the Starwood. He told me then of his need for new talent.

"Welcome, ladies," he said warmly, as he stood and stepped out from behind a large wooden desk. He exchanged a hug with each of us, then pulled two armless chairs away from the front of the clutter-free work surface.

"Please, here, have a seat, and we'll get the paperwork out of the way."

They appeared to be standard contracts, full of legalese. I barely glanced at mine before signing at the bottom. Nervous to find out exactly what I'd gotten us into, even this small amount of professionalism helped to calm my anxiety. Bruce and I made small talk while Danni took her time reading the fine print, but within a few minutes, she too was on board.

"So here's the deal," our employer for the afternoon said, taking the signed forms. "I make and distribute audio tapes for long-haul truckers. They're great repeat customers, if they like what they hear."

As he handed each of us an envelope containing our fee for the afternoon—in cash—Bruce continued, "Do this well and there'll be more for you."

I put the money in my purse and smiled. I'd never thought about what truck drivers did for entertainment on their cross-country runs and liked the idea of serenading them as the miles sped by.

"The guys are in the other room. Today's script has parts for two men and two women. Any questions?"

I looked at Danni and giggled nervously. "Nope. I'm ready."

Danni nodded in agreement. I enjoyed seeing her out of her element. Today's adventure was my gig, my connection.

I returned my attention to Bruce. "Let's do it."

"Okay," he said, sliding some pills across the desk. "If you're tense, these will help."

Our co-workers stood as we entered the room and Bruce offered introductions. "John, Lance, meet Debi and Danni."

We shook hands all around as I surveyed the studio. Being familiar with the recording industry, I had expected a sound-proof booth and a mixing board. The true nature of this audio recording outfit was obvious in its modesty. Two couches, at ninety degree angles, filled the corner directly ahead. A square coffee table in front of the worn seating displayed a plate of sliced oranges and the recording gear: a reel-to-reel tape recorder and a couple of mics. Several folding chairs and a bookcase stuffed full of magazines and audio tapes completed the contents of the small room. I pushed away the image of what else might be recorded in that space and perched at the edge of the closest lumpy, stained cushion. Lance sat down next to me, while Danni and John settled onto the sofa to my left.

"Okay, here's the script."

Bruce handed out four paper-clipped packets before grabbing one of the folding chairs and pulling it up to the table. "Each part is clearly marked. Debi, you're girl one; Lance, you're man one."

I blushed as I looked over the pages filled with graphic pornography. Glancing at Danni, I hoped for a similar reaction, but instead, she and John were leaning into each other, whispering their lines. I took a deep breath and hoped the sedative would kick in soon.

Our producer's voice broke my attention from the bawdy content. "It gets into the action quickly, and when it does, you can suck on these for sound effects."

That's when I realized the plate of orange wedges weren't simply a snack. Bruce's serious tone kept me from laughing out loud, but I thought, *You've got to be fucking kidding me.* I considered walking out, then remembered the cash payment. *Oh well,* I reasoned, *it's just an afternoon. And it's only my voice.*

The scene was hilarious, and somewhat frantic, as each of us read our appointed parts, the tension mounting in beat with the torrid script. As I sucked and slurped between X-rated lines, I wondered, *Do men really enjoy this crap?* Ironically, as the drugs kicked in and the passion built, I found myself getting turned on, in spite of the ridiculous setting. I actually walked out of that studio office several hours later ready for the real thing—or at least a nice bath.

17: Getting Out

Untangling myself from Danni was a sticky process, and ironically, my greatest ally in the transition turned out to be Margie.

The first few months I worked as a call girl, Margie and I were locked in the nonverbal feud that landed me at Danni's in the first place. While I didn't see my previous best friend when I returned to the abandoned studio—to get my clothes and beloved teal dishes—we did exchange visual daggers and zing back-biting comments toward each other at the Starwood. However, time and loneliness melted the tension between us, and we once again claimed our sisterhood.

Margie disliked Danni the moment they met. Although it wasn't spoken, I could sense Margie didn't approve of the power Danni had over me and wanted to regain her previous status as controller of my strings. However, I'd grown to like the lucrative nature of my new career, and hanging out with Margie didn't offer any cash. But she did offer musicians.

During the time we were estranged, Margie had become friends with another girl, also named Debbie. A well-liked and well-connected groupie, Debbie took Margie on as her protégée. As a result, Margie graduated from blowing rockers who performed at the local club to blowing those who played venues like The Fabulous Forum or The Hollywood Bowl. She had also become well-versed in the art of backstage entry, so by the time I joined their friendship, all I had to do was stand back and smile at the well-played security guard.

"I'm with the band" became the best sentence I'd ever spoken. I loved the exclusive, behind-the-scenes world the backstage pass provided. At the end of each concert, I would carefully remove the 3x4 inch stick-on patch from the denim of my jeans and reattach it in my hot-pink address book. Each of my cherished mementoes also bears the name of the band member I slept with, just in case I had the opportunity to see him again, though repeat performances were rare.

In addition to opening the world of concert-hall delights, my renewed friendship with Margie and resulting association with Debbie also led to meeting Fabib.

The girls saw the wealthy, middle-aged businessman as my way out of prostitution. On our first date, the three of us joined him for lunch on his thirty-foot yacht. Fabib, who loved to cook and had actually written a book on the subject, supplied a wonderful barbecued meal with all of the appropriate summertime fixings. I'd never eaten a grilled turkey before, and to this day, Fabib's rice dressing remains a tastebud champion. However, I wasn't as impressed with the man. If he had looked as good as his cuisine tasted, my life could have taken a distinctly different turn that day.

Fabib offered a straightforward proposition: I could move in with him and he would support me. I would have a room of my own and be free to come and go as I pleased. The only requirement was that I be available for sex at his desire.

Both Debbie and Margie saw his proposal as a major step up, and Debbie did her best to convince me of Fabib's attentive and kind nature, but his portly build and abundance of body hair spilling out from all edges of his shirt left me politely uninterested. I told Fabib I'd consider his offer but left the marina grateful to return to life at Danni's. Living with her, I sent my sex partners home after completing our business, and I liked it that way.

One day, shortly after I met Fabib, Danni took me on a field trip.

"It's a high-dollar party," she announced, "with lots of girls and a lot of wealthy men; you'll need to wear one of your Kamali gowns."

GETTING OUT

I didn't like the idea of taking business on the road, and hadn't done so since the threesome afternoon a few months before. I felt safe in my little bedroom, in control, but Danni insisted.

"This is a big deal; it's how we get new clients. But they'll only want more if you persuade them you're the best choice in a room full of sophisticated ladies. I've seen you be charming and sexy—I know you can do it."

Shit. Having men from Danni's "book" show up at the door for prearranged sex was one thing. Convincing them I would be the best choice in a room full of alluring options? That might be tough. I didn't feel innately sexy. Charm flowed in direct relationship with the drugs in my system.

Oh sure, I could play cute and sweet, but for the most part I felt awkward around the men who rode me for a few minutes. If a room full of potential tricks wasn't intimidating enough, I suspected the other call girls would see me for the shy, insecure rookie I believed myself to be. I needed the privacy and familiar setting of my four walls to play grownup seductress. Unfortunately, Danni didn't offer a way out. She had made a commitment and we were going, period.

Our ride, a friend of Danni's, showed up at about three in the afternoon. Relieved to see the fellow working girl wasn't particularly glamorous and seemed about the same age as Danni and me, my incessant *you won't fit in* fears calmed, but the inner critic was only placated for a moment. As soon as the three of us stepped into the afternoon sun, heading to the parked car, the nagging voice once again began its ridicule.

Those girls across the street are looking at us. See how they're whispering and giggling. They're Catholic girls, good girls. I can tell by their uniforms, and I'm sure they can tell we're hookers—only hookers walk down the street looking like this.

As a young teen, when I first started selecting my own clothes, Mom had warned me about looking like a hooker. She preached what I believed were well-established facts: only hookers wear black, and only hookers wear anklets. I wasn't wearing either that day, but I still felt a neon sign blazing over my head.

Once inside the anonymity of the Cadillac sedan, I relaxed and settled in to watch the fascinating parade of daily life on the streets of

Hollywood. Of course, there were the tourists, but tourists were nothing unusual. The locals were the most intriguing, like the group of teens who dyed their hair blue and dressed in silver lamé spacesuits. They were convinced they'd come from the stars and had their own language to strengthen their bond. Seeing a pod of them, I laughed, feeling less self-conscious of my own stand-out attire.

We had two stops on the drive across town, for two more ladies of the night.

The first stop was quick enough—pull up, slide across the back seat, make introductions all around—as another party-ready young lady expanded our trio. Not being good at girly chit-chat, I returned my gaze to the neighborhood, watching it switch from apartments to large, stately homes.

Enjoying the views of beautiful, manicured lawns and gardens, I became confused when we pulled into the driveway of a Spanish-style house and honked the horn. *Were we at the party? Surely this couldn't be the home of the last passenger.* As my mind turned over the possibilities, the front door opened and a stunningly beautiful woman—despite the hot curlers in her hair—stuck her head out.

"I'm almost ready," she said, beckoning us in. "Just a few more minutes."

Stepping into the entry way, I felt comforted by the home's warmth and coziness. Our hostess wore a kimono-style robe, loosely wrapped around her tall, slender body. Like the surroundings, her smile relayed a sense of ease.

"Please make yourself at home," she said, as her bare feet ran up the Mexican tile stairs. "There are drinks in the kitchen. I won't be long."

The photographs lining the staircase wall drew my attention, and confusion once again set in. This was obviously a family home, complete with school pictures of two young boys.

Hoping to allay my nerves, I joined the other ladies for a pre-party drink. Doing my best to appear cool and collected, despite my continuing uneasiness, I lined up with them in front of the bathroom mirror, to ensure a proper display of our top-dollar merchandise. When our hostess reemerged in her own formal evening attire, I asked about the pictures.

"Those are my boys," she said proudly. "They're staying with friends tonight."

Stunned, I felt my whole rule book on what it meant to be a prostitute blow apart. *Her boys? She's a mom? How is it possible a mom with a lovely house in a fancy neighborhood is a hooker?*

As I walked back to the vehicle, I wondered if the other residents on the quiet street knew of their neighbor's occupation. Then I returned to the rut of my internal chatter.

You have no business being here with these women. Who are you kidding? Look at yourself. You aren't poised or graceful, and you certainly aren't any sexual artist, ready to take men to heights of ecstasy. You're a backstage fuck-'em and leave-'em groupie. And even there you're more likely to land a roadie than a band member. You're way out of your league. These women are chic. These women are everything you're not.

By the time we arrived at the party, I had reduced myself to rubble, crushing what little self-esteem I had. I desperately needed some coke to boost my confidence, but didn't want to appear uncouth by asking the ladies if they'd brought along toot. At this penthouse gathering overlooking the grid of Los Angeles streets, I felt like an alien.

Unfamiliar with cocktail parties, I did my best to mimic what I'd seen on TV: smile and make small talk about the weather. After getting my rum and coke from the bar, I quietly separated myself from the twenty or so guests. Danni may have helped me refine the art of giving good head, but she missed the lesson on self-confidence. Plus, the men were old, father-age old. But they weren't like my father; these men were dignified—like the elegant women they were bidding for.

I hovered by the window, watching the early evening commuters navigate their way through the glare of the setting sun. Occasionally, I would glance out of the corner of my eye to check the status of the pairings. Since the women outnumbered the men, my plan was to linger somewhere outside of the selection pond, and then return to the bar, a fresh leftover, where I could pass time flirting with the cute bartender.

But Danni had no intentions of letting me go unsold, especially since a portion of my profits went directly into her purse. She caught my eye, marched across the room, and took my arm. Her nails dug into my tender skin as she pulled me over, introducing me to a gentleman with a touch of silver at his temples. I put on my best "so nice to meet you" face, forcing a smile, but inside my gut locked down. I knew I'd reached the end of my career as a "ho."

18: A Change of Venue

Margie and Debbie were ecstatic when I called to tell them I would accept Fabib's offer. Danni wasn't so happy. After the initial shock and a moment of protest, she became engaging, listing numerous benefits life with her offered. But this time, after seven months of call girl experience, I didn't bite.

Not willing to deal with the pressure Danni put on me to stay, I packed my clothes and called a cab the minute she left to run some errands. That evening, from the safety of Fabib's, I gathered my courage and dialed her number. It would have been easiest to run away cleanly, but I had to get the remainder of my things. That's when Danni got resentful, threatening to hold my belongings hostage.

I screamed into the phone, "You'll get yours," and slammed down the receiver in an uncharacteristic display of anger. Devastated at the thought of losing my teal-blue dishes, I burst into tears. I wasn't about to let Danni take my prized possession, handed down from Grandma, but didn't know what to do.

The next afternoon, Danni called and asked for directions. Wary of what might be a trap, I asked why. Surprised by her response—she had packed my boxes and wished to deliver them—I was relieved I wouldn't have to return to her apartment.

Pacing along the upstairs balcony, I wondered why Danni had changed her mind and even worried she might be returning broken china, but I assured myself I didn't need to be concerned about vengeance. As the taxi wound its way up the steep, asphalt driveway, I ran down to meet it. Danni climbed out and, before speaking, passed me two medium-sized packages, as well as a bag containing some toiletries I'd left behind.

"Okay," she said, "that's everything. Will you back off from calling the cops now?"

At first I didn't know what she meant. I didn't plan on being a snitch. Then I figured it out; she was referring to my comment from the day before.

I'd meant she would get her payback in a bigger context, in the form of karma, but Danni took it as an immediate threat. Telling her she didn't have anything to worry about, I gave her a hug before watching her climb back into the cab and drive away—never to be seen or talked to again.

Life with Fabib was more of a side-step than an exit from the world of trading sex, as I became girl number two in his harem. Fabib's number-one girl lived on the main floor and shared his bed; I took on the role of downstairs mistress.

My floor of the hilltop home, with its English pub décor of black leather furniture on red shag carpet, was comfortable, though far from my style. "The dungeon," our nickname for the space, came complete with medieval implements of torture adorning the walls and brick fireplace. A fully stocked bar, mini kitchen, and bathroom ran along the eastern wall, while my dark-wood, paneled bedroom occupied the western end of the large space.

Days in my new home—which generally didn't start until midafternoon when I'd crawl out of bed—flowed easily enough. I had permission to consume anything in the well-provisioned kitchen or wine cabinet, so I never had to worry about food. Fabib also gave me an allowance, enough to cover taxi rides to the club and back and other necessities, like cigarettes. There was only one house rule: no male guests, unless Fabib invited them. Because I didn't feel I had a choice, I agreed; then I snuck my lovers into the house. It wasn't really an issue, since the dungeon had its own entrance. Plus, the upstairs girl and Fabib's out-of-town business trips kept him occupied most of the time.

His visits with me were short and direct, much like his physical presence and personality. He'd climb on, pump for a while—sending me into wild, exquisitely rehearsed moans of pleasure—and then roll off, quite pleased with his virility. While I never looked forward to his every-other-day-or-so visits, they were easily tolerated, and washed away with a quick stop at the bidet. Then he discovered my fondness for receiving oral sex.

It was my fault; I got careless. One afternoon Fabib walked in on me and a forbidden visitor. He stood silently at the bedroom door, witnessing my unfettered delight, before throwing out my friend and returning to lecture me. However, never one to leave a girl wanting, Fabib finished the job, and from then on added face time to his repertoire.

I have fond memories of the nights Fabib opened the house for impromptu gatherings. Occasionally, when his favorite exclusive nightspot, Over the Rainbow, gave their "last call," a little before two a.m., he would announce, "Party continues up the hill," a blanket invitation for both friends and strangers to follow him home. As a result of going out with Margie and Debbie, I too had gained access to Over the Rainbow, an upstairs, private establishment on Sunset Boulevard, but I felt painfully aware of my non-status in that gathering place for stars and their entourages.

My inner Controller—ever vigilant in its quest to ensure I wouldn't be spotted for the impostor I felt myself to be—warned, *Have fun, be a party girl, but don't get sloppy. Don't embarrass yourself, and definitely don't embarrass the guy you're hanging on.* As in my life as a prostitute, I felt like a foreigner, someone who had only temporarily fooled the bouncer.

Most of the time, I enjoyed the casual, social events that filled Fabib's living room, and I often found stimulating conversations to listen in on. Sometimes, the party overflowed down the stairs, into the dungeon. When that happened, my room—and its only piece of furniture, the bed—became a magnet for our merrymaking guests.

Four hefty iron chains hung from a central point on the ceiling, attaching to each of the king-sized bed's four corners. This resulted in a spectacular adult play area that allowed—and encouraged—people to leap from the doorway onto the giant swing. Unfortunately, the swaying motion often left them—especially those who'd had a bit too much to drink—with a sour stomach.

Many who pulled themselves from the bed, back onto solid ground, stumbled into the small closet off my room. I kept quiet and held my breath once they stuck their head in the porcelain bowl, guessing how long it would be before they gasped and garbled "What the hell?" or other similar comment. You see, the bathroom and toilet were at the other end of the house—my room simply had a bidet.

Despite the relative physical comfort, I was an emotional wreck. Intense lows, consisting of excessive sleep and long crying binges, countered the highs of drugs, alcohol, and sex. My dream—to marry a musician and travel the world with him—routinely ended with my lover of the moment heading on to his next gig—and his next warm bed. By the time I lived with Fabib, I actually had two somewhat regular boyfriends who called when they came to town, but, inevitably, the tour would continue and I'd hit bottom, a little bit more devastated each time they left.

I came to hate my life—to the point that one night I decided to check out and swallowed a handful of downers. As I fell to the plush red carpet in complete surrender, my last thought was, *Finally, I'm free.* I blacked out with blissful gratitude flowing through my intentionally overdosed veins. When I awoke the next morning, rage replaced the bliss.

"What the fuck are you doing here?" I yelled, pushing myself away from a guy I barely knew lying next to me in bed. "How did you get in here?"

He stammered, "I called. You didn't answer. I was worried."

The previous night's eight Quaaludes appeared as a blurry memory.

I continued my outburst. "I didn't invite you here. And I didn't ask you to save me. You've ruined everything." Devastated, I began sobbing.

Shocked, my savior attempted to wrap his arms around me, explaining how he'd found me passed out on the floor. I guess he expected me to be happy or grateful, and in time I came to be, but initially I was just plain pissed to be alive. I pushed him away and curled into a fetal position, vaguely remembering how he'd walked me around and made me drink coffee before putting me to bed.

After I convinced him I wouldn't try again, the caring guy left, allowing me to return to my solitary misery. I felt like a failure, telling myself only a real loser couldn't successfully kill herself. Yet even in my depressed state, I recognized a miracle had occurred.

The guy—someone I'd screwed a couple of times—had no reason to be coming by for a middle-of-the-night visit. Well, okay, there's one reason, but even with my active sex life, guys didn't drop by for an unannounced quickie, especially at Fabib's.

And why did he let himself in? Did he just need to pee? Was that how he found me passed out on the bathroom floor? Perhaps, I reluctantly admitted, *he'd been guided by unseen forces.*

I never got answers to my questions. And I never saw the near stranger again. Primarily, I felt embarrassed by the whole thing—both the attempt and the outcome. So much so, I never told anyone of my intentional overdose.

In September of 1975, two months after moving in with Fabib, I once again decided it was time for a change. Margie had also grown tired of the Hollywood lifestyle and its empty promises. So, days before my nineteenth birthday, the two of us headed east to Flagstaff, where her uncle offered free rent and some fresh, clean, mountain living.

19: A Musician of My Own

Even though I'd had plenty of sex by the time we reached Arizona—and more partners than most people have in a lifetime—I was still clueless in many respects. An example of my naïveté: the free rent arrangement Margie had with her uncle. Sure they shared the bedroom—and the double bed—while I slept on the living room floor. That's just how it was in the upstairs unit overlooking the lake.

At the time, I never thought to question the agreement. Margie taking the edge off of her uncle's boners simply didn't occur to me. That perspective didn't surface until my "incest victim" retrospective.

Looking back, it's hard to believe I could be so naïve. But I also realize, at nineteen, I was in no way prepared for answers that may have led too close to my forbidden memory zone. Instead, once settled in our new home, I focused on satiating my highly charged libido—not analyzing how it came to be that way.

Although Flagstaff's laid-back night life was an abrupt change from Hollywood, Margie and I soon found our comfort zone in a small hometown hotspot. It offered our favorite ingredients, live bands and cute male bartenders who could easily be convinced to double our tequila sunrise or Seven and Sevens without the double cost. That's how I met Ed, and Margie met Mike, Ed's younger brother. Of course, they were musicians.

From that first night, we set our sights and our well-honed dance of seduction into play. I thoroughly enjoyed swaying to the band's pop-rock tunes, smiling demurely when I caught Ed's eye, and during breaks, oozing praise for their original lyrics. We didn't need to rush our charming glimmer, because the boys were locals, performing week-long runs on a regular basis.

On the second night, we upped the ante, sending beers to the stage for the guys' final set. That's when they changed from straight-laced, teetotaling musicians, into their free-spirited alter egos. Met with loud applause and delighted screams, "Hawk and the Pigeons" ran back onstage in complete "greaser" attire, immediately launching into their set of light-hearted fifties tunes.

Their foolish antics and consumption of alcohol led to outright flirting with us girls who lined the edge of the stage. The local ladies, who had previously hoped those good Catholic boys would be theirs, didn't know what hit them when we savvy—or loose—California girls showed up.

By the third night, Margie and I were more than ready for some after-hours action. Thankfully, the boys had picked up on our not-so-subtle clues, offering their hesitant, though straightforward invitation, "Want to come back to our place?"

"Our place" consisted of an older, two-bedroom home they rented in a quiet residential neighborhood. After the brothers set us up with a round of their favorite drink, a whisky and lemonade combination they called "pigeon puckers," we sat around the wood-paneled living room. Furnished in what nowadays would be labeled shabby chic, at the time I viewed it as thrift store furniture.

With the help of the tart beverage, our hosts relaxed, allowing their lack of familiarity with the situation to soften. I'm not saying the boys were virgins, but from the tension in the room, it was obvious they weren't in the habit of bringing girls home.

Eventually, after watching some silly television and making out on the sofa, Ed and I ventured down the hall to his bedroom. Once there, we both regained our confidence, behaving like sex-crazed bunnies.

I was happy as could be with my musician boyfriend, sitting front row during their nightly sets and proudly claiming Ed's attention during breaks. Heading back to their place became the norm, though after that first time, nightcaps were downgraded to a cup of tea. Disappointed our Arizona after-parties didn't possess the wild abandon of those I'd attended in Hollywood, I settled for the "lite" version of my rock 'n' roll lifestyle dream.

Soon, Margie and I were playing house quite comfortably with Mike and Ed. I found it easy to adapt to the brothers' mundane and somewhat clean lifestyle, and I even got to be friends with the remainder of their large family. I truly believed I was happy in a daily routine unlike anything I had lived before, though, as usual, I didn't look too closely.

It wasn't long before Flagstaff became too small for the band's big plan, so off I went with Ed and his musician buddies—all the way to Houston, Texas. Margie didn't join us this time. Instead, she returned home to Nebraska, bringing a silent end to our three-part saga of sisterhood.

In 1976, disco hadn't yet replaced live music, so Ed and the band kept busy around Texas with local and overnight gigs. I stayed busy maintaining the three-bedroom apartment I shared with Ed, Mike, and their band's roadie, Thom. It was fun cooking meals for my three appreciative guys, and I enjoyed being the lone woman under the roof. But soon, more pressing matters, like earning money, crept in.

The perfect solution presented itself in the form of a part-time job right there in the massive apartment complex. As I was only then learning how to drive, the location couldn't have been better. For the work itself, I already knew my way around bars and taking drink orders, so the skill set was also a cinch.

Although our over-the-rec-room bar didn't offer live music, they did play rock and roll, a blessing in that cowboy-centric town. The open, airy space also had a dance floor, and after taking care of my customers, I often enjoyed a solo spin.

I missed having Margie by my side, but I didn't let her absence—or my being in a committed relationship—slow down my party-girl persona, easily flirting with the guys who stopped in for evening drinks. I also fell back into virtually nameless quickies. Old habits are hard to break.

I knew it wasn't right to be drinking and sexing it up with one-night stands—well, one-hour stands. But when Ed was out of town, I staved off guilt by telling myself what he didn't know wouldn't hurt him. I felt confident *he* remained loyal, despite the continuous flow of easy-to-get females, due to a confrontation we had early on, when I caught him talking on the phone with one of his out-of-town "friends." The ferocity of my reaction—hungry lioness guarding her fresh kill—even surprised me; it definitely left an impression on him.

My wandering lust could also be blamed on my sex life with Ed; it had become routine, boring in fact. Without the physical attraction and charge of passionate sex, I found myself wondering if it was time to move on from our seven-month relationship. Then, one quiet, otherwise humdrum night, Ed decided to confide a childhood secret to me. This is how I remember another one of those "abuse survivor" warning signs etched into the rock of my gut. . . .

I was standing in the small bathroom, my face up close to the mirror, looking for imperfections ready to be picked. Ed was doing his own picking, at the strings of that goddamn guitar. Thinking It's hard to believe I once liked that twanging, I felt my jaw tighten, locking my mouth from screaming, "Shut up!"

Stepping away from my reflection, I leaned in the doorway and looked at the man I used to be madly in love with. He was sitting on the bed with pillows between him and the apartment's plain white wall. His feet, wearing equally plain white socks, were propped up, while his prized possession filled his lap. Ed remained focused on his fingers, as they idly plucked random chords. Softly, he began to speak. "Hey, Debi, have I told you about my friend Marty?"

Something about Ed's tone grabbed my attention, though I stayed silent, allowing him to continue.

"We were best friends when I was twelve. I used to go places, like baseball practice, with him. His mom would drive us around in her old, beat-up station wagon."

Ed became quiet. Curious to know more, I asked, "Yeah?"

My voice startled Ed and he looked up. The sadness in his eyes surprised me and I walked over, taking a seat close to the man who was usually light and happy. Ed returned his gaze to his hands before continuing.

"So one day, we were going for ice cream after practice. We had Marty's little sister in the back seat with us. She was about three years old, sitting next to me." After a moment's pause, Ed continued. *"Marty elbowed me and asked, 'Do you want to stick your hand in my sister's panties?'*

"At first I didn't know what to do, and I asked him what he meant, but he nodded and whispered, 'It's okay. I do it all the time.'

"I looked up front, to make sure his mom was busy driving, and then slid my hand up under his sister's dress. I pushed her underwear out of the way and felt around, pushing my finger up inside a little bit.

"She started to squirm and cry, so I pulled my hand out real quick. I looked over at Marty and he had a big grin on his face. He told me we were members of a private club and it was our secret."

At first, listening to Ed's story made my stomach hurt. I wanted to run from the room, to stop hearing the words coming from his mouth, but I was frozen on the bed beside him. A terrified voice inside me said, *This is horrible; Ed is a monster.* But as he continued talking, I felt myself relax.

Instead of being appalled, my reaction shifted to a feeling of safety and understanding, as though I'd been holding my breath for a very long time and circumstances had finally given me permission to exhale and resume a normal breathing pattern. Worst of all, I suddenly felt very turned on.

Crawling across the bed, I moved Ed's guitar and climbed into the space it vacated. Whispering, "Shhh, it's okay," I kissed him deeply, once again engaged and eager to satisfy my voracious appetite.

Why I reacted with lust to Ed's story of molesting a child didn't make sense to me. But instead of stopping to ask why, I added another layer to my ever-present blanket of shame, by telling myself I was disgusting. Then, as I had done with all of the other clues to my own abuse, I pushed the momentary blip of horror into the do-not-touch zone of my psyche—until the Incest TV show opened up a whole new way of looking at my past.

20: Dysfunctional Bliss

Ed and I tied the knot a week before my twentieth birthday in a small ceremony held at a nearby Catholic Church. I wasn't Catholic. I didn't consider myself a member of any organized religion, but Ed's faith, at least from a wedding perspective, was important to him and his family: eight siblings, plus mom and dad.

Thrilled their big brother was getting married, the clan broke open their piggy banks and combined funds, allowing them to pile into the family van and drive the thousand miles from Flagstaff to Houston. In addition to Ed's blood family, we of course included the musical family, which consisted of the remaining two band members, their wives, and Thom the roadie.

I told my mom and real father about the engagement, but neither could be motivated to join my big day. So, since I hadn't made any friends in our new town, the bride's side of the church remained empty. I ignored the sad vacancy—a skill I had become quite good at by that point in my life—and instead focused on the large, loving family I gained.

@

It was odd being married. Other than the dysfunctional modeling I'd witnessed growing up, the only guidance I had came from television, where brides cooked and cleaned and smiled through it all. Something inside was lacking; I didn't feel whole and complete—sensations I'd expected a wedding band to provide—but I played house as best as I knew how.

Looking back, I remember Ed as a sweet and generous young man, who loved me deeply and tried to make me happy, like the day he pitched in with the housework. Up until that point, I had been master of our domestic chores, but Ed thought he'd surprise me by cleaning the kitchen floor in our new, one-bedroom place. That's when he stepped into a spring-loaded snare, a trap set five years earlier....

My step-father came up with the grand idea one Saturday afternoon. Interrupting my favorite weekend pastime of watching Ma and Pa Kettle movies, he knocked once before throwing open my bedroom door and commanding, "Debi, help your mother. Mop the floor."

"What?" I protested. "I don't know how. That's Mom's job."

"Well, it's about time you learned!" he snapped back.

"Can I at least finish watching this?"

"No. Now!" he said, before disappearing through the laundry room into the garage.

I begrudgingly flipped off my set and went to the broom closet, finding it well-stocked with a variety of cleaning supplies. Although I'd never used the items stored there, I knew the routine, having watched my mom do the monotonous chore many times.

Pulling out the sponge mop and the bucket, I filled the blue vessel with warm water and added a scoop of TSP, the cheap powder cleanser we'd started using when mom re-married. I wished it was Pine-Sol, like Grandma used—at least that smelled good. But it, like lots of things I had grown up with, disappeared when my step-dad entered the scene.

Grumbling to myself, I began slopping the stinky water around the geometric-patterned vinyl. Why does Mom have to be sick? This is her work. And besides, the floor doesn't even look dirty. She does such a good job; it can go another week.

A steady creaking sound coming from the stairs interrupted my discontent as Mom slowly made her way down. Thinking she would be pleased with my uncommon behavior, I stopped muttering complaints, and instead focused on pushing the mop around.

"What are you doing!" she wheezed, before a coughing fit momentarily silenced her. Startled by her shocked tone, I looked around, expecting to see some previously missed mess, but all appeared fine.

"Dad told me to," I said in my defense, and for a moment, I couldn't tell who she was more annoyed with, me or him.

"Alright," she said, pulling out a barstool before perching on it like a buzzard waiting for the inevitable kill.

Despite her illness, Mom had no problem offering a steady stream of critiques such as "That's not good enough. Come back here. You missed a spot." Finally, unable to take my incompetence any longer, she grabbed the wooden handle. Taking the bucket back to the sink, she poured the barely dirty water down the drain and turned the tap to hot, ready to begin the process for herself.

I didn't mind passing over the task and getting back to my movie, but I was pissed she couldn't accept my efforts as good enough. When Dad came in a few minutes later and found Mom taking out her irritation with forceful repetitive motions, he yelled, "Joie, stop! Debi is supposed to be doing that."

Her response, passing clearly through my bedroom wall, left no room for debate. "I told her to get out. She wasn't doing it right."

When I saw Ed on his hands and knees, soapy dish towel in hand, I flipped.

"What are you doing?!" I shrieked. "Towels don't belong on the floor!"

He sat back on his heels, obviously stunned and confused. "I'm trying to help!" he yelled back.

I saw the surprise and hurt in his eyes, but couldn't stop myself from yelling back. "Well, that's not how you do it!"

I realized, as I heard the words flow effortlessly from my mouth, that Ed's method had served its intended goal, leaving a surface cleaner than when he started. But the aggravation with my mother had been festering for five years, and it was more than ready to claim its vengeance.

As if watching myself on TV, I knew I had gone too far, that my anger had nothing to do with my husband. I also knew I wouldn't admit it or bring Ed into the big picture. Vulnerability and emotional intimacy would not be entering our relationship. What entered instead was a voracious, power-hungry bitch, who liked having the upper hand. Although this toughened aspect didn't come out often, her presence was absolute when it did.

Another way I took control of our partnership came through finances. When we first moved to Houston—and split our expenses with roommates—Ed earned a sufficient living with the band, leaving my bar tips for fun things, like an occasional new pair of shoes. Then the demand for live music disappeared in favor of disco. Since Ed didn't know how to do anything except play his guitar or fiddle, he decided to go back to school and pursue his other passion, art.

This moved me into the sole-breadwinner position, something I couldn't do on tips and my meager hourly wage, so I entered the corporate world, getting a job in the management office of a nearby mall.

After adjusting my body clock to working days instead of nights, I fit easily into the small office and its administrative functions. I also enjoyed working around people who weren't drunk or high—a fact of life while working in clubs—though in reality, the massive amounts of coffee and donuts consumed by me and my office mates simply shifted our category of mood-altering substances.

That job's daily routine, answering the phones and helping the bookkeeper with her duties, held my interest for just under a year. Once boredom set in, I found the ideal new position—assistant manager in a nearby apartment complex. In addition to working in a lush, green environment, right off the Buffalo Bayou, my wages included an apartment, so once again Ed and I packed up our modest belongings, moving into our third place in less than two years.

By then, Ed had graduated with a certificate as a graphic artist and had also landed a job using his new skills. Curious about higher education, I signed up for evening classes at our local community college. As with my shift to working in the corporate world, I slipped effortlessly into being a student.

I loved school. Something about being in the classroom by choice really worked for me. And while I didn't like to admit it, my mother had been right about my talent for accounting. The system of debits, credits, and balancing everything made perfect sense, and I quickly took my place as one of the brightest students, easily earning straight A's and my teacher's admiration.

In my second semester, during a Business Law class, not only did I catch the eye of my professor, he caught mine. Along with his impressive credentials as Assistant District Attorney for Harris County, my new teacher was also young and attractive. His well-toned, muscular build presented a nice change from Ed's thin, almost bony stature.

I'd often stay after class, making up some excuse about needing more clarification on something from the night's lecture. By then, I had discovered my innate form of self-confidence, more powerful than drugs or alcohol ever were: intelligence. It didn't take long before Mr. Assistant D.A., who told me to call him Bud, was hooked by my brains and charm—or so I thought.

Bud's story was simple and compelling: his wife focused on her career, not him, and he longed for a child. I fell for it completely, and dreams of being his doting mate and mother of his children soon filled my head.

I'd tell Ed I had to meet a classmate for an extra-credit project and instead, Bud and I would go someplace small and out of the way for an after-class cup of coffee. About ten weeks into the thirteen-week semester, we made plans to take our relationship to the next level.

I took the afternoon off work, lying about a doctor's appointment, and met up with my man-in-need-of-a-good-woman in our usual diner. We then climbed into his white Chevy pickup and drove across town to a small house owned by a friend of his.

I knew I was about to cross a line I couldn't step back from, and momentarily questioned if I should be there as I climbed the stark concrete stairs. But Bud had laid out his "poor me" scenario so flawlessly all I could see was my part in rescuing a lonely, misunderstood man. The fact that my actions involved cheating on another man—one I had been faithful to since our wedding day a year and a half earlier—didn't enter my consciousness. Until the drive home.

I felt nauseated when I climbed back into my car, watching Bud drive off in his shiny, clean truck. Once home, I easily put on my good wife act and made dinner for my husband, but I couldn't eat a bite. My stomach had clamped down, aching in a most excruciating way.

I went to bed hoping for relief, but the next morning my gut still hadn't released its vise-like grip. After two days of no solid food and fitful sleep, I realized my only hope of relief would come from admitting my affair.

Ed was crushed. Then I announced the second blow of my one-two punch—I told him we'd be getting a divorce. In my mind I had broken a vow, leaving no choice but to split up. Counseling would not be an option.

While I felt awful about the finality of the verdict, I comforted myself with the fairy-tale world I had created around my new love. Bud and I would be married and I'd be a stay-at-home mom, raising all the wild, young offspring he wanted. Although Bud wasn't a musician, he still had, at least in my mind, a career with status. The only problem with the plan: convincing Bud to see me alone again.

Following the afternoon get-together, he became distant and almost cool during class. He made up a clever list of excuses—he needed to get home, his wife was sick, or work kept him busy with a heavier-than-usual caseload. I completed the course, proud of earning an A, yet sullen over my brief affair.

A couple of weeks into the next semester, I spotted Bud's truck at the convenience store near campus. Still hoping I could sway him to see me again, I entered the brightly lit space, figuring I would just casually bump into him and let things play out—in my favor, of course. But Bud's attention was already focused on another young girl when I entered the scene, so I stepped into the candy aisle and listened in on their conversation as it slid through the shelves of sweet delights.

I couldn't believe my ears when I heard Bud spinning a familiar tale to the fresh young bait. Not being the confrontational type, I kept my presence a secret, but managed to move slyly into a place that allowed me to get a closer look at the object of Bud's desire.

The true nature of my teacher's attraction became clear, as I realized I had simply been one of an ongoing string of coed targets. The same maternal hormones that had been ignited in my Bud fantasies kicked in, resulting in a need to protect the girl.

The following Thursday, I waited outside the Business Law classroom, and sure enough, spotted the pretty blonde, whom I followed into the restroom. She appeared quite surprised by my claim, but once we compared notes, it became obvious she was headed down the same sob-story path of desire.

I took pleasure in foiling Bud's plan and preventing another broken heart, but my savior role didn't stop there. In an effort to avert the repeated behavior, I went to the school's administration and made a formal complaint.

I felt embarrassed explaining the details of the previous semester's "relationship" over the cool Formica counter. Also, I didn't like the fact that I had become a snitch—a label far too close to that of narc, a designation I was often queried about back in high school—but the injustice of the situation left me no choice. Unfortunately, my "outing" never brought any consequences, at least none I could witness.

Although my love affair was clearly over, not being one to backpedal and tell Ed I had made a mistake, I moved on with ending our relationship, letting my inner bitch step into the ice-queen role she did oh-so-effortlessly. It was surprisingly easy to lock Ed out of my heart, not simply dismissing the good times we had shared, but refusing to acknowledge their presence.

Ruthless in the divorce, I took our jointly purchased Ford Pinto, claiming it as my own. I even took the stereo, the one I had faithfully paid for, week by week, until I proudly gave it to my husband as a birthday present. And finally, to signal my fresh start, I kicked Ed out of our ground floor, one-bedroom place, and promptly moved into an upper story, two-bedroom unit, in that bayou-side complex.

Although neither my real nor fantasy marriage had worked out, I excelled in my post-divorce life, balancing the action-packed hours between daytime assistant manager, part-time evening student, and weekend party girl.

21: Party's at My Place

I loved having a place of my own and promptly undertook the joyful work of nesting. First on the agenda: paint. Up until that point in my life, I had lived with white walls. Even at home with my parents—where rental companies who frowned upon altered spaces were not a consideration—my rooms had been boringly bland.

Since working in the apartment complex, I had found out that repainting happened between tenants anyway, so part of my bold new life included color. Ed's brother Mike helped with my project, not that we were close or anything, but I knew he had assisted his father in the trade. I also knew Mike, the proverbial nice guy, could be convinced—or bullied—into helping me.

I figured the bathroom, since it occupied the smallest square footage, would be the simplest first project, but within an hour of starting my cornflower-blue latex, I began to regret my choice. With my hand cramped around the brush's wooden handle, I cursed the seemingly never-ending angles, cabinets, and crannies. Mike's professional and perfectionistic nature urged me on, and being a good, industrious student, I persevered, absorbing tips and pointers I appreciate to this day.

Along with painting came furnishing my girl-on-her-own pad. Confident in my ability to make money and pay my bills, I applied for my first charge account at my favorite local department store. Since I'd proven myself as fiscally responsible with a previous layaway purchase, they accepted my application.

Shopping for my own sofa, matching loveseat, dining table, and chairs was a come-true fantasy. For the first time, I had complete freedom to bring home items I loved without discussion.

As a pre-teen, the first time I acquired new furniture, my step-father had made the decision, selecting a cheap French style—what he thought looked "girlie." Back then, I spent many a weekend sitting at my off-white-with-gold-trim desk, drawing up idyllic living arrangements.

After completing the floor plan, I would decide on the family who would inhabit the space, then sit down with the Sears catalog to compile the shopping list. My orders were always very detailed, including everything from kitchen appliances to socks and underwear for the home's imaginary residents.

So in Houston, at twenty-one years old, my contentment was palpable as I snuggled down into the reality of my boldly patterned, blue and brown sofa to watch TV. And I brimmed with satisfaction each time I pulled out one of the four matching honey-beige leatherette and chrome chairs to enjoy my corner view of the surrounding treetops while eating a meal.

For my bedroom, at the end of the hallway, I chose the perfect accompaniment to my free-flowing lifestyle—a waterbed. I also found an antique—Art Deco period—dresser, an item I lovingly stripped and refinished in my increasingly skilled handy-woman way.

The extra bedroom remained empty at first, a blank canvas used only for access to the second story balcony and my chaise, where I could lounge in the hot southern sun. In time, the space became a combination den and sewing room where I continued my creative call, whipping up a wide range of classic, conservative outfits, perfect for my up-and-coming accountant self.

I had worked in the collection of cozy, meandering apartment buildings for about nine months when workplace boredom once again set in. Used to free rent, I came up with a financially creative solution and presented it to my savvy boss. Though our relationship never touched on a maternal role, I had become quite friendly with this older woman.

The gist of the proposal included my collecting, reporting on, and depositing the monthly rent checks, just as I did in my full-time position, only I'd be free to do the work in the evenings or on weekends. In exchange, I'd be paid a small wage, enough to cover my apartment's monthly rent of $350.

Seeing the benefits of my ingenious plan, my boss agreed, and I switched into my next full-time career move—accounting assistant. The multi-state employer, headquartered in Houston, owned a variety of hotels, restaurants, and (what cinched the deal for me) nightclubs.

"I work at corporate" may not have sounded as exciting as "I'm with the band," but it gave me clout and free entry to their local clubs, Ciao and Élan. While both places offered everything you'd expect from a night-time hot spot—food, alcohol, good tunes and a place to dance—Ciao ended up being my favorite of the two.

Élan was nice, but since it had the distinction of being a members-only club, the snootiness of the regulars left me out in the cold. I hate to admit it, but I believed those fancy, well-funded customers were somehow better than me, and I imagined they whispered behind my back, "Oh, she's just the hired help."

Ciao, on the other hand, was more my vibe—stylish and hip without the arrogance. The club may not have been as exclusive as Élan, but it still commanded a line of eager patrons awaiting entry on Friday and Saturday nights. I of course strutted right past them, flashing my smile at the bouncers, who'd welcome me back as they stepped aside.

Along with my new job, I gained a new girlfriend, Linda. Although she had a college degree in accounting, we worked side-by-side in our cubical environment. Sharing a love for non-country on our desktop radios, we took most of our breaks together. Unfortunately, Linda wasn't all that interested in after-work activities. I convinced her to join me at the club a couple of times, but she always wanted to duck out early and head home to her solitude.

Luckily, one night after Linda left me unaccompanied at the bar, I met Karen. She smiled a large, warm grin as she leaned her abundant cleavage over the seat next to me, ordering a shot of tequila.

"Want one?" she asked, looking my way. Before I could answer, she directed the bartender, "Make it two."

After shooting the intense amber liquid and biting into the zing of lime, I introduced myself, offering thanks for the drink. Immediately fascinated with the voluptuous blonde, I accepted her invitation to join her and a couple of her girlfriends at a nearby table. From that point forward, Karen and I were disco buddies, hitting the club and its dance floor several nights a week.

Looking back, the ease with which Karen and I became friends reminds me of the comfortable group of friends I had in high school. Except, instead of being the good girls, we were hard-working-our-way-up-the-corporate-ladder ladies—who also knew how to have a good time.

For the first couple of months of my new single-girl lifestyle, I managed to keep school in the rotation. But by summer of 1978, rather than let my straight A record slip to a B or, even worse, a C, I dropped my classes, telling myself I'd start up again in the fall. Unfortunately, come September, I once again chose the bar over the classroom, withdrawing from my class load before flunking out.

Without school to take up my evenings, I fell into an uncomplicated routine. Mondays and Tuesdays were quiet nights usually spent at home or perhaps over at Linda's where we'd smoke pot and watch TV. I didn't like smoking marijuana alone but enjoyed the giggles Linda and I shared on those silly nights.

By Wednesday, Karen and I were ready to celebrate "hump" night, hitting the club early so we could grab a table. Depending on how late the festivities went, Thursday might be another at-home night, catching up on sleep before the all-important weekend. Of course, Friday and Saturday included the club. And since half the day Sunday could easily be taken up with sleeping-in, I spent many a wide-awake Sunday night at Ciao, perfecting my dance moves on the nearly empty wooden floor.

Unlike my previous best friend, Margie, Karen was quite different from me in appearance. Her long blond ringlets—requiring a head full of hot curlers—were held in place by incredible amounts of hairspray, and her makeup required at least thirty minutes to apply.

I'd often sit on the side of her bed watching the time-consuming routine. It puzzled me how someone who was attractive without all the fuss could put that much time into her appearance.

I've always been more of a natural girl. While curious enough about the process to let department store makeup girls do me up, I'd always head straight for the basin when I got home, more than ready to get that goop off my skin. For me, a quick curling iron to the ends of my straight, bleached-blond hair and a touch of mascara, shadow, and blush were all I wanted before heading into the night.

I'd never known anyone like Karen. Her love of life, unpretentious nature and reckless abandon spelled big-time fun. She could drink and dance and snort—oh yeah, cocaine had re-entered my life, though by then I no longer wore my spoon around my neck, opting instead for a pocket-rocket. That palm-sized cylinder measured out the perfect nonchalant blast, though everyone did blow, so discretion was hardly necessary.

The plentiful supply of coke also stripped me of any inhibitions the modest, good girl attempted to enforce. With an attitude towards casual sex every bit as enthusiastic as mine, Karen also loved to "get-down." I even gave her the perfect tee-shirt, whose message—"So Many Men, So Little Time"—blazoned proudly across her chest.

On a good night, the club would bring an abundance of cool, fun-to-talk-to guys who also loved to dance. Sometimes a guy would request my phone number, but dating rarely entered my life. For the most part, Karen and I would flirt and charm the guys that fell into the take-home category, and then invite two or more of them back to my place.

Between my room and the fold-out sofa in the den, we had plenty of mattress space for early-morning activities. During those wee hours, I would continue to drink and toot, keeping my performance in high gear. The only time I ran into trouble was when a guest pulled out a joint. Being a gracious hostess who didn't want to appear rude, I'd take a deep inhale, but without fail, I'd end up hugging the toilet, signaling the end of the party.

It was only a matter of time before my late-night, drug- and alcohol-infused hours crashed into my day-time, coffee-filled balancing act. Occasionally I'd stay up all night, dragging myself into the office with an aching head and a nose full of cocaine to fend off the exhaustion. On those days, my inner responsible girl would give the wild girl a stern talking-to, with the latter promising, *It won't happen again.*

Another such lecture from my prudent self occurred one morning when I got up to find my front door wide open, left so by a disrespectful guest. Although the entrance did not open directly onto the street, the blatant reminder of the previous night's abandon left my conservative self disquieted.

22: You Don't Want to Do This

In many respects, it was a typical Sunday: sleep until noon and then breakfast in bed with the *Houston Chronicle* spread out around me. My dog Buddy—a stray Basenji who adopted me when I moved into the two-bedroom place—kept a close eye on the meal, hoping for a bite of bacon or French toast. Like me, my curly-tailed companion enjoyed his independence, coming and going at his leisure throughout our quiet, bayou-side neighborhood. He was a good apartment dog, having the breed's odd trait of being bark-less.

Late in the afternoon, I got a visit from a tenant, a married cop who lived on the other side of the complex. Prior to that day we'd been friendly in the same way I was friendly with all the tenants, chatting about nothing when they delivered me their rent checks. I don't recall planning the quickie we shared that particular Sunday, but then again, I didn't plan most of the sex that went on in my apartment.

Evening brought its usual entertainment: meeting up with Karen at Ciao. By then I had also connected with a regular Sunday-night dance partner. I'd sit at my usual table-for-two, sipping on the Long Island Iced Tea—my favorite alcohol-packed drink—waiting for his arrival. Rarely disappointing me with a no-show, my guy would come along and sweep me off to one of the glowing, elevated dance floors.

I loved those dances. Something came over me when I hit the twelve-by-twelve wooden floor, especially with Disco Guy. I became carefree and could flawlessly glide into the moves of partner-dancing. With confidence, rhythm, and grace, I'd follow his lead, whirling and twirling like a pro, commanding that corner stage as ours.

Around midnight, contentedly worn out, I said good night to Karen and headed home—alone—ready for a decent night's sleep.

Walking into the four-unit building's foyer, I sleepily noticed the door of the vacant apartment below mine open a crack, but I brushed off the sense of not-right and climbed the stairs, happy to be home.

As I opened my front door, a wave of oven-hot air struck me. A split-second later, Buddy brushed past my legs and ran down the steps, anxious to gulp in the cold winter air.

Cursing at myself for not turning off the heater, I flipped on the light and went straight to the thermostat, where I moved the control to the Off position. Out loud, I reprimanded myself, "This is the second time this week. Look at it; it's over ninety degrees in here. Put in that repair order!"

Continuing to my bedroom, I opened the walk-in closet and stripped off my clothes. It was too hot for any nightgown or even a light robe. Walking naked to the bedroom window, I pulled back the drapes before sliding open the pane. With the drapes open, the exterior lights threw long tree-shadows across my bed. I quickly repeated the fresh-air process for the living room, dining room, and finally, kitchen windows—paying little attention to the voice of modesty.

After getting my favorite cartoon glass from the cupboard—the one with Natasha from *Rocky and Bullwinkle*—I opened the refrigerator. Grateful for the chilled air that fell on my feet, I reached for the milk and filled my glass. Returning the carton to the fridge, I stood in the dim light of the icebox, savoring the long, creamy swallows and the cool air. Despite the still-hot apartment, the icy beverage sent a shiver down my back.

I rinsed the glass and placed it in the sink before closing the refrigerator door and returning to the living room.

Since Buddy had been locked inside with the heat for several hours, I didn't bother to call him in before turning off the light and going to brush my teeth.

It was already cooler in my bedroom as I pulled back the covers and climbed onto my sloshing bed, pulling only a sheet over my naked skin. Still grumbling at myself for the sauna-like conditions, I adjusted the pillow and closed my eyes, wishing the waterbed weren't also radiating heat into my tired bones.

I'd only been in bed for a minute or two when I heard a violent crash from the second bedroom. In the heartbeat it took for me to sit bolt-upright, the intruder ran into the hall, where his dark frame stood illumined against the front window's diffused light. Before I had time to take a breath and scream, he was standing over me, telling me in a heavy accent he didn't want to hurt me, but he had a knife.

In disbelief, I snapped into mental clarity, repeating logic I'd heard on television dramas. "You don't want to do this," I said. "Please leave me alone. I won't call the cops; just get out of here."

Unzipping, he told me to shut up, then grabbed me and stuffed a rag—or was it a sock?—into my mouth. Fearful, I didn't try to dislodge it.

He yanked back the sheet and climbed on. Only momentarily surprised by the liquid mattress, he pinned back my arms and invaded my vagina, telling me again he didn't want to hurt me. As if it were a viable excuse, he said he was drunk and couldn't help himself. But his breath didn't smell of alcohol; it reeked of stale smoke—a stench he panted in my face in beat with his violating thrusts.

In shock, with time moving in extreme slow motion, I tried to make out his features, but only shadows appeared in the dim light. My mind looped between two questions: *Why me?* and *Why didn't I call Buddy back in?*

Continuing his admission of guilt, my rapist said he'd been waiting for me, sitting in the vacant apartment downstairs, thinking I would want to be with him. Then, as his grip on my wrists relaxed slightly, he told me he was sorry. Repeating that he'd had too much to drink, he also muttered, "It wasn't supposed to be like this."

After the invader climbed off and removed my gag, I once again spoke up, trying to convince him to leave by the front door, so I could see his face in the bright light of the stairwell. But he wasn't easily manipulated, insisting instead on retreating back through the den, and down the ladder he'd used to scale my balcony.

I threw on a robe and ran to my next-door neighbor's door. Knocking loudly, I cried out for Kay's help, only to be met by silence. Hurrying back home, I momentarily considered pounding on the wall of my walk-in closet, the one that backed up to Kay's, but decided against demanding her perhaps unwilling presence in my wide-awake nightmare.

With hands that wouldn't stop shaking, I dialed 9-1-1, telling the operator I had been raped and needed the police. Hanging up briefly, I then dialed Karen. Between deep choking sobs, I managed to tell her what had happened. She raced over, getting to my place a few minutes before the cops.

Right from the start, I felt guilty as the two male officers took down my story. I showed them the den's sliding glass door, explaining I had installed a floor bolt that kept the slider from opening more than six inches—enough space for safety that still allowed Buddy to step out onto the balcony.

Examining the heavy glass door, they told me locks like that were flimsy, and it looked as though the trespasser had pulled the door open with such force the latch didn't have time to engage. Internally, I scolded myself for not checking the lock before going to bed.

We also went downstairs, to inspect the ladder lying abandoned in the grass. Recognizing it as one that belonged in the apartment's cooling tower, I was hit by the premeditated nature of the crime. Thinking about the assailant's words—that he'd watched me and thought I'd like his advance—I wondered if I had enticed the attack, parading my nude body in front of the windows earlier in the week, the last time I'd forgotten to flip off the heat.

After the officers completed their paperwork and left, I still hadn't seen Buddy, but knowing he could fend for himself, I let Karen drive me to the hospital for the rape test. At least that procedure was administered by a woman. Still, spreading my legs into those stirrups to allow a closer look—and swab for semen—felt demeaning.

I figured the test would be worthless, since I'd had two men cum inside me over the past twelve hours. But rather than admit any promiscuous behavior, I kept that detail to myself, and went along with the process.

Around four in the morning, after I'd completed the necessary forms and tests, Karen and I stepped back into the night. My party-girl buddy proved to be a wonderful support, taking me back to her apartment and sitting with me. Bringing tea and tissues, she allowed me complete freedom to cry, question, and rant. With sunrise and the safety of daylight, Karen left me alone so she could get ready for work.

At eight a.m., unwilling to face the reality of the workweek, I called my boss. After sharing with her a brief recap of the break-in and attack, I then called Kay and asked her to put out some food and water for Buddy.

Curled up on Karen's sofa, I once again reviewed the night's events. Although physically and emotionally exhausted, I felt strangely comforted as I rolled the label—*Rape Victim*—over my tongue.

Welcoming the normalcy of life with Karen and her roommate, I stayed a couple more nights in their commotion-filled home, but by Wednesday, I longed for my beautiful, quiet, yet forever tainted, space.

Now, dredging this memory from the muck of my past brings with it a diversity of twisted reactions. Primarily, shame and guilt stand out along with deep sorrow; and there was also anger. Unfortunately, the anger wasn't directed outward toward the attacker, but pointed back at me—offering another not-so-subtle way I became my own abuser.

How amazingly easy it was to accept the role of victim. While one self-righteous inner aspect gleefully labeled me as a no-good slut who deserved what she got, another aspect actually felt empowered by the rape and occasionally flaunted a "wounded" status in her drama-queen orations. Beyond that, in keeping with the what-can-I-get-out-of-this mode that drove so much of my life, one morning I lied to my boss, saying I had to go to court for a hearing on the case when, in fact, the rapist was never caught—I simply wanted to sleep in that day.

Telling that lie took me one step lower on my self-evaluation scale. The detached, clinical voice who readily kept score of my offenses made it clear only a despicable human being is both a liar and a slut.

Fortunately, these days, that voice has become softer, like a distant echo drifting through a far-away canyon. Today I feel sorrow, both for the situation and the assumptions I made about myself as a result.

The now predominant aspect in me—the maternal, nurturing voice that becomes stronger each day—says, *Lighten up; stop the abuse. You've been in hell long enough.* This Divine Mother viewpoint doesn't try to understand why; she simply opens her arms, welcoming me and all my reactions into acceptance.

23: A New Track

    I'd like to say my life turned around after the rape, that a brush with the devil allowed the prudent, responsible, good girl to stand up and take control—but that's not what happened. Although my life did change, it was more along the lines of shifting to a train on a different track—whose ultimate destination remained the same.

    Linda had been bugging me for months to join her at the local drop-zone: a small airport south of town where skydivers gathered. Realizing her offer would bring a necessary change of scenery, I accepted.

    I'd always been fascinated by skydiving. When I flipped around the TV, images of people soaring through the air would cause me to stop, bringing my complete focused attention. Imagining I too was soaring through the air like a bird—wings supported by the currents I dipped in and through—gave me much pleasure, so I was excited to finally be awake and out of the house early enough on a Saturday to join her.

    Linda, who knew most of the spectators, introduced me to her older sister. They came religiously to watch Linda's brother-in-law, one of twenty or so tiny specks who would leap out of the old DC-3 once it reached the proper altitude.

    Skydivers, or jumpers, were unlike anyone I had met to date. Serious in their sport, they were also hard-core partiers, at least the ones in this group. With their motto, "Eat-Fuck-Skydive," I found myself quite at home with the new motley gang.

After free-falling solo, or gathering in formations for a few adrenaline-packed minutes, the men and women would engage their chutes, skillfully swooping back to earth. The whole process, from taking off, to feet safely back on the dirt, took about thirty minutes.

Everyone felt the rush of a jump, even those of us hanging out on the asphalt, peering up into the bright blue sky, trying to keep track of the aircraft. And all were jubilant, getting an easy contact high as we discussed the event afterwards.

Instantly star-stuck with the participants, my eyes were drawn to one of the particularly amped-up jumpers. Pulling Linda aside to ask the name of the sweaty-haired blond, she told me that was Dwayne, a wild and borderline-reckless guy who drove in from Louisiana.

Loving the attention I offered, Dwayne chatted easily as I watched him repack his chute, the most important task in skydiving. It didn't take long before we were an item.

Since Dwayne lived in Lake Charles, Louisiana, where he also held down a full-time warehouse job, our time together revolved around weekend visits. When he didn't have to work, he'd come to Houston, to my place, and of course to the drop-zone with its high-flying activities—and not just aerial highs. Dwayne and his cohorts also loved their coke, which they called "snow," often filling their noses between jumps.

One weekend—which we playfully dubbed The Blizzard That Hit Dallas—the Houston gang joined forces with jumpers from across the state. The daytime event was consistent with what went on at our local airstrip, except for a lot more planes and participants eager to jump out of them. By Saturday night, when thirty or more party-ready folks packed themselves into the largest tent, things really got festive.

At first the crowd huddled in small groups, sharing snow between themselves. Then someone got the idea to combine stashes. When confronted with the question of what could hold the blizzard, an auto mechanic told the group to hold tight as he stepped out of the canvas structure. A few minutes later, met by a rousing cheer, the handy guy reappeared with a window he'd pulled from the door of his car.

Holy shit, I'd never seen so much toot in one pile. It looked as though someone had dumped a bag of flour on the large pane of glass. Already sufficiently loaded, and possessed by the creative spirit, several artists in the group moved into position around the mountain.

With single-edge razor blades—a must-have tool for any coke lover—they chopped the snow into a fluffy powder before skillfully arranging it. Slowly, as those of us unskilled in coke-art looked on, the meticulously drawn design appeared: a skull-and-crossbones with a variety of small, equally threatening images surrounding it.

In a way, it was a shame to snort such a fine work of art. But gradually, the image disappeared into the early morning hours, bringing an eerie sense of playing at the edge of life and death.

Late Sunday afternoon we headed back south, speeding along country roads in Dwayne's 240Z convertible. Of course, he hadn't dumped his entire supply of the energizing drug into the shared pile the night before, so, as usual, we were buzzed.

Passing the time on the tree-lined highway, I reclined in the bucket seat with my eyes closed, absorbing the sun's rays and the rock tunes blasting from the radio. When Dwayne reached over to pull up my skirt and slide down my underwear, I didn't protest, since coke, in addition to bringing a sense of euphoria, sent my libido soaring while it erased the shy, reserved aspects of my psyche.

Completely uninhibited, I spread my legs wide, welcoming his adept fingers. We'd been traveling like that—with Dwayne's left hand guiding the sports car down the road, while his right drove me to multiple heights of ecstasy—when the sound of a truck's air horn broke my rapturous stupor.

Shocked, my eyes snapped open to see a trucker's partially toothless grin staring down at me. I looked to Dwayne, but he too smiled broadly, thoroughly enjoying the fact we'd been entertaining the stranger. Mortified, I snapped my legs shut and yanked my skirt over my lap, ordering Dwayne to speed up and lose the big rig.

On the weekends Dwayne had to work, I'd head east, making the three-hour drive after leaving the office on Friday, so I could be at his place early enough for drugs and sex before sleep. The first couple of times I made the trip, I passed time during the quiet weekend by reading or watching TV, waiting for him to get home. Then Dwayne suggested we meet up with another couple, Randy and his girlfriend Stephanie, a disc jockey at the only rock station in Lake Charles.

I hated her the first time I heard that soft, titillating voice come across the radio. *Shit, he thinks we can be friends?* Keeping my envious reaction to myself, I purposefully took my time the Friday night we were supposed to meet.

Letting go of frustration, I sat in line beneath the *Last Gas in Texas* sign. As the hour—or was it two?—ticked by, I told myself I was being safe, I didn't want to get stuck on I-10 in the middle of nowhere. And I was playing it safe, buffering myself from that temptress on the airwaves.

To my surprise, I loved her the moment we met, a few weeks later. By then, Randy had moved to Detroit, so it was just the three of us who climbed into my 320i for an afternoon drive in the back woods. Leaning forward from his perch in the back seat, Dwayne tried to join the conversation between us girls up front, but he'd become virtually unseen, acknowledged only for his steady supply of toot.

From that point forward, my visits to Lake Charles revolved more around spending time with my new best friend, and less about the guy I slept with. In fact, sex with Dwayne had drifted into the routine, and therefore boring, realm. One Sunday morning, as Stephanie and I sat at the kitchen table making plans, Dwayne acted particularly antsy and scattered as he prepared for a day at work.

Dropping a folded-up packet of coke on the table, he said, "Have fun, you two," before walking out the kitchen door. We didn't think much of it when, a few minutes later, he came bursting back in muttering some excuse about a forgotten item. Deep in conversation, we barely paid attention as he once again left the kitchen.

By the third time Dwayne threw open the back door, we began to take notice. Questioning what could be his motivation, Stephanie and I decided he expected to step in to find us entangled in each other's arms, rolling around on the kitchen vinyl, hungrily ripping off each other's clothes.

The vision sent us into gales of laughter, and we began to make guesses as to how many minutes would pass before another, by then expected, return. Like a record stuck in a groove, Dwayne repeated the odd behavior several more times before he finally gave up and drove to work—easily an hour late.

My auburn-haired friend and I shared many a good time in my cruise-mobile, sunroof open and wind blowing wildly around our free spirits. With the volume cranked, we'd sing along to our favorite bands, like The Cars. For serious conversations, we'd park in the lush green foliage of the bayou country, often fantasizing about what we'd do if we ever got our hands on Benjamin Orr, The Car's bassist.

One afternoon, I joined Stephanie at a party, where a guy friend of hers asked how long we'd known each other. Surprised when she told him we'd only met a couple of weeks earlier, he responded, "You act as though you've been friends for life."

I grinned widely and nodded in agreement when I heard her response, a line adapted from an album title: "We're twins from different mothers."

Within a few weeks of my meeting this newest soul sister, Dwayne came up with what he considered to be a grand idea: take out a loan on his house to buy a kilo of coke. By then, our plentiful supply—a half-gallon jar he'd gotten from a dentist cousin—was running low. Figuring the abundant quantity would allow sales, as well as cover personal use, he set about the paperwork.

As much as I loved blow, I drew the line at mortgaging the house for it. But Dwayne had made up his mind and my fiscally responsible arguments couldn't convince him to rethink his plan. Not wanting to be involved with a drug dealer, I broke things off with Dwayne—but hung onto my friendship with Stephanie.

By November 1979 I once again felt the need for change. I still enjoyed my friendship with Linda and occasional visits to the drop-zone. Some nights I would join Karen at Ciao, though more often I attended parties she threw in her home. Sometimes Stephanie would head west, joining me for weekends in Houston, but she too was feeling the call of something new.

Her inner compass pointed towards Dallas and the large-scale radio market it offered. I considered joining her in the move north come the first of the new year, but before that, I wanted to go home, to California.

In an unprecedented offer, my mom suggested a family Christmas in their mountain cabin. I suspected her invitation was related to the fact she felt bad about the rape earlier in the year. Nonetheless, the idea of family sounded good. It had been nearly five years since I'd left home.

My brother, who had joined the army, would also be home for the holidays, so somehow Mom had convinced Dad, and plans were made for us all to gather. Flying back to Orange County, I grew excited about my upcoming trip to Mammoth and the prospect of playing in real—falling from the sky—snow.

24: Here We Go Again

Standing in line—one of those long, back-and-forth type queues—I felt both exhilarated and worn out from a morning on the slopes. When my family and I had arrived four hours earlier, the combination of juggling skis without hitting anyone, and stomping through the lodge in rigid boots without falling, put me at the verge of quitting before I started. A single tear rolled down my cheek before I pulled it together, telling myself, *If Mom can do this, I sure as hell can.*

Once in my beginner ski class, surrounded by students half my size, I focused on the Levi's my step-dad had waterproofed with a can of spray-on repellant, gathering further evidence I didn't fit in with the stylishly attired, coordinated crowd. But then the class started, and I slowly made my way up the bunny slope, sideways, step-by-awkward-step. Miraculously, I made it back down that miniscule incline without falling.

After repeating the process a dozen or more times, my rubbery thighs were grateful to meet up with the rest of the family for lunch.

Chatting excitedly with Mom as we moved around one of the bends in the line, I jumped back, startled by a male voice just over my left shoulder. Looking up, I wondered where the tall, thin, bearded guy had come from. Dismissing my sense of alarm from being so close to someone without knowing it, I apologized for not seeing him.

The previously invisible man, who had a nice smile and soft, blue eyes, slipped easily into conversation with Mom and me. By the time we reached the front of the line, my entire family, which by then included three kids besides me, had been charmed by Mark, my second husband-to-be.

After ordering our meals, we followed him through the maze of long tables, where a guy he'd met earlier on the chair-lift held a seat. Piling seven people into a space for one took a bit of doing, but we managed to squeeze in and surround the easygoing, attractive young man named Dean.

Shyly listening to the conversation driven by my talkative step-dad, I learned that Dean lived further north and was in Mammoth skiing solo for the pre-holiday weekend, while Mark came to the trendy mountain resort with his parents, who owned a condo in town.

Barely involved in the lunchtime chatter, I was surprised when Dean offered an invitation for dinner that night. Uncertain I'd be able to pull off the chit-chat required on a date, but glad to have a break from the family, I accepted, giving him directions to our house.

Late that afternoon, completely done-in from my first day on the slopes, I regretted accepting the invitation, but without a way to contact my date, I resigned myself to the outing. I threw on some warm, dry clothes and a touch of eye makeup, then laced up my city-girl, definitely-not-snow-savvy boots, and was ready for the evening.

After more aimless banter between my dad and Dean, we stepped into the brisk night air. I walked carefully along the snow-covered path and then settled into the passenger side of Dean's two-seater sports car. As he turned on the engine, he said, "I hope you don't mind, I invited Mark too. He's meeting us at the restaurant."

Even without my usual mood elevator of drugs or alcohol, our dinner conversation went smoothly, and I enjoyed the attention from two good-looking, athletic guys. Dean and I did most of the talking between our mouthfuls of steak and potatoes, with Mark holding the quiet place I had occupied during lunch.

As he pushed back an empty plate, Dean asked if I wanted to dance, to which I uncharacteristically said, "No, but you go on."

Once Mark and I were alone at the table, we began the conversation, which in hindsight, flashed a neon warning of our perhaps fateful incompatibility. Offering me a cigarette, Mark posed his question: "In the Dessert Cart of Life, what do you want?"

After lighting the Marlboros, he leaned back in his chair, stretching his long legs out in front of him. Matching his relaxed posture, I took a long, deep draw. Watching my smoke rings float up to the ceiling, I answered, "I want it all."

"You can't have it all," he countered. "You have to pick one."

"No, I want a bite of each."

Neither of us was willing to budge from his or her position, and while the tension over the subject remained obvious, it didn't stop us from continuing to get to know each other. When I mentioned I was trying to quit smoking, and had brought along some joints to help take the edge off when I wanted something to inhale, Mark perked up.

"Do you have any with you?"

"Yeah, right here in my purse."

"Let's go for a drive."

Leaving money for dinner and saying a quick good-bye to Dean, Mark and I walked though the freshly plowed parking lot before climbing into his dad's Mercedes Benz. Opening the window a crack to keep the marijuana from stinking up the leather upholstery, I explained to Mark that my favorite drug was coke, but I didn't bring any along.

"Me either," he said. "But I've got a friend at home who always has it."

We passed the joint back and forth a few times while driving around the small community, then pulled up to the curb outside my parents' winter home. Sitting in the warmth of the luxury vehicle, Mark asked if I'd like to have dinner with him and his parents the following night. Though I felt nervous about the prospect of meeting his mom and dad, I said yes.

"Okay, tomorrow, five-thirty. We'll pick you up here."

Stepping into the clear night air, I took a deep, giddy breath before I stuck a piece of mint gum in my mouth and headed into the house.

When Mark was a few minutes late the next night, my step-father started in. "You've been stood up."

"No, I haven't. They're just running late."

"Can you call him to see if he's still coming?" Mom asked.

"No. He didn't give me his number."

"You've been stood up," my step-father said again.

Fearful he might be right, I paced the living room, occasionally stepping out the front door to peer over the snow bank and look for the dark brown sedan. Every five minutes or so, Dad repeated his proclamation, each time a bit more smugly.

By six o'clock he stated, "We're going to dinner. You can either come with us, or go hungry." Sullen, I pulled on my winter coat and followed my younger siblings out to the family car.

We'd been home from dinner for about an hour when the phone rang.

"Debi, it's for you." Smiling as she handed me the phone, Mom whispered, "I think it's Mark."

It turned out Mark had been running late, a trait I came to know very well in the years ahead. And he was quite surprised to discover I didn't wait for him. Looking back, I wonder if that unintentional act of independence prompted Mark to stay interested in the girl who lived fifteen hundred miles away.

My hopes we could take a rain check on the missed dinner were dashed when I learned that Mark and his parents would be heading home to southern California the next day. Unwilling to let go of the prospect of seeing the brown-haired, apparently well-off skier again, I brought up the idea of getting together down south.

After I mentioned I'd have a free night at the end of the week before flying back to Texas, he gave me his home number and we made plans to talk when I returned from the family ski trip.

Eager to see Mark again—and enjoy some of the toot he said was readily available—I talked my brother into driving me the fifty miles between our parents' home in Newport Beach and Mark's home in Claremont. Mark agreed to drive the return route.

Rather than meet at his parents' house, where my new love interest lived while attending college, we met at his friend Nick's, the guy with the coke.

As I watched excitedly, he chopped the white powder, then drew lines in the familiar, ritualistic manner; I told myself to appear cool and nonchalant. Pulling a crisp hundred-dollar bill from his wallet, Mark rolled a makeshift straw before passing it to me. I knelt over the charm-activating drug—served on the glass-top coffee table—and happily snorted my way into confident, talkative mode.

Although I had been born and raised in California, four years of living in the south had rubbed off in a southern drawl that poured from my lips, delighting my small audience. As the evening ticked by, we drank beers, drew lines, and laughed over stories, including the one of how Mark and I had met.

Around three in the morning—after purchasing a supply of toot to keep the cheerful mood going—we said good night to Nick. Walking to the curb, Mark assured me his parents would be sound asleep, so we climbed into his Trans Am and headed north, into the nearby foothills.

From the street, the house and its six-foot brick wall seemed unobtrusive. Opening the wrought-iron gate to the left of the triple garage doors, we were greeted by the family pet, a large guard dog named Pica. Instinctively comfortable with the beautiful German Shepherd, I reached down to stroke her thick winter coat. I then followed Mark into the garage, sorry Pica couldn't join us inside. Motioning for me to stay quiet, Mark opened the door into the laundry room.

Disconcerted, I looked past the washer and dryer down the long, carpeted hallway and wondered what the heck I'd gotten myself into. Still, I followed Mark past numerous closed doors. Knowing his parents slept behind one of them made my already-amped heart pound even harder, but eventually the hall made a right turn and opened into the main living space.

We continued across the tiled entry, past the formal living and dining rooms, before stepping down into the family room. Gently shutting the door behind us, Mark once again motioned for me to stay quiet as he disappeared into the kitchen.

I gazed out the picture windows, amazed at the spectacular array of twinkling lights—spanning a hundred eighty degrees. After verifying our privacy in the large, stately home, Mark returned, once again startling me as he came up from behind. Laughing quietly, we plopped down on the extra long blue and beige tweedy sofa.

Following a little refresher boost, we shared our first kiss. Fueled by passion—not to mention drugs—we wasted little time before stretching out along the cushions. Part of me—the prim and proper modest girl—didn't approve of getting hot and heavy with a near stranger, especially while his parents snoozed at the other end of the house. However, the horny me—with her nose full of blow—wasn't about to listen to sage advice and seized the opportunity for yet another conquest.

Although a year and a half older than I was, and thus I presumed sexually experienced, Mark appeared naïve and uncertain as our petting neared that point of no return. As though witnessing a predictable porn movie—where the innocent young man is seduced by the wanton woman—I slipped into well-practiced moves. With pulsing hips and my wraparound legs holding a vise-like grip, I left Mark virtually no option but to have sex with me—not that he seemed to mind.

Ever conscious that our love nest was the family's gathering spot for relaxation and television viewing, I made certain not to leave a tell-tale mess. Tightening my vaginal muscles—which were well toned and amazingly able to hold in liquids—I tiptoed back into the main part of the house to use the guest bath.

With dawn still a couple of hours away, Mark and I once again packed our noses, and after saying good-bye to Pica, got back into his seventies-style hot rod. Since I needed to get to Orange County for a flight later that morning, I suggested we drive to the beach, where we could enjoy breakfast at an all-night diner. Proudly displaying his vehicle's abundant horsepower, he raced along the nearly deserted freeways, and we arrived at our seaside destination in a flash.

I'd been to the Newport Pier many times in my youth, so I wasn't surprised to see a relatively full parking lot, even at this early morning hour. Grumbling about the small spaces, Mark drove toward the far end of the lot before pulling in and turning off the engine, hopeful his car's pristine paint job would remain safe in the semi-remote location. Eager to lighten his souring mood, I suggested a walk on the sand, which he declined, stating, "It's too cold."

"Well, how about breakfast? Charlie's Chili is right over there. It's really good."

Excited to introduce Mark to one of my favorite post-bar eating establishments, I led him down the boardwalk, where we were serenaded by powerful waves crashing on the moonlit beach. After stepping into the hubbub of the popular restaurant, we found a table and asked for two cups of coffee. With our meal ordered, Mark's crankiness increased. Muttering loud enough for me to hear him over the din, he began a string of petty complaints about the setting, its clientele, and, once delivered, our food.

Sorry I had subjected him to the raucous atmosphere, I ate my chili omelet and side of toast quickly. By the time we stepped back into the fresh ocean breeze, the eastern horizon showed signs of the impending dawn. Knowing my parents would be up soon, we drove over to the house so I could retrieve my already-packed suitcase.

Over hugs and tears, I stood on the concrete driveway and said good-bye to the family I'd felt estranged from for so many years. Dropping into nice-guy social graces, my step-father passed Mark my luggage, then reached out to shake his hand. As though congratulating Mark on a job well done, Dad's free hand reached around, patting my latest lover on the back.

Once curbside at what was back then a sleepy little airport, Mark and I shared a passionate good-bye kiss and one last blast of coke, forcing my exhausted system into another boosted overdrive.

On the plane—with out-of-control emotions gyrating between warm-hearted highs and sob-inducing lows—I reviewed the past week spent with family and the previous twelve hours shared with Mark. Little did I know, in less than a month, my life would take its most abrupt directional change yet.

25: Pre-marital Bliss, Take Two

"What the hell is wrong with you? I can't believe you did that! Is that how you were taught to behave in public?"

Mark's fury bites deeply into my moments-before-delighted psyche. Frozen—as the turbocharged engine rumbles hungrily at the red light—I absorb the full impact of his tirade.

Why is he so upset? I wonder. *All I did was sing and wiggle around a little bit. I wasn't even loud. It's such a happy, catchy tune, and The Flying Lizards' version is so much cooler than the Beatles'. How can he not like it?*

"The best things in life are free
But you can give them to the birds and bees
I want money
That's what I want . . .
Your love give me such a thrill
But your love won't pay my bills
I want money
That's what I want . . ."

Dumbfounded, I can't comprehend his fervor—and apparent glee—while he rips me apart. Watching hot tears drop silently in my lap, I stare at my motionless hands, demanding they take action. *Open the door. Get out. Run. Now! Before the light turns green.*

No. I can't. I don't know where I am.

Don't worry about that. You have to get away.

But my things . . . I've moved everything here. I'm scared. I don't know what to do.

Open the door. Now!

But I couldn't. I sat in submissive hell, part of me sensing I had sealed my fate with an abuser. As the sweet man I'd met skiing over the Christmas holiday ruthlessly detailed my flawed character traits, I didn't question his observations or defend myself. On some level—outside of conscious awareness—I accepted that I'd finally met someone who saw me for the truly despicable person I was, someone who could mold me into being a better person.

There had been several signs of Mark's sharp tongue in the weeks preceding my failed escape at the red light, like the time he flew to Houston to help me move back to California. . . .

It had been almost a month since we'd met—and shared that "quickie" of hungry, coke-fueled sex—and I couldn't wait to see the guy I'd gotten to know over the phone. Thanks to the 800 line on my desk, we had talked every weekday.

After dialing his number at straight-up five o'clock, we'd discuss our daily routine. I told him about my efforts to collect past-due funds for the hospitality firm and how many checks I had received as a result of my keen negotiation skills. In return, he told me about his grueling class load and hoped-for results from mid-terms at USC, the University of Southern California.

I'd first learned he attended the prestigious school shortly after we met, during lunch with my family in Mammoth. Mark's tale of a dual major—in economics and business management—greatly impressed Dad, who had graduated from the same institution many years before. I noted their camaraderie as a point in my favor.

Taking advantage of his spring break, Mark flew to Houston late in January, 1980, to assist me in loading up a U-Haul trailer with all of my precious belongings. Well, not all of my beloved items—though without hesitation I made sure the teal-blue dishes survived the cut.

He took one look at my 1920s dresser—the one I had lovingly refinished to its original mahogany richness—before stating, "That's not an antique." In a pompous tone, he continued, "Americans don't know the meaning of antique. Get rid of it." So I did.

I also got rid of my comfy living room sofa and loveseat, though thankfully the set went on to live a long and happy life with Stephanie up in Dallas. And Buddy, well, he too had to go. Fortunately, I found someone with a farm where he could run and not-bark to his heart's content. Sadly, some of my friends also fell into the expendable category.

Super Bowl Sunday was a big deal for Karen. Her annual bash included not only the game itself, but a lovingly prepared array of Bowl-worthy treats, like Texas barbeque and her famous hot cheese dip.

Arriving at her apartment with the well-attended event in full swing, I excitedly introduced Mark to my dear friend and several of the other guests. The fun-loving, talkative guy I had gotten to know over the phone turned quiet and borderline rude on the few occasions he entered into conversation with the football-crazed gang.

Embarrassed by his behavior and no longer interested in who would win the big game, I admitted defeat, slinking away from the party with an awkward excuse to the hostess.

"She's a cheap slut," Mark announced cruelly, as I drove us back to my place. "I can't believe you're friends with someone like that."

Sure, Karen wore heavy makeup and skintight tee-shirts accentuating every curve of her double-D boobs. And yeah, she slept around—we both did. That's why I liked her so much; she was my party buddy. And when the rapist broke into my apartment, she didn't add shame or blame to the ordeal; she sat with me, offering Kleenex and comfort.

But I kept those details to myself, betraying our friendship with my meek response, "Well, I don't know her that well." In another clear disconnection moment, I tossed Karen into the leave-it-behind pile. I wonder what ever happened to her.

With the trailer loaded and the apartment closed up, I said a teary good-bye to my home along the Buffalo Bayou and the wild string of adventures held within its walls. Climbing into my trusty Bimmer, we headed west, dawn barely breaking in the rearview mirror. Any sane person would have planned three days to drive the expanse between Houston and Los Angeles, but Mark wanted to make it in two.

Although I'd recently spent somewhat comfortable time with my family—Christmas in Mammoth—moving back into their abode was not an option. So instead, Mark's mom opened their home to me. In retrospect, it seems quite odd to move in with people—especially parents—I had yet to meet, but that's exactly what I did. Of course, I had my own room, though Mark and I shared a bathroom—not to mention middle-of-the-night "quickies."

From the twin bed previously occupied by his older brother, I spent many a morning staring up at a black velvet painting of a leopard. In many ways I felt as out of place in the finely furnished home as that stationary feline, though Mark's mom offered me nothing but the warmest welcome.

Once again settled in Southern California—well, living out of a few boxes that weren't held in storage—the reality of my new life began to unfold. First up, I witnessed Mark's true routine.

Turns out those stressful days filled with lectures and exams had actually been spent at his friend Nick's house kicking back beers and smoking pot. Amazed Mark could divert funds and deceive his parents so effortlessly, I stepped into the role of his conscience, convincing my bathroom mate he needed to come clean.

Blaming his habitual truancy on a love of drugs, he sheepishly agreed he needed a change of pace. However, instead of admitting the ruse himself, he asked me to play the role of whistleblower. Reluctantly, I agreed to talk to his mom.

Since I had no problem with our coke use, I limited my appeal that sunny, early February afternoon. "Mark needs your help. He's got a problem with smoking marijuana."

A startled reaction flashed quickly across the small woman's tastefully made-up face before she clicked into full-throttle rescue mode. Thanking me for my concern, my future mother-in-law picked up the phone, and with emotions in check, dialed her husband's office.

As I listened to one side of an indecipherable Norwegian conversation, I wondered if their answer would include a rehab center, though I hoped it would simply be therapy.

Nervous throughout dinner, I wondered when—and if—they would broach the subject. As I cleared plates and his dad prepared the after-dinner coffee, Mark's mom broke the tension.

"You're going to work for your father."

"I want you there full-time," his dad continued in a tone that left no room for debate. "You'll manage the workers."

"It's a great opportunity and we know you'll do well."

When they explained the new position would include compensation, I realized his parents would maintain their own habit—supplying financial support.

A few minutes later, as we sat around the kitchen table sipping the strong, unsweetened brew, I felt puzzled there had been no mention of counseling—let alone the drugs. I considered pointing out the omission, then thought better of it, figuring I had done enough.

With my boyfriend's time taken up by his Monday through Friday work routine, I expanded my own daily activities—primarily watching television—to include getting to know his mom. No, that's not true. The person I got to know was her sweet baby boy, number two of three, as seen through her loving eyes.

Listening carefully to the stories of Mark's childhood trials and tribulations, I offered understanding nods and supportive responses. Mindful that I wanted to fit into the good-looking Scandinavian family, I kept silent about my own past.

Armed with his weekly paycheck—and a good one at that—Mark and I simply limited our fun to weekends and partying at Nick's house, at least for the next few weeks, before his parents flew out on a long-planned vacation including a pilgrimage to Haifa, Israel.

After pulling a few strings, Mark's parents announced their son would join them on the tour of holy sites, though he wouldn't leave until a week after their departure.

I'd attended rich kids' while-the-cat's-away-type parties before in Newport Beach, but I had absolutely no experience in throwing such an event. Mark, however, was well versed in the art, and promptly after the automatic garage door signaled our unmonitored status, he got busy with invitations for a gathering.

With a steady stream of guys and girls showing up, booze and bathing suits in hand—not to mention coke and grass—unrestrained laughter filled the house, hot tub, and pool. Amidst the attendees, many of whom Mark had hung out with since high school, one mousy blonde, who obviously had a crush on Mark, eyed me warily as she flirted her way around the party. Unable to find my own easy-going groove, I slunk back to my room.

In solitary confinement, I grew certain my guy was cavorting with the bikini-clad females. Fueled by this drug-related paranoia, I crept around the rough stucco exterior to listen in on his conversations. I didn't hear anything incriminating from my peeper perspective, but the action itself encouraged the inner critic, who chastised me harshly.

Look at yourself. You've dropped to an all-time low, even for you. It's only a matter of time before he dumps you.

As I stood at the edge of the ivy-covered slope, my weak grasp on self-assurance slipped further away.

After returning from the family visit to their faith's sacred city, and steeped in time of prayerful reflection, Mark seemed happy and at peace. Wanting my own connection to salvation, I took up the family's religious beliefs. I actually believed I could fit into my new beau's world as I joyfully participated in large events they often held in their home with the beautiful views.

My parents had also been struck with the admiration bug, particularly my step-father. He and Mark's dad reveled in their upper-middle-class versions of good-ol'-boy exchanges whenever they were together—another point I took in my favor.

From my perspective, it seemed I finally had a chance to live the life I had grown up expecting. And for the most part, despite occasional criticisms from Mark, I performed my new role flawlessly.

By late spring—with my place in the family Jacuzzi firmly established—we began to discuss marriage.

26: The Next Big Day

"This is a mistake."

"What's a mistake?"

Startled by the question, I realized I'd spoken out loud. Tightening my grip on the steering wheel, I turned to Linda, who had flown in to attend the following day's celebration.

"Marrying Mark," I replied. "Marrying Mark is a mistake."

"Then don't do it," she stated practically.

As much I wanted to follow my friend's advice, I'd gone too far down the in-law hole to back out. By late August 1980, as Linda and I drove around doing last-minute errands, I saw no escape from the perfect life unfolding before me.

In the beginning, it was fun to play house with Mark. With his parents once again abroad, we enjoyed the early summer on our own, complete with weekend parties. Thankfully, after my first introduction to Mark's circle of friends, I'd grown more confident in my social abilities—or at least in my ability to play hostess—thanks to a steady supply of cocaine.

For true security and self-esteem, I returned to the accounting world, stepping into a full-time position at a local CPA firm—thanks to a friend of a friend of Mark's mom.

By July, with his parents back home, we got busy with the details of our upcoming ceremony. Excited to be planning a wedding a little more elaborate than the broken piggy-bank event I'd had with Ed, I shared my vision with Mark's mom.

Yeah, I know tradition calls for the bride's parents to do that part, but their involvement was limited. I received genuine enthusiasm when I told Mom and my step-dad about the engagement, showing off my pretty, tastefully modest diamond ring. But later, Mom made it clear they wouldn't be offering any monetary support.

She also made it clear that while they would be able to attend my second big day, they would only come if I didn't invite my real father. Although annoyed with my mother's ultimatum, I was also glad I wouldn't need to deal with the tension of having both sets of parents in attendance.

Mom's statement pissed off Mark, who had met my father and step-mother earlier in the year. In defense of honoring my Mom's demand, I reminded Mark that I didn't spend much time around my father because I felt creepy in his presence, prompting my fiancé into a mini-lecture on having respect for the man who had given me life. However, he didn't force the issue.

Although I had a few family members to invite, thanks to my mom's parents and my step-dad's side of the family, the only friends I included were my Texas sidekicks, Stephanie and Linda.

Earlier that summer, I had attempted rekindling long-silent southern California friendships, contacting Evie from the group of comfortable high school pals. Surprised, but pleased to hear from me, she gathered the group for dinner in a nice L.A. restaurant.

Mark remained silent as five of the original gang of eight chatted excitedly over memories and tales from our current-day lives. It felt right to reconnect with friends from a simple time in my life, and I left the restaurant happy, looking forward to seeing some or all again. Regrettably, Mark had other ideas.

As we drove home, he ranted about how rude they had all been, talking only of themselves, never once bringing him into the conversation. If they were truly good friends, he maintained, they would have wanted to get to know him. Accepting his criticisms as fact, I allowed his alienating tactics to seep in and do their dirty work.

With the wedding invitations printed and mailed, I shifted my attention to food and the all-important cake: a classic, multi-tiered design. Of course, the celebration would be held in Mark's parents' house, a space easily adapted to fancy parties. Trusting in her ability to plan the event, I made only one primary design request of Mark's mom: pink roses.

"You can't have pink," she stated flatly. "It would clash with our furniture."

"But I want pink," I whined.

"Sorry, they have to be peach; I've already talked it over with the florist."

Dejected, I agreed, then bowed out of all remaining preparations. At least I got to pick my dress—though I sheepishly accepted money from my future father-in-law for that, too.

In addition to setting us up with careers and handling our wedding plans, Mark's parents provided the down payment we needed for our first and only home.

Since the purchase was complete by mid-August, a couple of weeks before our legally hitched status, Mark moved in by himself—technically. As long as I was back in time to emerge from my room in his parents' home dressed differently for breakfast than I had been for dinner the night before, I felt all was okay in my role of "proper" daughter-in-law-to-be.

With a place of our own, where we could cut loose, our weekend party schedule began to creep into work nights. Our drug use had also expanded to include crank, a white powder similar in appearance to coke, but cheaper and with one hell of a punch and stinging sensation when snorted. Mark loved our speedy new companion and would often opt for it as our party drug. I didn't like the tension it created in my jaw and overall way-too-amped sensation, but when we didn't have cocaine, the crystal meth would do.

As we partied on the eve of our wedding—a bash that included Mark's closest local friends, plus Linda—I knew I had to get some sleep. But, in usual addict fashion, one line led to another. By four a.m., after saying good morning to Pica, Linda and I snuck into my almost in-laws' house.

Lying on the small bed for the last time, I knew I needed to close my eyes and get at least a few hours of sleep, but my eyelids wouldn't cooperate. Instead, my baby blues locked onto the motionless leopard who stared down at me as I listened to the inner chaos.

I'm scared. I know this is everything I've ever wanted, but I feel so lost and out of control. I don't want to be here. I'm living a lie. I love Mark, but it's happening so fast. I need to slow down, but I can't. How did I get myself into this mess? Now what?

Lost in thoughts wisely questioning my life, and with a gut crying out with familiar *don't-do-this* cramps, I drifted into quasi-sleep. The doorbell snapped me back to reality. After putting on my robe, I stepped into the commotion, already in full swing at eight a.m.—six hours before the ceremony. By noon, with a combination of exhaustion and doubt weighing heavily on me, Linda offered a little energy blast of cocaine.

Pleasantly perky after accepting her gift, I carried on the charade of last-minute blessed-union preparations, with only Linda knowing my secret. When Mark showed up an hour later, my "happy" mode in full swing, I didn't hesitate to fill my nose when he offered his pocket rocket.

As we stood in the hallway of his parents' home—with baby pictures of him and his brothers looking over our shoulders—I realized I had just snorted crank, not coke. The harsh powder burned through my sensitive nasal passages. Questioning Mark about his drug choice, he kissed me and said, "You'll be fine. Here, have another." So I did. Not long after, when Linda offered another pre-vows boost of coke, I said yes to that too, hoping it might take the edge off the speed.

I know from the photographs I looked beautiful for our blissful day. Framed by waves of golden blond hair beneath a wide-brimmed, cream-color hat, my face glowed with its summer tan. For most of the late-afternoon and early evening, a wide, ecstatic grin was plastered on my face.

Hoping the guests simply saw me as a nervous new bride, I repeated the best I could pull out of a brain in extreme drug overdrive: "Hi, how are you? Nice to see you. Thank you for coming."

A month later, my father pointed out my way-too-dilated pupils when I showed him those beloved photo memories.

"Look at your eyes! What were you on?"

Taken back by his directness, I did the only thing I could—lie. "Nothing. I don't know what you mean. See, I'm holding a bottle of Perrier."

27: Worlds Collide

From the curb of our professionally landscaped, picture perfect, three-bedroom suburban home, we looked like any other young professional couple. Monday through Friday I'd head off to my accounting job, while Mark played his part managing the family business. I even returned to school two nights a week, once again focused on my goal to become a CPA.

On the weekends I didn't sleep all day recovering from an all-night coke or crank fest, I passed my time on creative projects around the house, like the floor-to-ceiling loose weave drapes I sewed for the family room. Together, Mark and I tackled the backyard, laying sod, planting trees, and starting my must-have rose garden.

In many respects my new life brought joy and contentment. Even our social circle had grown tolerable, primarily due to spending more time with Mark's abandoned college-life friends and backgammon.

I loved the ancient board game and excelled in its combination of skill and number logic. It also helped delay the inevitable—going to bed with my husband.

It's not that I'd grown tired of sex, but after our wedding, things between us changed. Perhaps Mark became more daring. Perhaps I became more of a prude. Whatever the cause, we didn't sync up as well as we had in our adventurous pre-marital romps. The honeymoon brought my first glimpse into Mark's previously unspoken sexual desires. . . .

It was the morning after our wedding, and we were in the car, driving to Mark's parents' condo in Mammoth for part one of our post-marital celebration—part two would occur the next summer, in Europe. Still in big-time festive mode, we snorted coke as we sped along Route 395. Midway into the five-hour journey, my husband broached a new topic.

"I've got someone meeting us in Mammoth."

At first I couldn't figure out what he meant and wondered, This is our honeymoon. Why is someone meeting us? *Before I asked my question out loud, he continued.*

"A woman."

Sickened, but fairly sure we were pretending, I went along with the fantasy, asking, "Yeah, who is she?"

And so it began, the thought of a threesome dangling in the high-desert air between us—the first act of a tenacious game. As the miles clicked by, I indulged his daydream, batting back each line of his makeshift script. Although Mark knew nothing about my previous professional status, I instinctively slipped into call girl mode. While that aspect kept hubby happy, the blushing bride within felt lost, abandoned, and soiled.

Obviously I wasn't a virgin, but somewhere in my psyche I spun my own fantasy, one that included a gentle, caring, first-time lover. Expecting his elaborate story to go away once we settled into the condo and had dinner, I got scared when it once again surfaced.

"The doorbell is going to ring any minute now. Are you ready?"

"Yes," is what I said, but inside I cried, and shut down.

Although I'd enjoyed a few female encounters back at Danni's, sharing my husband touched off a huge wave of self-doubt and jealousy. Questions like, *What's wrong with me? Am I good enough? What if he likes her more?* and *How will we get rid of her?* whirled around my head.

The bell never rang, but a protective layer had clicked in. Whatever chance there had been of sacred union with my beloved passed by—not that I had a clue about such things.

About six months into marriage number two, Stephanie came to California. I'd been quite disappointed when my dear sister-friend said she couldn't make it to our ceremony, but understood her new life, working at a major Dallas radio station, took precedence. When she called in the spring of 1981 to say she'd be coming to town for a one-night industry gig that included accommodations, I told Mark I'd be away for the night.

After picking up my best buddy at LAX, we slid open my trusty cruise-mobile's sunroof and headed for one of Hollywood's most famous rocker hotels, The Hyatt House. It felt odd to once again be in a hotel I'd frequented back in my groupie days, but I puffed my chest and strutted across the lobby. Being with Stephanie made me feel legitimate in the music world. I wasn't just a nobody waiting for a security guard or roadie to offer me a chance at a rock star.

With the sun sinking low on the horizon, we quickly settled into our room and freshened up before heading down to the hotel's bar to meet up with the focus of Stephanie's trip, the band Franke and the Knockouts. The guys would be making their live television debut a couple of hours later on *Fridays*, our west coast version of *Saturday Night Live*.

After some initial tension—silently reminiscing at the leather-edged bar—I settled in nicely, partly due to some blow and a drink, but mostly because the band members were truly nice guys. Once at the television studio, backstage pass affixed to my jeans, I felt completely at home. It was a fabulous few hours with everything I loved most in the world—Stephanie, musicians, and television—all rolled up in one exciting event. If that weren't enough, the band's keyboard player, Blake, caught my attention.

After the well-received show, everyone celebrated at the band's luxury suite back at the hotel. I knew I shouldn't be flirting, but Blake had the melt-my-morals combination of tall, blond, and baby-faced. Once we started talking, my life in the suburbs seemed millions of miles away.

We sat close as we shared stories, and Blake's caring, authentic presence filled a void I didn't know I had. When Stephanie excused herself and said good night to the guys, I felt torn. As much as I enjoyed soaking up the male attention, I didn't want to miss a minute with my dear friend who had an early flight home, so Blake walked me to my room.

Standing outside the door, my heart did a little happy dance when he leaned down and kissed me. As the kiss lengthened and turned into a full on make-out session, I felt like a teenager all over again. After several minutes, feeling a mixture of excitement and guilt, I said good night, though I couldn't get our tender moments off my mind.

Once again back in my suburban dream—or was it a nightmare?—I felt lost without Stephanie and my new musician friend. By Sunday, knowing the band was still in town, I hit on a plan.

After calling the hotel to confirm Blake would enjoy seeing me again, I told Mark I was going to spend the day with my grandparents, a common practice for me. With my bikini hidden in my purse, I drove back to Hollywood to meet my cutie at the hotel's roof-top pool.

Although I didn't feel quite as vivacious without Stephanie, I remained captivated with Blake. Lying on a lounge chair next to him, I nervously smoked a cigarette, even though I had officially quit. With my heart beating wildly, I anticipated our next, inevitable move.

As it is with most of my sexual partners, the act itself has slipped from memory. What remains firmly anchored in my great-moments-in-life file is the shower we shared afterwards. That's the first time a man washed my hair. It's the first time anyone lovingly washed my hair. When I was a little girl, my mother made it feel like a chore, yanking my head this way and that as she scrubbed and rinsed my scalp.

Mark's form of loving attention differed 180 degrees from Blake's, literally. He focused on my feet....

We were sitting on my sofa in Houston after a long day of packing and carrying boxes up and down the stairs when he first offered me a massage.

After hoisting my tired limbs onto the soft cushions, I snuggled in and closed my eyes, and his strong grip worked its magic. When he finished, he announced it was time to walk. Not wanting to put any stress on my nicely relaxed feet, I said, "Not yet. I want to savor the relaxation."

Mark insisted I wouldn't be able to appreciate the great work he'd done without standing and experiencing the before and immediately after. Sensing his statement was more of a demand than a request, I gave in and stood up. Pacing the hallway, I feigned praise, though I would have preferred to stay seated.

I would have also preferred staying seated with Blake, but ultimately, I said a sad good-bye and headed home, knowing better than to think we were anything other than a fling. And unlike the affair I'd had while married to Ed, I kept that afternoon of bliss to myself.

Back in my life as if nothing had happened, I limited my contact with Blake to gazing at his picture on the album cover, wondering what life would have been like if I'd run away with him.

In November of that same year, the radio station once again sent Stephanie to California. This trip included both work—a rock 'n' rollers' bowl-a-thon—and relaxing play time. Of course, I took vacation from work and excused myself from a reluctant-to-be-left-at-home-again Mark, eager to start our next adventure.

In a restaurant overlooking the Malibu surf, we picked up our friendship, effortlessly sliding into no-time-away zone. Over a lunch of iced tea and oysters, I also met the man who had orchestrated Stephanie's visit, Josh, a record label bigwig responsible for the upcoming musician-filled bash.

After our meal, we drove up the beach to the home of Josh's friend, another music industry guy, where the four of us passed the late afternoon and evening. Snorting lines of coke in his oceanfront home, and later walking along the exclusive stretch of sand as we sipped Crystal champagne, I felt happier than I had in months.

True to form, I loved the attention I received from Josh's friend, Fred. That first night all we did was talk and flirt, but after I again opened the door of temptation, lust came flooding through.

The night of the event, not wanting to embarrass myself or my friend in front of her peers, I stayed in look-only mode while roaming the rock-star-filled bowling alley. Stephanie, accustomed to such sightings, mingled easily, though we did giggle and whisper between ourselves when we noticed Benjamin Orr from The Cars.

As the party gathered steam, I wound down with the familiar you-don't-belong-here tape playing in my head. While I was formulating my excuse to escape, Fred showed up, greatly elevating my emotional state with both his presence and his coke. Not impressed with what for him was a work party, he led me to his 1956 convertible T-Bird. We drove off to find a liquor store and some more Crystal, before heading back to the nearby motel where Stephanie and I were staying.

After that weekend, my life really started to get rough.

Since Fred lived only an hour away, I'd make excuses and be gone for the day. Thinking he could keep me home with more drugs, Mark upped our intake of coke and crank. Determined to hold my dream of becoming an accountant intact, I still worked full-time and managed to attend my morning college courses, despite staying up all night. Amazingly, even with frying brain cells, I pulled off a straight "A" grade point average.

In keeping with my unconscious belief, *why have a little chaos when you can have a lot?* I also decided to get a new job and became an assistant controller at a nearby medical school.

A few weeks into my new position I attended a conference taking place in Houston, my old stomping ground. The trip itself was boring, until I discovered that a band I'd met as a result of hanging around Fred would be playing in nearby Austin.

The name of the foursome has slipped into oblivion, but trust me, they were hot. A simple change of my return ticket later, I found myself once again in groupie heaven, backstage at their concert, and then sleeping with the cutest one.

The next morning I headed back to the airport, giving the guys, who happened to share my connecting flight, a ride. Before saying goodbye in Dallas, the now nameless musicians introduced me to a man from their record company, a somewhat creepy character who also lived in Los Angeles and was traveling home.

After promising he would take good care of me, "Creepy Short Guy" offered a pre-flight blast of coke, then asked the gate attendant for adjoining seats. With a little toot in my nose, the short guy seemed less creepy, and after adding a couple of airplane drinks to my empty stomach, he became downright fun.

Feeling obligated to thank my companion, I didn't flinch when he took my hand and slid it under the blanket laid across his lap.

An hour or so outside of Dallas, we made our way to the tiny restroom, where we once again filled our noses—and I became a member of the mile-high club. I'd like to say the cramped-quarter romp satisfied my own by-then-heightened libido, but it only fueled the fire.

Back in our seats, the blanket now in my lap, short guy fiddled about with acute finesse. Lost in a world of drugged-out sex, I was oblivious to the man sitting to my left, in the window seat, until he asked to be moved. I laughed it off, but part of me wondered if I had finally slipped over the edge, never to be proper again.

Once back on the ground, everyone on my inner committee encouraged me to say thank you and good-bye—everyone except the addict who could snort and have sex like nobody's business. The love note on my windshield also brought a momentary pause.

I miss you, sweetheart. Have a safe drive home. I love you.

Recognizing Mark's scrawl, I wondered how the hell he'd found my car in the sea of vehicles at LAX. Struck by a moment of tenderness, I considered going straight home, but opted instead to follow through on the plan offered by my in-flight playmate: more blow and a soak in a hot tub. Convincing myself it was a great idea, I waited at the exit for his sleek black Porsche. A few minutes later, as I idled at a red light on Sepulveda Boulevard, the inner debate heated up.

Turn right, go on, turn now! Your husband is waiting for you. Go home! You've already made a big enough fool of yourself today.

Green light, go! Stay close.

Shit, I'm still following him.

Don't lose him. This is fun, an adventure. Besides, we're going to his office. I can see the inside of a big label record company. Who knows what could happen there?

Haven't you had enough adventure for one day? I can't believe you were so shameless, the guy next to us on the plane actually asked to be reseated. How embarrassing!

After an uneventful stop for more coke, we made our way to a by-the-hour private hot tub place—something I didn't even know existed. Once we were settled in the small steamy room, my hungry nose and insatiable arousal took control yet again. After an hour (or was it two?) we dried off and redressed before stepping into the early evening air. Back in my car, I again felt possessed.

Okay, fine, can we go home now? Rush hour has passed, traffic is no longer an excuse. Besides, how much more blow can you snort?

Ah, come on, the party is just getting started. The evening is young. Stop your complaining. Once we get to his house, I'll call home and say the flight's been delayed. That'll buy us some time.

And I did just that, though with the latest Toto album blasting in the background, I was less than convincing. By midnight, my party buddy finally reached his limit, so with a nose packed for the road, I drove home.

Mark had also reached his limit. He didn't buy my story of a delayed flight. And, genuinely hurt I'd ignored his note, he explained the fluke of seeing my car when he'd picked up his dad at the airport, an explanation that tore at my conflicted heart.

After a few days of Mark's badgering and my guilt-ridden silence, he grabbed our Doberman puppy, Crystal, and headed home to his mom's. Nonplussed, I turned to a familiar solution: more sex, drugs, and rock 'n' roll.

Up until that point, the cheating wife had kept her festivities out of the ideal housewife's domain, but with Mark gone, I invited my new blow-supplying record label guy over for a night of wanton sex. I didn't say, "Come over and we'll fuck our brains out," but knowing it was implied, he showed up with a couple of his buddies.

I wonder if our nosy neighbor took a ringside seat, peering from his spotlessly clean sliding glass door down past our perfectly edged lawn and into the family room with its loose weave drapes. When I was on coke, I didn't care. When I was on coke, none of the voices that said *shame on you* mattered.

Having the world of the coke whore and the not-so-good wife collide—even if it happened in the guest room and not my marital bed—disturbed me. The fact that I got pregnant—and had no idea by whom—disturbed me even more.

Presumably the drugs had messed with my birth control, but being pregnant gave me an out; an affair presented an easy exit. It had worked with Ed, so it would work with Mark. Or so I thought.

28: Fresh Start

We were standing at the door of our house, Mark on the front porch, me just inside, when I broke the news.

"I had an affair."

"So did I," he responded.

Wham. My resolve to end the marriage flew out the back door. Instantly, the fact that I lived in an abusive relationship didn't matter. The jealousy monster had grabbed my heart and squeezed. Ready to shred the unknown female to bits, my fury was tempered by a voice in my head that screamed out, *Wait! You have to get away from this man. You need to get away from this man. He is out to destroy you. Remember how he yells, insisting he isn't verbally abusive. He has systematically degraded all your friends so you have no one to turn to.*

But it was too late; no way would I allow my husband to sleep with anyone else. As though slipping into a hypnotic trance, I returned to the game of love, becoming the model wife. And what better complement to my role—the perfect child.

No, not the baby from the unknown father; in another shame-on-me moment, I'd had an abortion even before I told Mark of the affair. But the brief time I'd carried a life within had touched off a biological instinct, and maternal hormones took over.

FRESH START

I loved being pregnant. I glowed. And in my renewed need to put my life back in order, I left the job at the medical school and returned to the accounting firm.

I also received acknowledgment for my scholastic endeavors, an invitation to join the honor student society Phi Kappa Phi. Good thing they didn't know about my life beyond the classroom, as "sound character" was a criterion for membership.

And finally—in my spotless new world—drugs and alcohol were no longer an option. No way would I intentionally jeopardize my unborn child. I even stopped drinking my beloved Earl Grey tea, to avoid the caffeine.

Without the all-night drug binges, I started throwing dinner parties to occupy our weekends. I'd made the mistake of preparing a feast for Mark's friends—once. I suppose I shouldn't have been surprised when it remained untouched. Before I got pregnant, I'd chosen coke over food, too. Unwilling to risk another display-only meal—and avoid any drug temptation—I invited family to subsequent next-phase-in-life gatherings.

Growing up, I'd had family dinners on Sunday night. That's when Mom, my brother Jimmy, and I would go to Grandma and Grandpa's house. Those memories with Mom's parents bring a smile to my face. . . .

We'd have special food, stuff we didn't keep around the apartment: appetizers, like potato chips and dip, and cocktails, like Coke or 7-Up. The adults drank scotch and water or gin and tonic, depending on the season. There was dessert too, baked from scratch in the afternoon by Grandma and Mom—and me when I got old enough. I loved taking Grandpa his fresh slice of love, like hot apple pie. Not à la mode. He preferred that after-dinner treat with a slice of sharp cheddar cheese.

I'd walk carefully through the living room, balancing dessert in one hand and coffee in the other, before proudly setting the dishes on his desk otherwise covered with amateur radio equipment. I never got a hug or a kiss from Grandpa. I knew he loved me by the way his eyes would light up when I walked into the room.

Even cleanup from the weekly meal brings fond memories—Grandma washing, me drying, and Mom putting away. With the kitchen once again in order, we girls would return to the dining room table to play poker.

In my life with Mark, there wasn't any after-dinner poker. We were too sophisticated for that. Instead, we would retire to the living room, drink coffee—herbal tea for me—and chat.

My step-father probably only attended those dinners because it gave him a chance to visit with Mark's dad, but I didn't care why he came. It felt good to believe I had finally gained his approval. Plus, something about pregnancy and babies brought out the nice in him. Like the time when my half-sister was born. I was eleven. . . .

That Christmas, we lived in Sherman Oaks, and while Mom spent a night recuperating in the hospital, Dad took Jimmy and me for a drive to look at the lights. I knew letting my guard down around Dad would be risky, especially with his explosive temper, but I did, and amazingly, we had a fun night looking at sparkly things.

Childhood dinners with my step-father were never happy, and they were never family. By the time we lived in Newport Beach, children ate first, before he came home. And if he came home early, the first husband's kids were hidden away in ground-floor bedrooms; we simply weren't allowed in the "family" room.

Heaven forbid I should get caught playing with my little sister upstairs in her room. I had about fifteen seconds to reach safety from the time we'd hear the automatic garage door opener start to grind.

For a moment, we'd both freeze, then the four-year-old's alarmed voice would snap us back to reality with, "Dad's home!" signaling the start of my precision dash.

Peer over the banister and out the front window to be sure the car had pulled into the garage. This step was imperative. If he looked in those picture windows and saw me coming down the stairs, well, it never happened, but it would have been ugly.

Once the diesel Mercedes slid inside the garage, I bolted two or three steps at a time, then quickly U-turned and sprinted the remaining twenty feet to my bedroom. Many a day my door clicked quietly—never slammed—just as the back door directly opposite squeaked open.

Mom warned me about being found upstairs, but with resignation in her eyes, she let me break the rules. Although I was afraid of my step-dad's wrath—and fist—I also enjoyed the adrenaline-pumping, risky edge of teenage rebellion.

Come the holidays, Jimmy and I were clearly non-family members. Like our first Thanksgiving in Newport Beach, at fifteen. Mom actually thought it would be a

FRESH START

treat for us to eat Swanson Turkey TV dinners—something she didn't ordinarily buy—while she and the "family" went out to dinner. Maybe Mom was hypnotized too, intent on her good-looking life with its socialite-focused family.

Another way I occupied my time while pregnant: I indulged Mark in his every sexual whim. As my belly grew round, I enjoyed our frequent unions, often initiating the lovemaking. Maybe it was the pre-natal vitamins.

With our daughter's birth—a New Year's Day, early-morning surprise, three weeks before expected—my joyful life continued. Saying good-bye once again to friends and colleagues at the CPA firm, I became a stay-at-home mom. My baby cried incessantly at first, but we soon found our rhythm, one that included her crib next to our king-sized bed and long, leisurely mornings sitting in Mark's recliner, me sipping tea with my daughter at my breast. That's where this story began.

The fact that I had returned to being a willing and eager sexual partner, up until the Incest TV show, probably accounts for some of Mark's frustration at losing his resident whore. After that morning, as my world fell apart, I asked for what I wanted, just like the counselor in the Incest Survivors Group told me to do.

"I need you to be a friend. And I need to be a safe little girl, a child who isn't sexual. I want to hold your hand and trust that you love me enough to let that be as far as we go for a while."

"What's a while?" Mark wanted to know.

"Thirty days? Can I have at least thirty days?"

About halfway through my requested time-off, Mark got tired of waiting. It's hard to say if he thought I slept through his middle-of-the-night intrusions from behind. We never spoke of them, and I played dead.

I wonder if that's a trick I learned as a toddler. Lie very still and pretend to be asleep. Pretend you don't know what's happening.

The flashes I've had—images surfacing as a result of delving into these details—go like this. . . .

"Shhh . . . it's only me, Princess," Daddy whispers as he stops at my crib for his good-night kiss. Gently stroking my hair with one hand, the other reaches down and strokes his eager cock.

"It's time for our special game. Open up like a good girl and let Daddy put his magic wand in your mouth. You've been such a good girl. I've been saving this up, just for you."

As I imagine his words, my jaw aches and the mental picture makes me gag. The fact that I know my mother slept across the room makes the scene even more appalling. But it explains a lot. And I see a pattern.

I'm not saying my mother was awake and aware of the bedtime routine. But I'm betting she'd mastered the skill of shutting out the obvious while sleeping in her own parents' bedroom—until she was five.

For myself, with Mark, I would lie there night after night in silent agony, taking his intrusions. I felt horrible knowing he could just as easily be humping a blow-up doll, but I didn't resist. I became a human shield, protecting my precious child—as I had not been protected—our baby who slept just an arm's length away.

The logic sounds crazy, but in some warped world—for the first time visible—it fits. Another piece of my life's puzzle falls into place.

In an alternate reality, I'd be one of those outwardly angry women who know how to protect themselves. In that fantasyland I would reach back, grab Mark's prying erection, and shove him back to his side of the bed.

"*Get the fuck off me*," *I'd say, and turn on the bedside light to confront him. The powerful, able-to-protect-herself woman would stand up and glare down on her assailant.*

"I've told you I need a friend. Rape is never okay. I can't believe this is how you treat the person you claim to love most in the world. If you don't learn to listen to me, to honor me, you're going to lose me."

Instead, at twenty-seven, I went numb. I became the walking dead. Eventually I even stopped the silent tears.

Just tolerate it, I told myself. *He'll be finished soon. . . . You don't want to piss him off. And you can't just walk out.* Slowly but steadily, I became my own abuser, locked in an internal hell. That's when I began to smoke marijuana on a daily basis.

I could smoke my joint and go to the happy realms, where being an incest victim didn't nag at me. And the weekly Survivor Group meetings offered just enough support to help me believe I was getting better, whatever "better" meant.

29: Recovery?

Mark had his own ideas about my path of healing, and encouraged—or badgered—me to spend time with my "real" dad. Once again bolstered by pregnancy hormones, I bowed to my husband's pressure and agreed we could spend the upcoming Thanksgiving holiday with the paternal relatives—whom I barely knew.

When I was a child, the drive along the winding roads of the Hollywood Hills to my father's boyhood home seemed like a mysterious adventure. We even passed a sign reading *Mount Olympus*, adding to the sense of otherworldliness.

Once we'd parked on a street so narrow locals knew to limit their travel to a single direction, we were greeted by a set of two large, deep blue porcelain Chinese Fu dogs, who kept a watchful eye over the curbside entrance.

Next, the exhausting fun began: a climb up the one hundred—of course, we counted—cracked and weathered brick steps weaving up the tree-covered hillside. In the dozen or so times I'd visited that home, I never made it all the way up without taking a break to catch my breath; that November in 1984 was no different.

Past the massive, oak front door, my grandfather's collection of Asian artifacts loomed menacingly. After we walked gingerly past the

Samurai warrior suits of armor and up another flight of concrete steps, the dim and dusty living room offered its familiar welcome.

Although I rarely visited the home, its large open room appeared just as I hoped it would, and I was glad to see the overstuffed, dark-green, velveteen sofa still held its stately—albeit well-worn—position.

Instead of the hushed silence of my previous visits, laughter drifted into the space, and the wooden floors creaked as offspring of cousins—relatives I hadn't seen since they were the age of their children—ran past.

Toward the back of the house, we found my father and step-mother sitting with Grandpa in his library. To this day, when I think of that perpetually cold room, I smell wood smoke and see the man with the wild, straight-up white hair tending the fire.

Accompanying us to help with introductions, my father walked to the kitchen, where two of my cousins helped Grandma with the festive meal's preparation. The elderly woman looked every bit as frail as I remembered, so I hugged her thin frame carefully. After offering a helping hand—which she graciously declined—I passed my daughter over to Mark and excused myself.

Part of the reason I had gone along with the idea of a family holiday was the nagging sensation that something had happened to me in that house. With the confidence I had gained in my support group and a desire to uncover the truth about the abuse, I decided to be daring and sneak up the narrow wooden staircase to the upper-floor bedrooms.

Alone at the top of the stairs, my hand shook as I reached for the door to the right of the landing, the room calling to me like whispers from a bad dream. As I held my breath, I turned the glass handle, cautiously opening the dingy door.

Peering into the room aglow with the setting sun's rays, I saw a desk, more bookcases, and a side chair, but nothing sinister. Relieved, I told myself I'd been making up scary stories and closed the door. After creeping back down to the celebration, I relaxed and joined in the fun, unaware a sleeping monster stirred.

As we sat around the ten-foot-long dining table—needing every inch of space it offered us—I enjoyed this first-time holiday meal with relatives ranging in age from Grandma and Grandpa's eighty-eight years to my daughter's almost two. Until my father reached for the potatoes.

As I watched his long, slender fingers stretch out towards me, my throat closed, catching on the turkey halfway down. After coughing and clearing my throat, I briefly pondered the wave of fear, before brushing it aside. The following day, in addition to writing a thank-you note to my grandparents, I wrote a letter to my father.

Dear Dad,

It was nice spending Thanksgiving with you and the family. We enjoyed ourselves. But something has been bothering me a lot lately. Something I think you might be able to help with. I have a sense that something happened to me as a child there in Grandma and Grandpa's house. In fact, I even went up to the room at the top of the stairs when we were visiting and peeked inside, but it didn't look scary.

Yet, while you were serving dinner, something about your hands bothered me. And I have to ask you. What happened to me as a child? Why do I fear your hands?

I hope you can help.
Love, Debi

Mark didn't approve of my query, telling me I needed to get past anything that may have happened. But I needed to ask the pivotal questions, so I dropped the embossed stationery into the mailbox. Nervous for days afterwards, I finally calmed down, accepting that my father would not be replying. And, in a way, I was grateful he didn't.

Despite a lack of clarity regarding any abuse, the Hollywood Hills visit stirred up internal chaos. From that agitated place—pregnant, and in the thick of the frenzy surrounding home-made holiday delicacies—I again found my husband and our life together intolerable. So, three years after our first separation, Mark once again packed his bags, returning to his parents' home. That's when we started counseling.

Our therapist, a friend of his parents, talked about the Madonna and the Whore archetypes, and how some men see their wives as one or the other. Though she didn't know anything about my call girl days, some of her discussion of black and white thinking, and integrating the two, made sense. She also told me I needed to start offering my body kindness and care, and suggested a simple exercise of rubbing lotion on my legs.

At first I got mad, finding the process an uncomfortable chore.

Begrudgingly, I would slap the greasy liquid on as fast as I could, cursing my dry, cracked, winter skin. But eventually I slowed down and learned to enjoy the process and the almond scent of Jergens lotion.

Of course, Mark and I both avoided talking to the professional about our drug use, but, willing to give the flawed relationship another try, my husband moved back in two months after moving out.

With our second reconciliation, I released my grand illusions about our marriage. Instead, I focused on completing our beautiful home.

In my quest to have every inch of our space reflect perfection, I painted, wallpapered, and sewed to my heart's delight, completely immersed in the final stages of my pregnancy's nesting hormones.

When not decorating or taking care of my two-year-old, I filled my time with studying for, and then passing, the CPA exam—all while continuing to smoke pot.

I knew I shouldn't be stoned, especially while pregnant—I did stop briefly around the time my son was born—but I honestly didn't think I could live without my self-prescribed medication. On the rare occasions we ran out, I became almost frantic, and Mark's suggestion to drink a beer instead just left me more anxious.

While high, I had abundant energy and channeled a wonderful, creative flow. I even started my own mail order company, specializing in natural baby products and clothes for nursing mothers that I designed myself. Ironically, my home-based business, called The Whole Family, pushed Mark and me further apart.

So even though I smoked on an almost daily basis, I functioned well. I raised my daughter and son, entertained family, and ran a business, all within the walls of our ideal, happy-home illusion. The only lingering issue: sex.

Convinced my problems with intimacy were Mark's fault, I fantasized about an unselfish lover, one not voraciously hungry for multiple orgasms in a single day. That man wouldn't have a stack of porno magazines in the garage. And he wouldn't start each day with a little meat-banging session at the workbench.

If I could find a man like that, I would be healthy. I wouldn't need to get high and sneak one of the girly magazines into the bedroom, where, with my husband away for the day, I could safely explore my own sexuality.

With the perfect lover, I wouldn't need to find just the right picture, of just the right woman, with just the right alluring look. And I certainly wouldn't need to imagine I was the guy, with a rock-hard erection, sliding it into that willing and wanting crevice. All I needed was the right man. The one who would treat me like his princess.

30: Confrontation

"I think there is hope for your marriage. It's a good sign you don't hate him."

The therapist's comment, several months into our counseling, struck me as inherently wrong. If I hated him, at least there would be emotion. Hate, like love, has passion. And that wasn't the thinking of a smoke-induced reality. In fact, the twelve-step meetings I had started attending actually helped me see I was living a lie.

The pastel-colored pamphlets encouraging a "clean and sober" lifestyle had first caught my eye when I attended the Incest Survivor group meetings. A quiet voice within—one I occasionally heard when the pothead wasn't in total control—said, *Please check this out.*

I showed the hope-filled literature to Mark, but he boldly stated, "I don't have a problem."

Recognizing that I did, I attended my first Narcotics Anonymous meeting, held in a church basement, in the winter of 1986.

At first, all I did was sit and listen, terrified of speaking up. But something about the open and honest shares of the dozen or so people in the room kept me coming back every Tuesday night.

I'd ride the "high" of the meeting for a couple of days, but by the weekend, I'd return to my trusty friend, pot. Determined to make a lasting change, come Tuesday, I'd return to the fluorescent-lit room and the comfort it offered.

Attending those meetings—filled with people who lived a life without drugs—gave me a glimpse of unconditional acceptance. For perhaps the first time in my life, I felt a glimmer of real confidence, not speed- or coke- or weed-induced charm. I even convinced Mark to join me once, but instead of seeing recovery, he saw a class of individuals far beneath himself and refused to go again.

By April, after expanding my meeting schedule to three or four a week—and able to string one, then two "clean" weeks together—I realized there was nothing left between my husband and me. No love, no hate, just cool indifference toward the person who shared my life.

When I told Mark of my insight, he got furious. Slipping into one of his insult-hurling rages, he let me know just what a vile and untrustworthy person I was. I'd learned previously, in an early attempt to speak up for myself, that pointing out the verbal abuse of his rants only led to an extended—and louder—lecture, so I remained silent. But something within me had shifted. No longer more fearful of the world on my own than of that in my beautiful home, I packed up the kids and left.

Feeling a call towards the wild, we settled into Wrightwood, a small country community on the back side of Mt. Baldy, the mountain which had loomed behind us for the past six years, sometimes completely smothered in smog.

From a small cabin backing up on the Angeles National Forest, I settled into a daily routine of caring for my one- and three-year-old children, running the somewhat successful cottage business, and, most important, attending meetings and working the steps.

For step four, "made a searching and fearless moral inventory," I filled a one-subject spiral-bound notebook, recounting my life and its myriad twists and turns. For step five, "admitted to God, to ourselves, and to another human being the exact nature of our wrongs," I turned to the woman who supported me in working the program, my sponsor, Jeanne.

She seemed a bit surprised with the length of my work, but nonetheless sat with me as the sun's midday brightness shifted to long, late-afternoon shadows. Always on a quest for perfection, I didn't want to leave anything regarding my recovery to chance. I took the same tack with steps eight and nine, "a list of all persons we had harmed . . ." and "we made direct amends to such people wherever possible, except when to do so would injure them or others."

I didn't think making amends to my father about walking away from the furniture he had supplied for my studio in Hollywood would cause either of us harm, so I called and made arrangements to see him.

Dropping the kids with Mark's mom on my way to my father's place in L.A., just down the street from Chippendale's, I felt nervous about the upcoming discussion, but determination held strong. I'd already made amends to Mark's dad, admitting I had stolen quarters out of his five-gallon bottle of loose change in the early days of my relationship with his son. That had gone well, so I prayed for the same with my dad.

Climbing the weathered wooden stairs to the same apartment he and Liesl had lived in since I was a teen, I opened the door to the living room that never seemed to have enough air in it.

My father sat in the corner across from the front entrance, on the well-worn, large-gold-floral-design sofa. As usual, he was on the air, talking to someone in some part of the world, on his ham radio. My visits, though rare, were always introduced to the unknown voice on the other side of the connection as if it were no big deal.

"My daughter just got here, Joe (or Jed or Fred). This is W-6-zed-R-zed signing off."

It's always seemed odd to me that someone could talk for hours on end with a faceless voice. But it was also familiar. My mom's dad lived in that same pre-Internet-though-connected-to-the-globe world.

But there was a difference between Grandpa and my father; Grandpa never felt compelled to announce what was going on in the room to his invisible friends. His way of honoring those world-wide radio buffs was to paste their call letter postcards around the "radio room" like a wallpaper border.

Technically, my father used the second bedroom as his radio room, a space filled with all sorts of dusty old electronic equipment. But most of the time he was here on the sofa with a cat nearby. Being allergic to cats gave me a good excuse to not stay long.

Ordinarily, my father jumped up to greet me, but that day he stayed seated, fiddling with dials. Standing on the worn carpet, I silently surveyed the room's seating options.

I can move to the sofa, next to my father and the cat.
No. Too close.

I considered one of the black leather stools to the left of the front door—part of the too-ornate-for-my-taste, black walnut bar that opened for business at three p.m. sharp.

No. Too far away. And besides, that painting would be behind me.

"That" painting, the one with the woman lounging seductively on her side, naked from the waist up, had always made my stomach crawl, and having her in my father's line of vision while he talked with me wasn't a good combo.

Finally, I decided to pull up one of the three aluminum kitchen chairs, and place it a safe, yet not overtly rude distance from the man who lived in short-sleeved plaid shirts. But I didn't sit down. Instead, I stood behind the vinyl-covered chair like a lion tamer, ready to wield its legs for protection if the beast got out of hand.

"Can I get you anything to drink?" offered my step-mother. "We've got apple juice, or I could make you some tea."

"Water is fine," I replied, knowing that later in the afternoon the offering would have included a cocktail—something I had also given up.

"I'll be back in a minute, sweetheart," my father said, depositing a sloppy kiss on my cheek as he slipped into the short hallway leading to the bathroom.

"He wants to talk to you about the letter," Liesl said in hushed tones, as she handed me a washed-to-the-point-of-being-foggy glass of chilled water.

Oh shit. The letter. I forgot about that.

Remembering the Thanksgiving letter, I began to pace, suddenly the caged animal.

"Okay," Liesl said in a normal tone as my father walked back into the room, "I'll let you talk to your dad alone." Her exit—punctuated by the slam of the self-closing-a-bit-too-hard screen door—made me jump.

Not one for social niceties, my father plopped back down on the sofa and dove in. "So what's this about you thinking I did something to you as a child?"

His words were slightly curt, unusual for the man who often refers to me—in just a little too sweet a tone—as his princess.

So there it was. My open invitation. On the table. Not a clean, shiny table, but a grimy, littered surface. Someone else might have started crying, or yelling. I stayed in my head, treading lightly down what I suspected to be a pitfall-ridden path.

Speaking candidly was new for me. Especially with him. And honestly, I'm not sure I wanted the light-of-day reality. Suspicions and unanswered accusations—along with victim or survivor status—were enough to hold in those early days.

"Well," I began tentatively, stepping around to the front of the chair and sitting at its edge. "I saw a TV show a couple of years ago. About sexual abuse. And, well, there's this room in Grandma and Grandpa's house. Upstairs. It pulls and scares me at the same time."

My father sat quietly, his eyes focused on his hands, gently petting the cat stretched out on the cushion beside him. My father might lack human skills, but the feline purred in grateful recognition.

"At Thanksgiving, I decided to be brave and check it out," I continued. "The door was closed, but I knocked gently and then opened it. It didn't look scary. It was just a room. A desk, a chair, bookshelves, the same wood walls as the rest of the house."

"Which room?" my father asked.

"The first one, at the top of the stairs, on the right."

"That's my old room." His blue eyes finally shifted to meet mine.

Looking down, I sat in awkward silence, before feeling compelled to keep talking.

"I don't have any clear memories," I blurted, in a slightly apologetic manner.

I knew I was side-stepping the images that were there, etched in stone.

Like the time I was fourteen. When Liesl was gone for the night and he invited me to sleep with him. And the time I was fifteen. When Ingrid broke the spell about kissing on the mouth. But that day, at twenty-nine years old, I didn't have the courage to speak of memories. Instead, I focused on my hands lying in my lap, busily picking at dry cuticles.

"Well, I know father had sex with my sisters," my father said, more talking to himself than me.

I snapped back to attention. *What! Did I hear this right? Grandpa had sex with his daughters?*

It was only later—after I'd had time to absorb the magnitude of his statement—that a recurring dream from my childhood began to make horrifying sense. . . .

I'm in the backyard of a dream house, but I know it belongs to my grandparents. I never saw the inside, but it's a nice structure at the top of a grass-covered hill. There's a swing set in the yard, and at the bottom of the green slope sits my grandfather's workshop.

The dream always starts with my swinging happily, gently pumping my legs. Then I lose my balance and fall backwards onto the grass before rolling down the hill and coming to a stop outside the shed.

Slightly dizzy, but otherwise unharmed, I get up and go inside, where I'm fascinated by the neat organization of grandpa's things.

On the wall to the left of the door, a number of wooden shelves line the wall, and hanging beneath them are a series of baby food jars, each attached to the shelf above by its lid. Inside the clear glass containers is a collection of screws in various sizes.

In other versions of the dream, I am playing with Anna, my step-niece. The two of us roll off the swing set and down the hill. We step into the workshop, and I show her the screws in the baby food jars.

So there I sat, in that stuffy, second-story apartment, receiving the first real, waking life confirmation that things were twisted in my family. Not simply dreams leaving cryptic clues about screwing babies.

"Actually, Pat would never admit it," he continued. "But Franny told me Father would have sex with her."

Aunt Franny, my father's older sister. She's the one who died of uterine cancer when I was a teenager. While I didn't know anything about the disease, something inside me clicked. Like an accurate twist of a combination lock, a piece of the crazy puzzle now fell into place, and I knew her death was related to the abuse.

I'd never met my father's younger sister, Aunt Pat, since she and her family had moved—or escaped—to Alaska before I was born.

As I sat in stunned silence and attempted to formulate a response equal to the enormity of my father's statements, I watched him shake from head to toe. Not just a little twitch, but a full-on jolt, as though an icy poker had just shot through his spine.

Then, suddenly, he began talking again, louder, on another topic, mid-sentence, as though I'd walked out of the room and returned a few moments later. It was the oddest thing I'd ever witnessed. Riveted to my seat, I silently cheered and screamed at the same time.

Part of me wanted to coax my father back to the subject of abuse. I wanted to know exactly what had happened, naïvely thinking it would provide a miracle cure. However, the part of myself I know today as my small, still voice said, *Let it be. This man is broken.*

31: Fundamentals

In addition to working the twelve-step program, I added something new to my single-mom-living-in-the-mountains lifestyle, a tool Ed and I learned back in 1976 while living in Texas: meditation. . . .

At first I teased him relentlessly about wanting to study transcendental meditation, also known as TM, yet something inside urged me to explore the foreign practice. Met by teachers who spoke as softly as the folds of fabric wrapped around their bodies, Ed and I were ushered into separate rooms for our indoctrination.

I don't recall their exact questions, but after the brief interview, I was awarded my own sacred—and secret—mantra. I doubted that two simple, everyday words could offer any magic, but I followed their instructions to close my eyes and silently repeat the chant. Twenty minutes never seemed so long; and twice a day, no less. But I made a commitment to give it a try for thirty days.

About a week into the new routine, I noticed I no longer dreaded turning off the lights—or the TV—and that once I was in bed, sleep came easier. A month or so later, by then enjoying the respite meditation offered, I also realized I hadn't had any nighttime panic attacks—something I'd lived with for as long as I could remember.

When I was fifteen, after we had moved to Newport Beach, my startled waking—generally within five to ten minutes of falling asleep—became chronic.

Occasionally a nightmare precipitated the waves of terror, but most of the time I simply had a blank mind and racing heart.

Once awake, I'd toss and turn, sometimes for hours, adrenaline pumping through my system. The solution—which worked quite well until I moved away from home—involved my brother Jimmy.

I'd gather up my pillow and blanket and lie on the floor of his room, the only other first-floor bedroom in that upscale, coast-side community. Unrelenting in my quest for relief, I'd pester my sibling with questions about his latest passion. Once I had him good and conscious, he'd ramble on with monotonous details. If I'd paid attention—instead of letting his long-winded drone lull me back to sleep—I could have learned mesmerizing intricacies about stereos, cars, and airplanes.

Although meditation helped soothe my psyche as I pulled together a new life, the Wrightwood cabin my children and I called home, with its unseen rodent tenants scratching around the wood-paneled walls, brought back my night terrors. Thankfully, while looking through magazines suitable for marketing my small business, I came upon an advertisement for a natural, flower-based stress reduction remedy. Immediately intrigued, I called the number. After a nice chat, I made an appointment with the friendly practitioner, who also worked from home.

As I sat in the grandma-aged woman's stylishly furnished dining room, I poured out the facts of my recent life. About twenty minutes into my tale, she commented on my lack of emotion. Her statement seemed odd to me, since I'd grown up hearing I was too emotional.

I honestly thought, while reflecting on her comment, that my upbeat, keep-it-together attitude regarding my various traumas was a good thing. The counselor, on the other hand, did not. While selecting my prescription from her choice of thirty-eight Bach Flower Essences, she told me she was including Agrimony, the remedy for those who hide behind a cheerful face. As a result, she mentioned, I might find myself crying more.

Holy shit ... I cried for days. Almost incapacitated by grief—though I did manage to feed the kids and myself—I sobbed deeply, acknowledging years of skirted-over pain.

It was as though the watery nightmares—ones I'd had off and on since childhood—had found my waking state. In those dreams, I'd either be standing at a precipice with skyscraper-size waves breaking directly in front of me, or I'd be in a house with glass walls, again at a cliff's edge, while the stormy seas rose and churned around me.

In both versions of the dream, my situation felt tenuous, as though one wrong move would bring the wall of water crashing over me. While I wouldn't say I welcomed my waking experience of anguish, I survived the torrents without turning to drugs and began to trust my previously unrecognized emotional capacity.

After the inner storm broke, I marveled at how a few drops of water infused with flowers and herbs could make such a difference. And, in my familiar attitude of why-pay-someone-to-do-what-you-can-do-for-yourself, I ordered a full set of Dr. Bach's remedies.

With my meditation practice and flower essence therapy—fundamentals I still rely on for alignment and attunement—I felt ready to step confidently into the unknown. Until Mark told me he planned to fight for custody of the kids.

I couldn't believe it. I'd felt devastated during our first separation when he pried Crystal, our Doberman puppy, out of my arms, but I saw his threat of taking the kids as a new depth of heartless revenge.

With seven months clean and sober, I felt I had my life together. My attorney, however, a man I'd met in the NA meetings who had been around long enough to be called an "old timer," warned that anything under a year would carry little weight.

On the morning of our court date, fear-based thoughts tried to take over my mind. I told myself to stop obsessing. Instead—after taking a dose of flower essences designed for highly stressful situations—I focused on the love and devotion I felt toward my precious babies. Of course, I assured myself, they would continue to live with me. My NA sponsor shared my belief and helped to bolster my confidence when I dropped the kids off at her place before continuing down to the Ontario, California courthouse.

My bravery held while I met my lawyer in the lobby, and I even remained calmly self-assured as we joined Mark and his high-powered legal advisor, funded by his mom and dad. Once inside the courtroom itself, which was presided over by a stern-faced, gray-haired, male judge, I felt my confidence waiver.

When I'd divorced from Ed seven years earlier, I'd simply gotten him to sign papers and then presented them to a judge in an otherwise empty courtroom. Walking into the Ontario space, filled to near capacity with others who'd come to plead their cases, I felt that everyone turned and focused on me.

In my head, they were all thinking, *There she is, that poor woman who only has seven months clean; too bad for her.* Standing in the back of the room, I took a deep breath and watched as the attorneys approached the bailiff.

While waiting for them, I heard Grandpa's voice clearly in my head: *Don't air your dirty laundry in public.* Growing up, I'd heard this disgusted tone and statement often, in response to the television or a ham radio operator's conversation, though I never heard Grandpa confront anyone directly.

Relieved when the lawyers returned and escorted us out from under the guilt-proclaiming eyes, we were told our case would require a session with the court's mediator, for just Mark and me. Wandering the courthouse in search of the unbiased party, I felt renewed in my ability to confidently speak my case and in my commitment not only to stay clean and sober but to care for my kids. That is, until I met the mediator—yet another male—who wasn't much older than we were.

He listened intently, scribbling notes, as I answered questions, telling my side of the story. Focusing on recovery, my love for my children, and my marginally supportive business, I refrained from any negative commentary regarding my husband, wanting to keep the testimony above reproach.

Mark, on the other hand, didn't possess such scruples, and when it was his turn, he slung every muddy event into the previously pristine room. While I listened in shameful disbelief, he cataloged all my faults and unmotherly past behaviors. Though my voice within encouraged me to speak up, to defend myself, it—and I—had been beaten into submission. Though I hadn't been physically beaten, my husband's verbal abuse had etched itself firmly into my self-esteem, leaving its invisible mark.

I believed Mark still used, but I didn't point that out. As part of my program, I'd decided to be holier than any saint I may have prayed to back in the nights of too many drugs in my system. So instead I allowed scorching, silent tears to drip into my lap.

After weighing both sides, the mediator may as well have said, "Debi, I commit you to death," instead of his real words, "Mark, I think you've got a good case for custody. Just tell the judge what you've told me here."

In utter disbelief, I couldn't stop crying as we wandered back into the cold, marble lobby, to rejoin our lawyers. Was it really possible I'd have to listen to Mark once again recite my inalienable character flaws; and worse yet, in front of strangers? That's when the previously unthinkable popped into my head, and before I could veto the decision to speak, it came out of my mouth.

"Okay. You win. You can have custody."

My life took an unalterable detour that regrettable day. And I need to pause for a moment to acknowledge long-held emotions: the agony of my pronouncement, and the ache I've carried as a result. . . .

In my mind's eye, I return to the me of nearly twenty-five years ago, and catch her as she crumbles. The words she has just spoken shake reality to its core. Holding her with strength rooted deep in the earth, I whisper, "I'm sorry, oh, so desperately sorry." With a blend of compassion and wisdom, traits I have gained with time, I hold her in my arms able to understand inconsolable grief.

She wails. Time stands still. The death blow has been thrown.

Anguish transforms into rage. This younger me lashes out, "How could you let this happen?" Guilt sets in. Excuses won't do. I've condemned myself to hell.

The elder me speaks again. "Sweetheart, you did the best you could. You truly believed the children would be better off in a financially stable home. There is no doubt you loved—and love—them ferociously. Please stop making yourself wrong. Please consider opening your heart. Please allow a space for peace."

The shock of my words struck us all, and for a moment no one spoke. My attorney, pulling me aside, asked, "Are you sure? I think you've got a case."

Too late. The door of my heart and mind had snapped closed—and with my clarity-providing flower essences left at home, fear gripped me. Buying into all my glaring failures, I grasped onto the only plan I could see, Mark's. Suddenly the benefits he'd listed—not the least of which was his parents' money—seemed to determine the best option for our daughter and son.

Flooded by emotions—primarily relief that I wouldn't have to return to the dreaded courtroom—I signed over physical custody, accepting joint legal custody as my heartless consolation.

Stepping back into the brightness of the noonday sun—and reeling from shock over the outcome of the past few hours—I attempted to soothe my devastation with the belief the kids would be well cared for.

And besides, an excited inner aspect pointed out, *without them, there'll be more freedom to play around with guys from the twelve-step meetings. Like Dave, that cute construction worker who walked me to the car last night.*

32: Unseen Help

Back then "protection" was limited to my daily birth control pill. I didn't know anything about defending my aura or energetic field.

I knew about auras in concept: the bubble—visible to some—surrounding the physical body about an arm's length out. I'd learned of the energy body, and other esoteric wisdom, thanks to Grandpa's well-stocked and abundantly diverse library.

Growing up, we often spoke of spirits, and Mom, though she couldn't confirm the sightings, had a friend who saw and spoke to ghosts. I would often tell Grandma and Grandpa that when the day came for them to "cross over," they'd be more than welcome to stop by and visit with me from the other side.

So when Jeanne, my NA sponsor, told me we'd been invited to a spiritualism class, I didn't wonder if she had started using again.

"Two women came into the restaurant today," she shared excitedly, "saying that Spirit had sent them, and we're supposed to start attending weekly meetings in Riverside."

Never questioning the source of the invitation, every Thursday night I'd head down from my achingly empty mountain cabin and drive an hour to the modest home of Susan and her husband, Harry. Once there, Jeanne, myself, and about six other men and women would study a variety of metaphysical tools, including meditation and channeling.

Although most of the other class members slipped easily into trance, I would listen to the unseen guidance, then run any messages they offered through my logical brain to censor anything I thought might sound foolish when spoken aloud. I knew my editorial practice frustrated the teachers and spirit guides on the other side of the veil, but I refused to consciously step aside and let someone else control the helm.

This need to be in charge was somewhat of a paradox, considering how many times in my life I'd given my power away. And with the lack of respect I'd had so far for my body, it seems odd I would hesitate to slip fully into trance, but I held my mind in higher regard than my existence from the neck down.

Although I never lost conscious control, I enjoyed the lessons and camaraderie of the spiritually based group; we all heard voices, and we were encouraged to do so. Finally, I felt free to acknowledge—and hone—my "third ear," a gift I had done my best to ignore while living with Mark. Only once did I make the mistake of mentioning to him those random, faceless visitations, touching off one of his what-the-hell-is-wrong-with-you rampages.

Susan and Harry taught us the basics of being a medium. One of my favorite lessons was "Just because someone is dead, doesn't mean they have any superior intelligence." Sure, they've stepped out of the bounds of our time and space realm, but in many respects, they're still Aunt Sally or Uncle Ed.

During that same time period, I decided to attend Sunday services at an esoteric, "new age" church in my previous stomping ground of Upland. Part of their morning inspiration included a healing ritual where they projected a huge image of Jesus Christ on the wall behind the pulpit.

The guidance for working with the somewhat intimidating icon was straightforward. Open yourself to healing. Whatever calls for assistance, simply ask the "Light of Christ" to come and comfort your needs.

As I sat gazing at the gentle, caring eyes looking out over the congregation, I felt my back radiate electrical pulses of hair-raising fright that shot out from my spine. It wasn't a new experience. Similar to my past nighttime panic attacks, the swiftly hitting—and just as quickly retreating—sense of being a scared Halloween kitty had been with me for many years.

New to the world of healing services, yet enveloped in the grace of a hundred or so people slipping into meditation, I offered a silent prayer, asking Christ to remove the fear from my body. As tears began to slide across my cheeks, I felt a nurturing, warm sense of compassion emanate from my heart and flow throughout my being. Basking in the tender glow, I sensed my prayer had been answered.

Later that afternoon, my penchant for alternative-based explorations continued in the form of a massage and "breathwork" session. The practitioner, who came highly recommended for her gift of healing, guided me in deep and focused breathing as she worked on various points in my body.

While I lay stretched out on the massage table, she worked her way up my back, stopping when she reached the area behind my heart.

"Jesus Christ is here," she said calmly, "up there in the corner. And he has someone with him, a young man."

Although I couldn't see anything when I turned to look with my physical eyes, I had the impression of the same wonderfully comforting image I had prayed to earlier. But in my mind's eye, instead of both arms being relaxed, with palms facing toward me as they had been in the healing service, the robed savior appeared with one arm wrapped gently around the shoulders of a slim, pale man in his mid-thirties.

"This man has been with you for a long time, and he holds a lot of fear, but he's leaving now," continued the practitioner. "Jesus is escorting him to the other side. But before they leave, he wants to know if you'll be okay without him."

I realized this wayward spirit thought he'd been serving me—and as a result I felt a conflicted sense of gratitude. However, I was relieved to see him go. "Thank you," I said, through a gush of tears, more to Jesus than to the disincarnate being. "Thank you, I'll be fine."

As the vision faded from consciousness, my body felt lighter, as though a physical weight had been removed from my spine. I also felt an emotional shift, a feeling of deep calm. And, most impressive, the shock of electrifying fear never happened again.

In retrospect, my open-door policy—or Swiss cheese aura—may have started with my first joint, back when I was fourteen. Or maybe I had inadvertently invited a hitchhiker in while playing with a Ouija board, something I'd done to pass time as a kid. Or maybe the damage happened even earlier, during those childhood years that eluded me for so long. Any of these possibilities would explain a lot about the voices and inner battles for control that have been so prevalent in my life.

But did I question who, when, or how back then? No, even with the events on that humbling Sunday. Similar to the disregard I had for my physical body, recognizing—and especially honoring—my spiritual skin remained a foreign concept.

33: Loving Kindness

As my passion for new, potentially healing experiences continued, I stumbled onto Esalen Institute, a haven for consciousness studies in Big Sur, California.

My mother told me about the cliffside property after reading an article on it in the Sunday *L.A. Times*. I found it ironic that a woman who didn't have a clue—or care—about my inner workings, and who adamantly blamed her parents for all of her life's challenges, would pop up with a suggestion like Esalen that forever changed my life.

After signing up for a weekend titled *Letting Go and Moving On*, I drove up the beautiful California coast, ready for my latest transformational adventure.

The *Times* article had focused on the natural beauty of Big Sur, and quoted seminarians who'd reveled in their personal breakthroughs. I had no idea Esalen was also well known for its clothing-optional hot tubs, tucked into the rugged hillside.

When I arrived on Friday afternoon, feeling brave and somewhat adventurous, I decided to pass the time until dinner with a stroll around the property. Enjoying the warming rays of the midwinter sun as it contrasted with the cold, though incredibly alive air, I wandered the lush garden and open grassy areas. Grateful for someone to talk to, I accepted an elderly gentleman's invitation for a tour "down to the baths."

Somewhat entranced by the sound of the ocean waves' steady cycle, I followed the self-appointed first-timers' guide down the steep, gravel-covered path, continuing to marvel at the rugged perfection and postcard-worthy views of the California coastline.

Near the bottom of the trail, edged by a low, wrought-iron fence offering the illusion of safety, sat a small-house-sized structure. Rather than continue down the trail and onto the steps that led inside the wooden building, my escort stopped and peered over the rocky edge.

That first glance over the cliff, down to a variety of steamy pools—and bare-assed people—caught me off guard, and had I not been trying to appear cool and confident, I would have turned and run back up the steep hill. I probably didn't sound nonchalant as I declined my guide's offer of a soak, but I don't think he noticed the sheer terror in my voice as I muttered an excuse about wanting to get settled before dinner.

Later that night, in the workshop's first session, the leader, a kind, though I sensed no-bullshit-allowing, woman named Mary offered a solution to my tub fear. She suggested that the baths were generally quiet—and dark—after the evening session, and explained that those new to the property might find it a good time to explore the relaxing, natural sulfur waters.

The thought gave me a furious headache, but damn it, I'd come to push myself into unknown territory. I wasn't going to let a little thing like nudity get in my way.

Without being spotted, I managed to get down the hill and into the building, which turned out to be a dressing—or undressing—area. Still alone, I took a deep breath and assured myself I would be okay. After hanging my clothes on the nearest wooden peg, I obeyed the sign—"One Only Please"—and wrapped a single skimpy towel around my torso. I did my best to appear composed, despite my temples throbbing in protest, as I walked into the chilly night air.

I stepped down into the first open-to-the-night-sky, rocky pool I came to. With my feet in the hot—really hot—rotten-egg-scented waters, I glanced up and realized I wasn't alone. Of course, it was a man, about eight feet away, in the tub's opposite corner. I wanted to back out. But, feeling committed, I reluctantly placed my towel over the railing, and in an attempt at modesty, forced myself to submerge all the way to my shoulders. The sudden submersion into heat amplified my screaming pulse.

Closing my eyes, I did my best to slow my breathing, in search of a peaceful calm. With the Pacific Ocean pounding against the rocky shore thirty feet below my perch, I felt like a cat having its first bath.

Terrified to move to a vacant tub and thus show my nakedness, I sat, quietly willing the guy to leave me in peace. After watching the stars twinkle and stubbornly not move across the darkness, I was relieved when he finally did step past me, and out.

When the time I'd allotted for him to dress had passed, I too climbed from the tub into the blessedly refreshing night air. Aware that all the pools were empty and I was completely alone, I allowed myself to relax and take in the beauty of the surroundings. Tossing my towel over my shoulder—and throwing caution over the cliff—I walked back inside to get dressed, only to find the guy sitting on the bench, tying his shoes.

Silent the whole time we'd been sharing the smelly waters, he smiled and said, "Hi."

Hi? His tone was so matter-of-fact, like he sat fully clothed in front of dripping wet women every day. I managed a "Hi" in return, before stepping into the showers to give myself some space.

When I went back to the dressing area, my tub mate had disappeared, allowing me to dress in precious solitude. My head still hurt, but I'd survived my first Esalen "soak."

Not only did I experience a daring new level of physical exposure that weekend, but I stretched my emotional and mental states of being as well, almost to the breaking point.

Sure, I'd suspected the workshop might bring up rough spots, but Sunday morning, as I fixed my gaze on the waves churning far below me, I felt the nearly unbearable weight of personal growth. I seriously considered throwing myself over the precipice—a literal "letting go," but decided to pull myself together and go to class, willing to "move on."

You'd think, with an introduction like that one, I'd be hesitant to return. However, those medicinal waters and insightful seminars have a magnetic quality to them even today. Once past my initial fear, I learned to enjoy—and eagerly anticipate—my many visits to come.

Esalen became my favorite place for learning, where I soaked up wisdom ranging from spiritual studies to lucid dreaming, from shamanism to breathwork. Sitting at the feet of masters in their fields such as Joseph Chilton Pearce, Stephen LeBurge, Michael Harner, Stanislaus Grof, and many others, I steeped my body, mind, and spirit in new thoughts.

In addition to gathering knowledge at the cliffside oasis, I gathered men. One-night, or maybe, if they were good, two- or three-night stands. Until I met Bjorn—on Valentine's Day 1989.

Bjorn looked like any number of long-haired, blond surfer dudes I'd longed for back in high school, except he hadn't grown up in a beachside community. That adorable Norwegian—I'm a sucker for Vikings—had grown up in Texas, with a cutting edge psychologist father. As a result, he'd been coming to Esalen since he was a teen. At twenty-three years old, those awkward years weren't that far behind him.

I fell for his boyish, light-hearted charm, not to mention his hormone-rich, gorgeous body. And he fell for me. I didn't dwell on it—or perhaps even accept it as fact—but I often heard comments about being "hot." Although I'd had two children and what many would call a hard life, my thirty-one-year-old form showed no signs of wear. In fact, Bjorn often commented on, while gazing at our reflection in our mirrored closet doors, what a good-looking couple we made. The vanity of that statement, while charming, always left me disquieted—though I never said so.

By the time we met, I'd let go of my cabin in the woods and sold off my mail-order business—no longer able to tolerate *The Whole Family* and its cohesive message.

Back in my original girl-on-her-own stomping ground, Costa Mesa, California, I moved into a spacious, one-bedroom duplex. I even had a private backyard, complete with a play area for my kids' every-other-weekend visits. And while Bjorn never acted like a father figure to them, he enjoyed my children, as they did him. In many respects, we appeared the model family.

In addition to our surface attraction, Bjorn and I shared a love of the inner world. Although I'd dropped meditation before I met Mark, it was easy to slip back into a daily routine with my new love, who had moved in with me shortly after we hooked up at Esalen.

We met our spiritual and physical needs with mornings focused on a heart-centered meditation and nights ending with fabulously satisfying sex, though the concept of bringing the two together into sacred union remained unknown. I'm not saying our sex was heartless, but it certainly didn't take on the form of an erotic, conscious practice. What did creep into our relationship was Bjorn's interest in porn.

The first time I walked in on him watching an X-rated video, he quickly ejected it. After blurting a startled, somewhat unbelievable excuse, he promised it would never happen again, assuring a tearful me that I more than satisfied his needs.

The second time, after I found a hidden tape, he got mad. Not at me—at himself. It seems that in his quest to be a good, spiritually centered man, he'd prohibited himself from whacking off to dirty movies. Something about knowing that flipped a switch in me. Instead of being dismayed, or righteous, or supportive of his ban, I chose to become the instigator, suggesting we watch the smut together. Yikes.

The illicit nature of porn lit a fire in me. Watching the shameless acts with my boyfriend opened a floodgate of unbridled passion. I found myself living the mundane life of an accountant during the week, then come Saturday, when I wasn't playing Mom, I became voraciously horny.

Like those cocaine-filled nights of ravenous moans and insatiable groans I'd shared with lovers back in the drug days, Bjorn and I would suck and hump for hours in front of skin flicks, with quick breaks for food, drinks or bathroom visits.

The day after, similar to nursing a raging hangover, I'd waddle around the house, sore to the bone from the previous day's workout, wondering what on earth had come over me. Like Bjorn, I'd tell myself I wasn't interesting in doing "that" again. Until the next time.

Pushing away anything that questioned our robust non-mommy weekend activities, I told myself we were just having fun. Fortunately, before our sexual binges broke something, the opportunity to take a workshop with two of Bjorn's favorite teachers, Stephen and Ondrea Levine, offered a different kind of deep experience.

I'd studied meditation before, even en masse, but I'd never experienced a room of several hundred people breathing in resonance. Talk about intoxicating. While Stephen did most of the talking, I preferred the quiet presence of Ondrea.

Sitting on her meditation pillow, eyes closed, she simply filled the space with love. I don't know any other way to explain it. The sensation was palpable. Like Bjorn, I was hooked, attending day or longer sessions whenever they were offered on the West Coast.

Regrettably, while Bjorn and I attended one of those "loving kindness" events—a week-long gathering in the hills outside Monterey—I came up against love's polar opposite, a rage-filled, dare I say evil presence.

About a hundred participants listened intently to the discussion held in the large gathering room. The topic: Healing from Sexual Abuse. I paid close attention—as best I could over the voice in my head determined to distract me.

This is bullshit. You can't heal. You're damaged for life. Even your children are in danger around you. Someday you'll crack. You can't escape passing along the family's legacy.

Taunted by despicable and incessant thoughts, I considered voicing aloud to the group my fear I could abuse my son. But after hearing others spew merciless venom toward their real perpetrators, I decided to keep my crazy—and imagined—proclamations to myself.

Hoping some fresh air would clear my head, I told Bjorn I'd catch up with him at dinner and went outside. Unfortunately, that only made things worse, leaving me alone with the insanity.

I knew from experience that once the ruthless invader got control of me, there would be no option but to comply with its wishes. Basically, to cause bodily harm to myself. I knew because the same thing had happened years before, early in my marriage to Mark. . . .

We were out on a double date for a night of fun—at least Mark's best friend and his wife's idea of fun. In a brazen new venture, they had jumped into the mud wrestling craze, him as a referee, her as a wrestler. I wasn't the slightest bit interested in seeing women roll around in the mud, but those were the cocaine days, so I'd fill my nose and sit and watch this low-life form of entertainment.

We sat ringside—well, pit-side—in VIP seats, and watched as bikini-clad women, two at a time, stepped into the slop and began a good old-fashioned brawl. Uck.

However, much to the distress of my prim and proper self, part of me found the display arousing. Determined to alter my focus—and suppress my libido—I slipped my hands under the small round table.

Slowly and systematically, fully intending to inflict pain, I began to dig my long, beautifully manicured nails across the back of my right hand. It hurt like hell, but I listened to the voice chastising me for getting turned on, and, following its bidding, continued my punishment. By the end of the "show," I'd carved a series of deep, bloody grooves into my hand.

I hid the damage easily enough that night, but the next morning, I felt completely mortified with the obvious mutilation. My excuse—that I had fallen against the stucco of the house, with my arms full, thus explaining the unusual placement of the injury—deterred questions, but I carried around physical and emotional scars for years.

As I sat under the dense spruce canopy at the mercy-offering retreat, I knew better than to make the damage visible. So I hiked up my ankle-length skirt and dug into my right thigh, again scratching long, calculated rips into my flesh.

Mesmerized by the cutting words echoing in my head, I slipped into a trance of repetitive motion and accepted the hateful statements, acknowledging I didn't deserve to heal. After an indeterminate amount of torture, I snapped back to lucid consciousness, and tears streamed down my cheeks.

As I looked down at the bloody mess I'd made of my leg, I felt horribly ashamed. Oddly, I also felt at liberty to offer myself the very thing the workshop offered, loving kindness, as though I was only worthy of receiving nurturance after reaching the depths of despair.

At first, I didn't tell Bjorn about my lapse into self-abuse. When I did, he reacted in a cool, detached manner, not the ah-poor-baby-let-me-make-it-better response I'd hoped for.

Here's a snapshot of hell from my journal. . . .

December 31, 1989
End of another year, another decade, too. I'm not feeling very happy about it though. The struggle goes on. The pain goes on. What the fuck am I doing? What is this day-to-day bullshit called life?

Here I sit at Esalen, a beautiful, magical place. Incredible view of the ocean, the sound of crashing waves. Here with Bjorn, someone who loves me more than I think anyone ever has, and still I'm miserable.

He's pushing to get married, to set a date. I'm so confused. Sometimes I hate him; I want to beat the shit out of him.

I want him to be strong, to take care of me, but he can't.

Then he clings to me, needs me to be strong, or loving, or I don't know what. I get so scared.

I can't take care of him. And I resent the fact that I support him. Then sometimes I treat him like he's my property. I'm so confused. I don't know what I'm doing with him.

Is it really going to work out? Can our love really heal all this pain? Or am I just scared and holding onto him because I'm afraid to be alone again? Or afraid to hurt his feelings? I don't know.

Sometimes I think we will be together always, and sometimes I think it's just a big mistake. I don't want anyone close, ever again. It just hurts.

Back and forth, love and hate, the days whirled in a blend of chaos. Even moving into a beautiful, four-bedroom house in the quintessential, planned community of Irvine—a dream home in many respects—the nightmare continued, eroding our bliss. . . .

March 1, 1990
Went to sleep last night very tense, wondering what the hell I'm doing with my life, doing with Bjorn. I asked my dreams for some clarity:

I'm driving across railroad tracks as a train comes. It smashes into the back of my car and sends me spinning out of control. I'm scared I'm going to hit someone walking by, but I don't. When the spinning stops, I get out of the car, shaken and scared. I sit on the curb, dazed.

In my waking life, the animosity gained fury, erupting one night after dinner.

As though trapped in a classic crazy-bitch role from a bad movie, I grabbed a plate. After chasing Bjorn through the house and into the front yard, I slung my weapon Frisbee-style at him.

I missed. Horrified, I watched it disappear into the line of Italian Cypress separating my driveway from that of the neighbors. In my head I screamed, *No, not the plate, now you don't have a full set,* as the inevitable crash of pottery on concrete broke the silence. Thankfully, it wasn't one of the teal-blue dishes. Relieved there weren't any witnesses, I quickly cleaned up the evidence and slunk back inside.

Bjorn reached his breaking point, as well. The next day he packed his bags and left, standing firmly in advice he'd received from Stephen Levine, "Physical abuse is never okay. You must get out."

In attempts to "make it work," we started dating, getting together a few nights a week, hoping to build the foundation we'd skipped thirteen months earlier. While we stopped fighting, the grooves of mistrust and doubt persisted. When Bjorn moved back in a couple of weeks after moving out, we continued to question the wisdom—or lack thereof—behind our decision. Even our sex life and its passionate loving embraces had moved into the foreseeable realm of monotony.

Hopeful a tropical breeze would put the spark back in our relationship, we headed off to Hawaii—a trip we'd planned for several months. . . .

March 29, 1990 5:30 P.M.

So here I am, sitting in a beautiful hotel overlooking Waikiki. Why am I so down, so heavy, so depressed? Feel the need to alter my mind, get drunk or stoned.

Part of me wants to walk the beach—alone—while Bjorn meditates. Part of me wants to shop; part of me wants to sleep.

Feel crazy. So many times today I've felt enraged or closed off toward Bjorn. Then sometimes I want to be with him, have babies, make a home.

Then there are the times I just want to be single, but I'm afraid of being alone in my big house. I'm so mixed up...

9:30 P.M.

... Bjorn wanted to make love—as he calls it. To me it was sex. He was horny. I was accommodating, doing my "duty."

I just wanted him to do it and get it over with, so I could be left alone, safe, not pursued for a day or two.

Bjorn knew something was wrong. He saw my tears, but his cock won any debate as he continued to pump into me. I saw myself in the mirror, terror on my face.

I feel so violated. I don't want anyone in my body.

The voices tonight were clearer than ever, "I'm sorry Mommy," and "...just finish, then leave me alone." Who am I talking to? What happened to the little girl in this body?

Once he cums, I'm safe again. He goes to sleep, and I can nurture myself.

A wonderful, hot bath—with bubbles—and a washcloth filled with soapy froth. It felt so good to gently rub my whole body, even my toes, and then soak. Carefully drying myself, I felt like a little girl, dwarfed by the oversized, fluffy towel.

Afterward, I sat down and rubbed lotion over my skin. Not mechanically, but lovingly. Feeling the softness, enjoying the touch. Hugging myself. Loving myself.

It's going to be okay, Debbie. I'm going to take care of you.

And I did—as best as I knew how.

It took a few more months of struggle, but by summer, Bjorn and I broke it off for good. We parted amicably, sharing a loving-kindness meditation as we gazed softly into each other's eyes for the last time.

Without a partner under my feet, I once again clicked into I-can-do-better-for-myself mode and signed up for a photography class at the local junior college. I loved my view of the world through a camera, learning to see ordinary things in a new way. With my sandals enjoying life around a campus, I expanded my higher learning with a couple of speech classes.

First, inter-personal communication, where I gained an ability to speak up before my peers. Encouraged by my professor who had also become a friend, I ventured next into a course on intra-personal communication, a fascinating opportunity to crack the code of my inner workings.

Thinking back on the wide array of self-reflective tools I tasted in that course, I'd found my very own help-yourself *Dessert Cart of Life*. Of course, I got straight A's in everything.

34: Ecstatic Dance

With my bag of self-help tricks full to the brim, I decided to manifest a life unlike anything I had lived to date, including a career change; I wanted to become a shamanic artist. Never mind that my creative abilities were honed in the realm of home décor. In my bold, new world, anything was possible. After giving away my corporate attire and selling my home in the pristine Irvine community, I once again put my belongings——with just the creamer to represent the teal-blue dishes—in storage. By then my Mom's mother had passed on another complete set of Asian design, blue koi tableware, and a single girl on the move, especially a logical one like me, can only justify so many place settings. I trust the beloved teal-blue set found the perfect home via my local Goodwill charity.

Armed with advice from a highly recommended psychic—trust your feelings, allow them to guide you—I drove north, in search of my bliss.

While sitting in a hotel in San Francisco, compliments of the owner—a guy I'd met during a dance workshop—I fine-tuned the parameters of my desire: five acres, rolling green hills, near water, and dark at night. Oh yeah, and a $50,000 price tag. I landed in Lake County, a sparsely populated, rural area north of Napa and its famous vineyards.

Once the sale closed, I chose to ponder my upcoming life from the best place I knew for doing such things—Esalen.

After a three-month hiatus—once again steeped to near perfection in the healing waters and abundant workshops—I stepped into my next expression of Self. I even claimed my given name, Debra, a name I had never used. Debra was punitive, a label I'd only heard in combination with Jean, signaling Mom had reached the breaking point. But then I came across a woman who inspected my Akashic record, which is kind of like the soul's DNA.

Before the cosmic specialist would answer any of my questions—about a guy I hoped might be the new "him"—she told me it was imperative I go by Debra, stating that my soul needed the vibratory frequency of Ra. She went on to tell me about a powerful lifetime I'd had in Egypt and my alignment with the teachings of the Sun God.

She further explained that ancient wisdom and past-life allies would have a hard time finding me without my name's full power, so I figured I had better hedge my new-life bets, and thus dropped Debi when I moved onto my land.

At first I loved playing pioneer woman, living in a VW camper, drawing up my starter house plans, and then acting as owner/builder for the project. But with the home's completion, nine months after I arrived on my piece of earth overlooking the creek, I began to detect holes in the dream.

In one of those classic, grass-isn't-really-greener moments, I found myself alone and without friends—having opted out of continuing a relationship with any of the good ol' boys who'd helped on the house.

And my naïve goal—to have my children join me for fresh country living—met with extreme opposition from both my ex and his parents. Fortunately, Mark was willing to modify our arrangement, allowing the kids extended visits during school holidays and summer vacation. So during spring break 1992, coinciding with both my son's seventh birthday and an Easter egg hunt unlike any we had shared to date, I celebrated my home's final, move-in-ready approval.

After a heart-wrenching good-bye to my kids, and with the promise of summer on the horizon, I pushed aside loneliness and got busy on the finishing stage of my girl-on-her-own project.

Occupied with painting, laying tile and hardwood floors, digging a garden, and moving—literally—a ton of rock, I fully embraced my creative spirit. With the delivery of my belongings—what had previously filled a four-bedroom house—I somehow managed to cram everything of importance into my compact seven-hundred-and-twenty-square-foot nest. For overflow items that I simply couldn't part with, I purchased a shed, another meticulously organized space.

When exhausted from physical activities, I'd shift my attention to the mental realm: reading, writing, and self-empowering affirmations.

As much as I wanted my northern California lifestyle to follow a direct path embracing *"complete trust and clarity"*—a phrase that appears often in my journals at the time—before long, my days more closely resembled an ambiguous loop.

There were some bright moments when I reached out to my new small-town community: the service I provided to Hospice as a child grief counselor and the after-school program I started at the high school.

I'd first connected with teens back in Orange County, where I'd ventured into a local nonprofit organization for girls. Working with a group of about a dozen twelve- to fourteen-year-olds, I taught them to pay attention to their bodies, and their subtle—and not so subtle—ways of communicating.

We played with the "knowing" of their sixth sense, so often present, yet ignored. Not only did the teens understand and benefit from our group interactions, I felt empowered by both the girls and the games.

In my new small-town community, I presented an after-hours program at the high school: one focused on writing from the heart in an unedited, authentic manner. Four brave young women showed up that first afternoon. When they left, ninety minutes later, each seemed a bit brighter and eager to explore her new creative outlet.

I, conversely, went home overwhelmed, feeling as though I had overstepped my role as a teacher and guide by sharing my own spontaneous words. The anger and frustration that flowed from my pen needed an outlet, but reading my outburst aloud to the girls shocked and, I think, even frightened a couple of them.

The following week, I used the weather and its light dusting of snow as an excuse to cancel class. Two weeks later, I came up with another excuse. Bottom line, I never went back.

As I review my journals from nearly two decades ago—the written records of my mental and emotional state—it's easy to see my flailing energy directly related to my old friend marijuana.

At first, my "clean and sober" designation accompanied me in my next chapter of being. But, as any regular twelve-step member will attest, if you stop going to meetings, you're playing on a slippery field. It's not like I didn't seek out recovery, but I had a string of excuses as to why I didn't return, like the hour-long drive—each way—to the only NA meeting in the county.

There were AA meetings closer to me—Alcoholics Anonymous seems to be everywhere—but I didn't have a problem with drinking and, being a purist, I wanted to stick with my own kind. Of course, I told myself smoking would be limited to "just a little" when friends—like a couple I'd met at Esalen—came by for a visit. However, like any good addict, before long I accepted their offer to leave some of the herbal companion behind.

In the beginning, I only smoked after completing my daily chores, convinced I deserved a treat. That's when I discovered the magic of dancing myself into ecstatic bliss.

First pulling up energies from the earth herself, I'd channel the pulsing waves through my body, then out my hands. With my inner eye wide open and mesmerized by the colorful display, I'd weave ribbons of light around my body, easily orgasmic to a depth I'd never risked with another.

Dance had become a major part of my days since just prior to my move north, when I'd discovered Gabrielle Roth. Unlike the disco or rock 'n' roll gyrations of my youth, her workshops encouraged movement from a deeper, more authentic place. From her week-long training titled *God, Sex, and the Body*, where I danced for hours each day, I became inspired with the design of my new home, especially its wooden floor. I'm not saying Gabrielle encouraged us to smoke before dancing. That was my addition, easing me—or sometimes hungrily hurling me—into sexual passion.

Before my ride of smoke-enhanced bliss reached its inevitable burn-out, I'd imagine I had a room full of honored patrons, guests of the temple priestess—a captive audience who rode the ecstasy with me, taken by the Goddess who inhabited my body.

Stimulated by my dance performances for my invisible guests and an Esalen workshop on transformational video productions, I took my first action steps toward becoming a shamanic artist. After purchasing a camera, an editing deck, and an Amiga computer, complete with a *Video Toaster*, I put together a thirty-minute tape.

With a combination of dance that I recorded using a tripod, poetry, and music I loved, I wove a psychedelic, cutting-edge—at least at the time—multi-media presentation. Nine years into what I'll loosely call "healing," this series of vignettes exposed my relationship to sexuality.

On the back cover—of course I had packaging, too—I added the following invitation:

It's sacred dance. Viewing it is meant to invoke a willingness to go within oneself, to go beyond the surface of sexuality, beyond the surface of eroticism.

The only problem with my first production was the content. It scared most people I had the nerve to show it to.

It might have been the nudity, but more likely it was the section where I growled and hissed like a caged tiger. In fact, that's what I called it: Caged.

Looking back, I think it's curious how close the word "sacred" is to "scared." I was scared, terrified in fact, but I wasn't willing—or perhaps able—to stay present with myself long enough to ask why. I simply forged ahead, in the same way I had pushed myself with school, determined to produce.

My original intent had been to create a sensual blend of calming nature scenes overlaid with erotic imagery, something beautiful, so I too was surprised when rage demanded equal time. But, compelled to reveal an accurate picture of what I believed to be my inner truth, I included pieces like this:

Slowly she approaches
crazed grin on her face
she taunts, closes in
shuts out all others
I know she comes
to devour me
to shred me apart

Alone with my insanity
as bare hands
rip out my guts

It's painful to go back and read—or watch—my desperate words, but that's the harsh reality I lived in. Anger can only stay ignored for so long. As much trouble as I'd had expressing mine—at least toward others—I can see the value it holds. Living a life where I held myself hostage, albeit in a beautiful prison, I'm not surprised my art burst forth in furious rants.

Thankfully—and that's an understatement—the madwoman didn't have complete control; delightful moments snuck in too. Those polar opposite extremes, what a psychologist (if I'd had the nerve to see one) might have called "manic behavior," were clearly related to my drug use.

From today's world—and wisdom—it's clear I was addicted to sex. Or at least the feel-good chemicals orgasm sent rushing through my system. Passion and pot, my two downfalls. Yet, with that said, I don't want to toss out my search for sacred union, however wayward my path may appear.

Sometimes it was a matter of days, while other times weeks would pass, but eventually my desire for the stony, creative fog would lift. Once again promising myself I wouldn't do "that" again, I'd swing—or crawl—back to the clean-girl lifestyle and a morning routine of meditation and writing, instead of lungs full of smoke.

Teetering at the edge of a space where I believed I was good enough and deserved something better, I would search for motivation, for something deeper that I could give back to humanity while avoiding a run-in with my fuck-it-all, disowned-step-child depression.

When my non-drug-fueled energy and zest for life returned, it still focused around dance and creative expression as a means of presenting myself in the world. Not just me dancing at home, alone. I imagined taking what I had learned with Gabrielle Roth—and from my own body—into the world and teaching others.

The others I wanted to teach? At-risk populations, like teenage girls who lived in group homes, or those who had already tipped the scales of justice and wound up in jail.

But none of that came to pass, because in addition to causing viewers to squirm uncomfortably, producing my dance video ate up the last of my financial resources, sending me back to the predictable—and relatively emotionless—world of accounting. Not such a bad place to be.

35: Boundaries

August 1996. I felt the need for something different, a new chapter in my routine life.

For the past three years, on Sunday nights, I'd been packing my bags and driving two hours south to San Francisco. A friend of mine, Chip, the same guy who'd put me up during my transition north, owned a group of hotels and restaurants there.

Back when I'd run out of money, Chip had found himself in need of an accountant, so, as often happened in my life, I simply stepped through the easily opened door.

Working for the hospitality firm was enjoyable, with perks including not only a well-appointed, complimentary room, but full access to the vegetarian restaurant that shared a roof with our offices. After three or four work-packed days, I'd climb back into my car and once again escape the hubbub of the city, replacing nights of street lights and sirens with millions of stars and crickets.

With the summer preceding my fortieth birthday rolling by in hundred-mile stretches, I began to feel the familiar pull for something out of the ordinary, a fun new adventure. I considered buying another camper—I'd sold my temporary home after the house was completed—and turning into a modern-day gypsy, but before I made the purchase, my next phase in life came via my thirteen-year-old daughter.

"I want to move in with you."

Her statement wasn't a complete shock. One of the things that had kept me from all-encompassing depression after giving up the kids was knowing that once they got older, they'd be able to make their own choices about living arrangements. Her request about where we would live brought the real surprise.

"I don't want to be a country bumpkin. Can you come back down here?"

I said yes. And while Orange County—where the majority of my blood relations still lived—would never have been a stop on my gypsy caravan, I felt drawn there for my role as mid-life mom.

I dove in completely. For the first few months, I supported myself as a stay-at-home parent by living off loan proceeds from my country home. Driving back and forth to junior high and helping with homework, I bonded deeply with Amy, making up for lost time. We even joined a local Goddess-centric women's center and explored some teen-friendly events.

Being back in Southern California also allowed me more time with my son. Though he didn't follow his sister's decision to move in, I made sure he had his own bedroom for weekend visits.

All in all, those months following my return "home" were fabulous, some of the best I'd lived to date. But times change. As Amy made friends in school, and I took a full-time controller position, our relationship grew sticky, prompting me to look outside the home for companionship.

In the five years since Bjorn, I'd certainly seen men—or screwed around with them—but my couplings consistently lacked any depth or fulfillment.

Thinking the Internet might offer something, I did a search on "sacred sexuality," and discovered an organization with workshops that focused on love and "intimacy"—a term I approached with hesitation.

The first time I'd heard that word—back when I was eighteen and seeing a counselor at the suggestion of a friend—the *into-me-you-see* breakdown sent me reeling. With my insides freaking out—if they'd been able to run without me, they would have—I remained courteous for the duration of the session, yet never returned.

Now, at my somewhat mature forty years of age, I felt sturdy and confident in my ability to explore new, more intimate ways of relating, so I called the number listed on the site.

After a pleasant and fear-allaying phone call with the group's office manager, I decided to be bold and signed up for a weekend course, even though I wouldn't know a soul there.

The preparatory instructions had been clear: arrive by 6 p.m. for dinner, and no admittance after 8. Shit. It was nearly that when I pulled off the freeway and headed into the Santa Barbara hills, searching for self enlightenment. Already stressed from beyond-awful traffic, I maneuvered the dark, winding roads, putting out a silent prayer, *if it's meant to be.*

Part of me hoped my daring adventure into foreign territory with a bunch of potentially strange people would be thwarted, but I continued on, acknowledging the risk of being turned away. Fortunately—an inner voice of today says that's debatable—they allowed me into the room thirty minutes late.

The large, open, mellow space directly opposed my traffic- and hunger-induced craggy buzz. Eighty or so people—in a wide range of age, color, shape, and stages of undress—were scattered about the maroon, plush-pile carpet. A couple of heads turned to see who had come in late, but most focused their attention on the couple at the front of the room who I guessed were the workshop's leaders.

I did my best to also tune in to the speaker's words, but the sight of so many partially naked people momentarily overwhelmed my remaining senses. I'd been told the workshop would be "clothing optional," but hadn't expected so many of the participants to select the option.

As I stood by the door taking in the reality of what I'd stepped into, a kind-faced young woman silently directly me toward an empty spot. Not wanting to stand out, I slid off my shoes, jacket, tee-shirt, jeans, and yes, even my bra—I held onto my panties—before wadding everything up and stuffing it into one of the empty cubbyholes lining the back wall.

I'd just settled onto the floor, getting as close to comfortable as I was going to get, when the leader caught my attention, announcing it was time to get up.

"I'd like you all to push your things off to the sides of the room," he announced in his gentle, yet authoritative voice. "It's time to pick your buddy for the weekend." Whatever calm I'd absorbed from the room immediately fled as he continued, "This person will be your best friend throughout the workshop and you'll have several opportunities to check in with each other."

Motionless, the proverbial deer-in-headlights, I watched as my fellow participants, who'd had time to meet and mingle over dinner, smiled and shared loving embraces as they wove about. *Fuck*, I thought. *I'm in the wrong place. A weekend buddy. This is awful.*

I watched as pairs rapidly formed, before I commanded myself to move about the room, dreading the thought of being stuck as a leftover. As luck—or perhaps fate—would have it, every time I approached someone, I got cut off; either that or they were already spoken for.

With the selection pool dwindling—the leaders had asked for those remaining without a partner to raise their hands—the universe provided just the right buddy.

I knew George, an older, gray-haired guy, was a perpetrator the instant he got close. While he didn't creep up and snarl, "I like to hurt little girls," I knew. I could feel it in my gut. Just like I had, several years before. . . .

My stay-away-from-this-man alarm first went off when I lived in cookie-cutter suburbia, aka Irvine, California, during the Bjorn days.

Being the friendly and outgoing type, my seven-year-old daughter quickly got to know the other girls on the street during her weekend visits. One lived next door with her mom, grandma, and little brother—ideal playmates for my children—and another, two doors down, lived alone with her dad.

The kids usually played at our house or next door. But one Saturday, the girl from two doors down rang the bell and asked if Amy could come over to play. As I was being the responsible mom—albeit part-time—it seemed obvious I should meet the new friend's dad before allowing the girls to play indoors.

The thirty-something man who opened the door didn't look dangerous, but a chill shot through me causing me to reach for my daughter and take a step back. Stumbling over words of introductions, my survivor mind screamed: "Do not let your child into this house!" So despite the social awkwardness of the moment, I made up an excuse about us needing to get home, dragging my confused child away with me.

Once back to the safety of our green lawn, my daughter and I plopped down to join my son in Ninja Turtles play. She asked the inevitable, "Why?" Figuring my best option would be the truth, I explained how I believed her friend's daddy was a bad man who might hurt children.

My baby girl, far too wise for her seven years, asked, "Did a bad man hurt you when you were little?"

"Yes," I replied simply, relieved she didn't press me for a more detailed answer.

As far as I know, both of my kids heeded the warning to never step foot across that neighbor's threshold. I pray I'm right.

Without my children, I was outside of my protector-mommy mode that night in the hills above Santa Barbara. I stood silently for a moment considering George's "buddy" invitation. Looking around the room I noticed the glaring lack of upheld hands—and an alternative—so I suppressed my perpetrator fear and answered, "Okay."

As I sat politely during the introductory exchange, I allowed my pal for the weekend to go first, doing my best to focus on his words over the din of my interior outrage.

Interrupt him. Tell him you made a mistake, you didn't mean to say yes. Listen to him, he's carrying on about his unfulfilled relationship with his daughter. You don't want to play nice girl with this man. And you definitely don't want to get into any sexual father-daughter projections with him. Cut it off now!

When my turn to share came around, I smiled sweetly, skimming the surface of who, why, and what, telling myself, *to hell with any intimacy for this man.*

Later that night, with the opening session over, I settled into my rustic cabin—a shared, campground-style accommodation. However, instead of enjoying sweet sleep induced by fresh, mountain air, I felt an inner fury that kept me tossing and turning for most of the night. When I did doze, it was fitful, with dreams of fire and destruction.

At daybreak, I knew I had to do something even if it meant going buddy-less for the weekend. That meant I would have to confront George and tell him he was fired. The choice between having my weekend ruined or speaking up for myself weighed heavily on me as I walked down to breakfast with the other participants.

While I was enjoying my fruit and yogurt and a lively conversation with a cute guy sitting across from me, George approached. I could feel him hovering over my right shoulder. While I would have preferred to swat him away like the annoying bug I felt him to be, I offered a brief—and slightly curt—"Good morning" before returning my focus across the pine table.

Soon we gathered in the workshop space and partnered up for a morning check-in. George sat cross-legged in front of me.

"I don't like how you ignored me earlier," he sulked. "I'm angry you were talking to that other guy."

Something inside me snapped. Perhaps lack of sleep sent my nice girl packing. But damn it, I'd paid good money for the workshop, and I sure as hell wasn't going to let some menacing man tell me who I could and couldn't talk to.

"I'm done, George."

"What do you mean, you're done?" he asked in a puzzled tone.

"I mean I'm done. We're done. I can't, I won't be your buddy any more. I'm sorry." And with that, I got up and walked away. I'd set a boundary.

George got another companion, a workshop assistant. I also got a new partner, that same young woman who had pointed out the open floor space the night before. She turned out to be a fabulously supportive—as well as understanding—weekend buddy.

By Sunday evening, as I drove the return route home, I felt vibrantly alive. I'd survived not only the expanse of bare skin, but had also expanded myself to share in a variety of gentle, respectful, and loving exercises, some with individuals, some with small groups. I'd even grown compassionate enough to give George a good-bye hug—after I'd put my clothes on.

All in all, my first exploration of intentional intimacy went well.

36: Connecting with Heart

At forty-two—a birthday I believed would lead to an insightful year—I felt marginally satisfied in my roles as mother and accountant. Yet clearly I was on a quest for something more, something to fill the emptiness that crept around my attention.

After several more workshops and a couple of short-term relationships, I still hungered for an elusive ingredient in the realm of partnering. So, once again playing at the edge of "normal" sexuality, I accepted an invitation to an "oil party."

About forty people lounged around the living room or mingled in the kitchen of the elegant home in Coto de Caza, a prestigious community in south Orange County. I knew a few of the other guests, individuals and couples I'd met at intimacy workshops, but I still felt nervous. What did the evening have in store?

After straightening up from the pot-luck dinner, clearing the family room of all furnishings, and laying out plastic sheeting, the guests gathered in a large circle—naked.

The premise was simple: fun-loving, pleasure-seeking adults getting together for an open-hearted, sensuous adventure.

As soothing music filled the charged air around us, we each stated our name and anything else that seemed important. Then the leaders, a good-looking, fortyish couple who routinely opened their home for such events, told us the "safe-environment" guidelines. First up: no open-mouth kissing. Darn.

On one hand, that primary rule brought relief; on the other hand, I yearned to be kissed, deep and hard. But that would be a different party. This gathering centered around trust and touch. Luscious, flowing touch facilitated by warm oil.

We broke into groups of four, temporary tribes to begin the ritual. I went first, receiving a silent, loving embrace from one of the married couples I knew and a guy friend of theirs. Then came the oil: an unscented, pale amber liquid that could have come from the same bottle they'd used for cooking earlier in the day.

It was hard not to giggle as slippery hands passed up, down, and around the body parts. Oh yeah, another rule, no fingers dipped inside dark crevices—it was a surface pleasure party.

At first it was as awkward as it sounds. But I quickly diverted my attention away from anxious thoughts and into the delightful experience of six warm hands gliding gently over my appreciative skin. Applying the oil turned out to be just as much fun.

Although reluctant to release the bond of our initial four, we joined the large group for the next phase of instruction: make two concentric circles, men on the outside and women on the inside. Yikes, face to face with strangers—men, no less. I wanted new experiences, but something about looking into a man's eyes felt too intimate.

Once in place, with women I knew on both my left and right, I stared into my first partner's foreign, dark brown irises across from me. Following the suggestion to close our eyes—relieving both the discomfort with looking and worry about being seen—I could more fully appreciate the delicate play of fingers, both the men's and mine.

With about five minutes per shift around the slippery sphere, I gently explored a steady stream of unknown faces, shoulders, and arms. Even round bellies and hairy backs were vast territories to be explored via this modified Braille method. Although penises were obviously present, it wasn't about jerking them off. They were simply part of the territory in the human safari.

At first—ever the logical accountant—I followed a routine for every frame: top to bottom, front, then back, wanting to make sure I didn't miss anything before moving on. As the evening continued, I relaxed and found myself enraptured with the diversity of each new exploration.

In some cases we stood, tentatively touching. With others, we knelt or sat. And with a few bold adventurers, I found myself rolling around on the floor, our bodies slipping and sliding in an erotic dance of sensual delight.

All in all, it was a good night—definitely an event to remember. I would have gone back if I hadn't met Don.

Thanksgiving weekend, 1998. I'd returned to the love and intimacy workshops for another weekend session, one with a focus dear to my heart: spirituality. Only this time, instead of being surrounded by people I'd gotten to know over the past two years, I went to Northern California and gazed upon mostly unfamiliar faces.

After my first partnering calamity with George, I'd learned to weed through potential partners—a process occurring numerous times throughout each weekend.

Clearly taking my time, I'd stand quietly and check with my insides, making sure "Yes" was really the answer I wanted to utter before I spoke. If not, after an unapologetic, "No, thank you," I'd continue around the space until I felt a good match. When no one passed my "taste test," I'd sit alone and write in my journal or do the exercise solo.

In the room of about sixty men and women, I didn't notice my next heartthrob on Friday night or even Saturday morning, but Saturday afternoon he definitely caught my attention. I'd graciously declined several offers, and then I turned around, nearly bumping into him.

"Do you want to be my partner?" he asked gently.

While I found his long, straight brown hair and sweet smile enticing, I felt a bit put off by his pierced nipples. However, before saying no, I decided to follow my deep-breath check-in routine as I gazed into his soft, blue eyes.

Before I could hear an internal no—or yes—I "saw" a small cord of light extend from his chest, as though he had thrown out a fishing line.

In fact, he had done just that. The energetic cord landed right in the middle of my own chest, in my heart. Watching in amazement, I let this previously unknown man reel me in.

Within minutes after finding a seat on some pillows and snuggling up close, really close, we were having sex, deep, hungry, all-consuming intercourse.

Part of me said, *Hey, what's going on here?* That part looked around the room, noticing other couples weren't taking the exercise—on exploring the sacred nature of sexuality—quite so literally. But it was too late. I'd been hooked.

Giddy and totally smitten, I felt the familiar rush of lust flood my body. The voice of wisdom that said, *Proceed with caution*, was easily dismissed with, *Not now, I've got it under control.* Yeah, right.

While I'd had sex with absolute strangers before, I'd never been so vulnerable and open. Of course, that was the workshop's design: let go of boundaries, connect deeply. And I did. Like a puppy, love-struck with its new owner.

During the meal breaks I learned a bit more about Don. Things that ordinarily would have led me to close down and back off, like the fact that both he and his girlfriend—yes, girlfriend—were bikers, complete with Harley Davidsons. That alone presented a clear, do-not-cross line, but then I heard his tales of woe.

He played the perfect hand with the girlfriend—he first spoke of her as a housemate—who didn't appreciate him. How he slept on the sofa. And how he wanted to break it off.

If that didn't have me yearning to step in and rescue him, his cancer did. After he told me the story of his numerous scars, some uncomfortably fresh, I became his ideal combination of love, strength, and hope. Ready to battle the dreaded disease with him, I swore if he had a recurrence, I'd be there every step of the way. Unlike his current girlfriend who, he complained, hadn't even visited during his last hospital stay.

What I didn't pay heed to was the tiny voice inside, whispering truths.

Careful of stepping into the rescuer game. His relationship can't be as bad as he says. If it is, why has he stayed in it? Looks a lot like you're taking an "I'll rescue

Daddy from Mommy and her distance" role. And yes, this looks a lot like you're playing out your life at two, before the divorce.

I briefly pondered that questioning voice later—and many a sleepless night thereafter—as I sat in bed with my trusty journal.

December 5, 1998

My heart is so filled with emotions: expansive love and constricting fears. I need to remember, no matter what, I have myself...

... God, I love him. I want him so badly right now. I haven't felt this deeply in many years—perhaps ever. I'm so open, the core of my being is so accessible. I've laid out the red carpet for Don to enter deeply into my soul. And now I get to sit with myself and see if it's okay if he doesn't choose to stay.

This touches deep grief, staying present, in love with myself, while sitting in the place of not knowing. I hear a voice inside that says, "It's okay. He does love you deeply, and you will be together. Please have patience. Please allow your own healing to take place. Stay present with yourself through this time of shadows. Use this as a living meditation. Breathe; focus on letting go, trusting, sending love. Not only to Don, but to yourself...

"... You can focus on questions, doubts, fears, but why? Open to the bliss. Fill yourself with love."

Looking back over my freshly smitten words of adoration, I'm pleased to see the commitment I made to myself, or at least *offered* to the woman so enamored, but further review of my journal also reveals a crack, an early indicator I'd placed Don in a savior role: *I feel cherished and precious. I'm learning to see what Don sees in me.*

In addition to my wanting a man to open my heart to, there was a mundane reality in my quest for a partner: I needed someone to help with my daughter. At soon-to-be-sixteen, she possessed the same penchant for anti-authority I'd had at that age—though, unlike me, she always got caught. So with a new job requiring me to travel, generally a week at a time, I didn't need a baby-sitter—I needed a warden.

Besides needing day-to-day help with my life's responsibilities, I'm embarrassed to admit I also wanted a ring on my finger. A tangible sign of my lovability, so people I met in airplanes or hotels wouldn't look at me as another one of those sad, middle-aged women without a mate. I know, pitiful. Of course, I could have bought myself a ring, and pretended to be hitched, but that seemed even more pathetic.

And perhaps the fact that Don was a biker, a scary tough guy—though he really wasn't—helped tip me into my own reckless, rebel mode. That and the sex.

For the previous thirteen years, sex had been a roller coaster, some satisfying, some mediocre, and some downright humiliating.

Don and I had phenomenal sex. That first time, surrounded by others in the "intimate" space, had reawakened my wild-girl fire. By the end of the weekend, it didn't matter that Don lived with a woman he'd been committed to for several years—ironically, the person who'd given him the workshop as a birthday present. It didn't matter that I lived five hundred miles away. It especially didn't matter that we were both single parents of perilously aged, teenage girls.

That's the biggest regret I have from the Don days—the effects of our relationship on those around us. But at first, nothing mattered except the intense need to be together. Our seemingly endless well of passion had to be explored.

We were apart three weeks before I went north again to visit, taking advantage of his girlfriend's absence. Although, according to Don, she was fine with him having relations on the side.

The first night of my short pre-Christmas visit, we sat under the stars, each lost in our own world as we enjoyed a soak in his hot tub. Gazing upward past the crescent moon, I skipped gleefully amidst the shimmering stars, high on their dust, as I silently invoked the Goddess. Asking for her blessings, I professed my undying love for Don, an uncharacteristic move so early on, even for me.

I knew better than to create ritual space and invoke a sacred vow without so much as a hint to the recipient. But something came over me. In a way, I fell into a trance, encouraged by my own—or were they?—unspoken words.

The following day, excited to expose me to his world, Don pulled out his pride and joy—or was it a dirty little secret? There in the back of the dresser, wrapped in a shirt, was a shoe box full of self-portrait photographs. I'd seen a lot in my forty-two years, but never anything like that. Before the shy, prudish aspect of me could grab my brain and blush, the logical aspect wondered how the hell he'd gotten the pictures developed. I was so stunned by the images of self-inflicted pain that all I could say was, "Oh."

Then there were the porno magazines.

I'd seen plenty of X-rated imagery before, but that day I was introduced to the world of he/she's and bestiality. Feigning interest in the glossy images of naked men with breasts and women having sex with animals, my mind shut down. I refused to acknowledge the shock racing through my system and disconnected from my body, the very thing I'd been trying so hard to befriend.

If I could go back to that me of yesterday I'd play it a bit differently. . . .

"Wow," the confident, sure-of-herself woman would state as she thumbed through his images of self-abuse. "I've never seen anything like this before. Does it give you pleasure to be in pain? It had to hurt, right?"

Not waiting for an answer, I'd continue, "I'm really glad you feel comfortable showing me these. But I have to tell you, I'm not okay with the practice of masochism. And I'm not interested in playing the sadistic role either, even with a caring heart.

"As much as I've grown to love you over this past month, I need to end our relationship—here, now. I hope you understand I'm not judging you or your way of finding erotic pleasure. I simply have a different path."

Ah yes, how my life would have been different. But the compulsive fires had a hold on me. I was sure I'd found the man I had been looking for—the one whose love would inspire me to look at, deal with, and release all of my demons. In reality, it was less about inspiration and more like force. I'd jammed my heart into high gear, and damn anyone who stood in the way of my race toward nirvana—even me.

37: Is This Love?

As I look back, I see obvious signs we were forcing an oil and water mixture; a passing glance would have told you that. But I took it all—from Don's horrible grammar, to his skintight boot-cut Levi's, to the country music whining from his lowered Chevy truck—as an opportunity to expand my world, to open to love.

Of course, things were wonderful at first. How could they not be? Young love—well, mid-life lust—liberated all. It's not like I'd put on blinders regarding what lay before me. My journals from that time clearly reflect concerns. Yet they also gently brush my questions aside as I focused on the bliss.

Just days after Christmas I got the best present I could imagine.

At first speechless when Don asked if I was serious about opening my home to him and his daughter, I quickly recovered and answered, "Yes, absolutely."

Ignoring the thud that kicked in my gut, I tossed the voice cautioning, *Wait, give it time,* into solitary confinement. Thrilled I had won the me-versus-her battle—her being the old girlfriend—I gloated. In hindsight, if I'd taken the time to talk to Don's soon-to-be-ex and listen to her side of his unappreciated-in-relationship story, I could have saved myself a lot of grief. But I didn't. I knew everything, insisting my saint-like heart was big enough for all of us. Yikes.

So, just after New Year's, a mere five weeks following our first meeting, the next crazy chapter of my life began to unfold—or unravel—with him and his sixteen-year-old joining me and mine under my three-bedroom condo's roof. Talk about a brazen—and risky—new adventure. The girls hadn't even met.

Now, with more than a decade of post-Don wisdom, I can offer myself some breathing room. I honestly didn't know how to take it slow. Date. Get to know a guy. Introduce him to family. See if you have common interests, morals, ethics. It all sounds great; it just wasn't for me.

Reflecting on my avoidance of the gentle, meandering path of relating, I wonder if I've come by my attack-and-conquer method naturally. Or perhaps biologically. . . .

I returned to using my maiden name about a year after my divorce from Mark, something I hadn't done following my split with Ed. Surprised to be getting mail in my reclaimed name—especially what I at first considered to be junk—I was confused when inner guidance said to open it.

I'd never heard of the Association of Pre- and Perinatal Psychology, but their annual conference was coming up in nearby Newport Beach, and after reading through the information-packed brochure, I felt certain I had to attend. An accountant has no need to understand birth and its potential for trauma; my interest was personal.

With a scholarship trade in place—I ran the Association's audio recording equipment—I was able to attend back-to-back lectures and even some experiential sessions. Each new topic, from conception through birth itself, brought fascinating insights.

Similar to my life of thirty-plus years, my gestation and birth weren't calm. According to the people I met during the conference, my life choices related directly to my existence in—and inevitable exit from—the womb.

When a guided visualization took me through implantation from the egg's perspective, I felt magnetic and welcoming. Of course, those pollywog-like swimmers were drawn to me, and I, once they came knocking, selected just the right one for entry.

The sperm's reaction, however, witnessed the next day during another inner journey, brought a distinctly different viewpoint. Swimming along with the frenzied masses, I allowed myself to be drawn toward the ultimate goal. But when I felt my head being sucked into the unrelenting mass, I wanted to scream. If my body in sperm form had possessed arms, I would have done my best to push away from the gigantic, life-sucking beast. I wiggled my tail furiously, to no avail. I was trapped.

In addition to going on mental journeys led carefully by the experts, some participants, myself included, stumbled into spontaneous physical reactions. At one point, I ended up in a presenter's hotel room, going through an unwanted—at least consciously—re-birth experience. Fortunately, the expert had seen such cases before and was skillful in navigating my response, which alternated between rage and grief.

The way my mother tells it, at three weeks past her due date, the doctor decided I needed a little encouragement and administered labor-inducing chemicals. Personally, I think I'd changed my mind about being born. Though it occurs to me that perhaps the second thoughts originated with Mom, and I was simply being a good co-dependent.

When the chemicals weren't enough to push me out, the doctor resorted to forceps, literally pulling me into life. I've even had a memory flash of the doctor's upside-down face, while I released my first wrathful scream.

So, there it is, an oddly comfortable and somewhat logical reason as to why I tend to ram myself full-force into questionable situations—like opening my home and heart to Don.

Although I did my best to cultivate and nurture the love I professed for the man *du jour*, it didn't take long for the spark to waver. In a matter of months, what I'd originally seen as his devoted behavior registered as neediness and clinginess.

With my work schedule taking me on the road four to five days at a time, he'd grow restless and bored, almost desperate for me to return. While I too counted the days away, what I craved most was private re-entry time, at least a few hours. I explained how I felt and asked for what I wanted—that much I'd learned about relating—but Don either couldn't hear me or was unwilling to change his behavior.

Around the time of our six-month anniversary, my journals display a markedly different tone from that of expansive love. In fact, I'd even taken to writing in the middle of the night while Don slept, the only time I could find for myself and my inner support team.

Sunday, June 20, 1999

> *Two strangers*
> *Each hiding behind a wall of silence*
> *Each blaming the other for cold indifference*
> *Wallowing in self-pity*
> *Each retreats further*
> *Soon there will be no lifeline left*
> *No connection*
> *No memory of what drew them together*
> *Silent strangers they will once again be*

How long will we sit in this passive hell? What can be learned from this? How do I find the love in this too? See the perfection of the moment?

I believed you when you said you'd go into darkness with me. Was that a lie? Or have we simply hit the edge where you are no longer willing to share? So many questions roam around the barren desert of my mind.

As our first anniversary approached, we'd settled into a routine, outwardly complacent and inwardly devoid. Unable to communicate effectively with my mate, I continued to turn toward my journals and their smooth, blank, uncomplicated pages.

Sunday, November 7, 1999 midnight

Lying here in bed; staring at the walls for two hours now. Don sleeps next to me, yet further away than I've ever felt him before. He's slipping away, distancing, sedating, hardening. Or is this simply what I feel in myself? Perhaps it is both of us, mirroring each other's discontent.

I feel as though I'm going numb. I hear him say he loves me, and I respond the same. Yet I don't feel it; they are empty words, spoken to avoid rocking this already shaky boat. My heart feels as though it's covered by a veil. I don't know how to fix it, and quite honestly, a part of me doesn't want to. I want Don to fix it. I want Don to want to fix it, but he seems content to keep living this lie.

What happened to the loving, kind, open-hearted man I met a year ago?

I'm drowning, slowly but surely dying. I look into your eyes and melt, yet that's something we rarely do anymore. No time for basking in sweetness, or looking into the darkness that resides there as well.

Is it possible that love isn't enough?

I want you, yet I'm afraid—afraid of needing you, afraid of being needed. As soon as you need me, I'm in a position to let you down. I move into the role of power, the space of the abuser. I can give or withhold love, make you a puppet on a string.

I become the frightened child who had these things done to her, who developed a fierce guardian spirit that seems to be willing to do anything to protect me from hurt, protect me from hurtful love. Don, you just happened to slip in through a crack when my heart was open, when I actually thought I was strong enough, or healed enough, or safe enough to give love without any restraints.

Now I feel attacked, and the vulnerable little girl feels unsafe. The protector spirit is back and more crazy than ever. She feels she's been tricked into a corner. Tricked into sharing her space. Tricked into losing her privacy, except in strange beds in strange cities.

Help me please, dear God, Goddess. I feel so lost and confused, and the man I thought could help me is hidden away somewhere. Am I once again alone in the dark? Am I once again drowning in drama? I feel the demons crawling around in my belly. The dragon in my gut once again restless. Where do I find solace?

And yet, this seems to be my solace. Just exactly this; sitting up in the middle of the night, a quiet dark house, me and my pen once again trying to figure it out. Hoping my mind can be the solution for my heart.

Sorry, doesn't seem to work that way.

Feeling lost? Then feel it. Feeling angry? Then express it, move it. Stop stopping yourself. You've got yourself boxed up so tight the rage comes spewing out. Dance it, move it, ask for what you want.

Stop playing the martyr because he doesn't figure it out. Take a risk. Jump on it. Ask for what you need.

Stop using Don as the excuse for you not living your life. He's not the one holding you back. You are. Your life. Your drama. He just happens to be one of the players in it right now. You want him here? Great. Then be here with him. You *don't? Then cut him loose. He's only your puppet on a string if you keep holding on. Take your power back. Take your passion back. Be big. Be bold. Haven't you done the poor-me whiner long enough?*

See your light. If Don can't see his own then . . .

Then what? Show him? Teach him? I want an equal, a partner, not a student. Am I even seeing Don for who he truly is, or is he simply a product of my imagination and reality no longer matches the fantasy? Questions again. Too many questions.

After nights like that I'd build up my resolve; yes, I could follow through and get out. I'd state my case with firm reason. But determination would wane with the break of dawn. The hypnotized part who believed she had to be a good, loving wife took over.

Oh yeah, I forgot to mention we added marriage to the mix about four months in, so it wasn't just a simple move out. I'd become not only wife, but step-mother.

As children so naturally do, our girls soaked up the drama, then played it out in their own cranked-up hormonal way. My daughter's antics included middle-of-the-night disappearing acts, temper tantrums, and the classic, "You can't tell me what to do" shout-offs. Don's daughter—whom I never encouraged to call me Mom—took the balancing role of quiet defiance. So quiet that she was six months pregnant before we found out.

Amy, who noticed she was the only one using the previously shared tampon supply, brought the new life to light. It turned out Don's daughter had intentionally lied to a boy—and us—about being on birth control. In her mind, a baby would command center stage, making everyone happy, but I knew of Don's rule, the same one my step-father had threatened me with: get pregnant, and you're out of here. So after high school graduation, despite my husband's backpedaling, I stepped into the role of evil step-mom and enforced the eviction. Fortunately, soon-to-be-mom and forthcoming late-summer baby were welcomed by long-time family friends who cherished their savior role.

Shortly after our shift to a household of three, the balance between Good Wife whose mantra was "Make it work" and another aspect, let's call her Freedom Seeker, who routinely said "Enough already; get out" tipped in the direction the latter.

I announced my proclamation firmly one bright, sunny morning. "Don, I want out."

Apparently unaffected by my statement, or perhaps anticipating it, he responded, "I'll stick around until you find someone else."

What?! Did I hear him correctly? Stunned, I wondered if he expected to hear a reply from Good Wife. Something she might utter from her mushy heart space. *Oh, you love me that much? How sweet of you to stick around.*

And then there's the response Freedom Seeker clearly demanded, though I didn't have the nerve to say it aloud. *Are you fucking kidding me? What makes you think I want anyone in my life? This time with you has driven me to the point of insanity. I don't want anyone. Get the hell out! Now!*

What happened was . . . nothing. A big fat, sitting-on-the-bed-with-the-sun-gently-warming-my-back nothing. Good Wife took control again, though she didn't utter any reassuring words. Bewildered, I simply stepped back into the make-nice muted routine of our life and went downstairs to fix breakfast.

38: Enough Is Enough

Life with Don was not all bad. A certain fringe element from our time together taught me a few things—like how to strap on a dildo and thrust it deep where the sun don't shine.

I thought I was way out on the edge with acts like that. But when we talked about our sex life and sexual histories, Don called me vanilla, a term I guessed meant I was plain and lacked an adventurous spirit. I never told him about my Hollywood days.

Something in me wanted to open deeply with him, wanted to continue the lessons we had learned on sex and intimacy, not only in the workshop where we'd met, but at subsequent trainings. But Don's idea of a loving union included pain, and after some reluctant play with clothespins and rope—no, he didn't have a laundry fetish—I came to accept how truly different our bedroom desires were.

I craved a witnessing and blending of our essential, true selves, starting with foreplay along the lines of synchronized breathing and gazing softly into each other's eyes—practices I'd learned and enjoyed in pre-Don tantra workshops. While Don would occasionally indulge me, it was obvious he simply went through the motions as an absentee player—a real buzz kill.

Eventually, when the distance between us had reached an intolerable point—and not a minute sooner—the committee I call me came to an agreement that life with Don had to end. Enough was enough.

Yet, even with a commitment to break up, our boundaries were entwined in a firmly knotted mess. I knew what I wanted, but standing firm in my clarity was another story. Then Don got sick. The committee had a great run with that.

"You're stuck now," said the inner judge.

"Yeah, now you get a chance to show what a good nurse-maid you are," added a gloating cohort.

"Ha, ha. Bet you wish you hadn't criticized his old girlfriend for being uncaring when he was sick. Now you get a chance to be doting."

"What kind of a person kicks someone out when they're battling cancer? You certainly can't divorce him when he needs your medical insurance. You're stuck."

Those inner voices were right. I was stuck. Despite the conviction that I had to reclaim my life, I couldn't kick out a potentially dying man. Like it or not, I had to deal with caring for someone whose presence I had come to loathe, so I put on a not-so-happy face and dealt with it. Fortunately, the doctors caught the recurrence quickly, allowing a swift recovery.

A few months later, unwilling to put up with any more delays, I once again announced my decision. "We're done." Really. I had no more room for Mr. I'll Hang Around.

"You owe me," Don protested. "I moved my whole life down here for you. Where am I going to go? What am I going to do?"

Ah, the guilt card. I'm a sucker for it every time.

"Well, I suppose you could go live in the Northern California house."

Holy shit, my internal team came to attention with that offer. *Are you nuts? That's your pride and joy. That's your heart and soul, your solace. What're you saying? Let Don move to the country just to get him out of here?*

Yep, that's exactly what I did. The big compromise. The lingering effects of the good-girl trance. Co-dependent big time.

Don loved the idea.

For him it was a deal made in heaven: a quiet home with lots of land to tend and tinker with—all rent free. "I'll be your caretaker!" he said. For me the arrangement fell at the other end of the spectrum, but at least he was out from under my everyday feet.

After setting some guidelines—do's and don'ts he *promised* he'd adhere to—I assured myself he couldn't get into too much trouble. I felt pumped up; good girl did a good deed.

It turned out that long-distance relating was worse. Since I was out of sight—and probably out of mind—my wishes were blatantly ignored. Don even started having his old girlfriend up for weekend visits. I had become a pawn in my own play-nice game.

Looking back, it's obvious the hook from our first meeting was still in place, despite the distance. In a way I'd slipped in deeper.

In a constant state of aggravation—grumbling at Don's camping-out status in *my* escape space—I turned my discontent into fuel. Slowly and painfully, inching along our cord, I gnawed my way through and dissolved our unseen bonds. Ironically, our end point came by bringing him back to stay with me in Orange County.

I did not want to work on the marriage; divorce papers had been filed, and I was in the waiting period for official freedom status. But after a few months of banging around my country home with no paying work, Don went a bit stir crazy.

He may have had a roof over his head, and a nice one at that, but fortunately the accountant in me had not fallen for the love trance, and I'd kept our finances untangled. Bottom line, I didn't give him an allowance.

So there we were, twenty-seven months after that fateful weekend of exploring spirituality and sex, sharing the same roof. I'd been clear when he came back it would be temporary. Just until he saved up some money and could get his own place. I meant it. Problem was, Don didn't hear me. In his mind, we were on the road to recovery: this time, everything would be grand. Stalled in my own deep rut, my journal repeated verses from a muted hell.

February 24, 2001

Don's back. He's been here for a week.

I leave tomorrow for ten days up north. Five days with clients then up to the house, but the house Don-style. I feel I've been inundated by my shadow. I'm afraid

I'll find sex everywhere: his pornos, his magazines, his pictures of fantasy air-brushed women all over the walls. Not sure where to even begin with spiritually disinfecting my home; the weight is almost unbearable. I hide behind a façade of control, keeping it together, but cracks are beginning to weaken the structure.

Last night we had sex. The kind of sex that comes from knowing I'd better pay the piper. Didn't want to deal with Don's moping dejection, so I gave him a bone, or rather let him give me one. That would be funny if it weren't so sad.

As I lay there in the dark, tears starting to flow, I continued to wonder why I didn't speak up. Why am I so unwilling to ask for the type of pleasure I want, instead of allowing him to probe and poke and pound and squeeze the way he wants? Is it my fear of letting him into my world or my fear of discovering what my world really is? Do I even know what pleasures me? Am I willing to take the time to discover my innermost yearnings? Not the drug-induced, hungry, compulsive fantasies that I've indulged in to take the edge off. Where is my energy? Where is my sexual power?

It appears to be about control. I'm still playing the prostitute. It's a business deal. I'll give you the sex you want, but not get emotionally involved. Keep my heart out of it; keep my vulnerability far from the bedroom. If I dole out just enough sex to keep you on a leash, then I've got the upper hand. I've got the handyman when I need him.

But is this worth the price I'm paying? Feel my soul heavy this morning. Don't even want to look at him. Feel ashamed, guilty. This man loves me truly, as clearly as he can, and yet I deceive him. Repeat his "I love you," though it doesn't come from my heart. It's a conditioned response that comes from the head. A lie? No; a logical response. I must love him on some level to have agreed to these lessons of shadow watching.

I long for lightness, joy, a dance to my step. I feel like my feet are sunk in concrete.

◉

It's frustrating to go back and read my journal pages. The pain, the conflicting voices of rage and self-care, fear and tenacious hope weave a continuous thread. And yet in retrospect, the Don years were a fruitful time—well, maybe more of a deep-in-the-compost-pile time—of transformation.

When we finally detached completely, late in the spring of 2001, I snapped back into my essential nature like a strung-out rubber band, relaxing into a period of intensely focused inner reflection and healing.

I was even willing to ask for a psychiatrist's help, choosing a well-respected teacher in the spiritual community I'd swept in and out of. In sessions that were truly insightful, I felt safe selectively opening my world to him, being seen. Until the afternoon I mentioned sex.

"I'd like to hear more about that next time," he commented as our session came to a close.

I never went back.

39: My Own Best Friend

With Don gone—and my bed once again a solo sleeping space—I hoped for freedom from nighttime wakefulness. Unfortunately, the questions and insights stalking my middle-of-the-night mind had grown comfortable in their routine.

May 28, 2001 4:30 A.M.
It's terrible to not feel safe in your own home.
> *Perpetual tension*
> *Nowhere to turn*
> *Tears come*
> *Tears go*
> *Washing me through the world*
> *I hide out*
> *But always, it finds me*
> *The tension gnawing away at my gut*

It's worse in the night; the dreaded middle of the night. Father's lies creeping into my dreams. The little girl who can't scream. The little girl who has nowhere to turn.
Lost, lonely, afraid. She turns to a blanket that will never tell the horrors locked up inside. A friend that will comfort her—me—when all else fails.

A vein of terror is always present. Sometimes more visible than others, it keeps me hiding in the shadows, afraid of the light, afraid of seeing and facing my attacker head on. So I hide in myself, distract myself with thoughts. Look beyond the obvious and ignore my pain. Look the other way. Please don't make me see what's going on.

I want to sleep, want to disappear into dreams. It's survival. Hide inside so no one can see from the outside, see the hollow shell I call home.

I keep trying everything they said would help: a home, a marriage, a family—all broken. Please, someone, fix it. Fix me.

Keep flashing on Daddy, yet I want to scream NO at the image, turn my thoughts elsewhere to distract, disconnect. Coping mechanisms I've learned well.

But what about the scared little girl?

I want to call Don, cry, and be comforted. But I stop myself. I don't want to continue needing him. And I don't want him to believe there is anything to us.

Hum, song in my head, though the lyrics are slightly changed, "Lock the doors in case they attack." I wonder, do the attacker and the comforter come in the same package? Is that what's driven me so insane over the years?

I didn't call Don that night, and when we did talk—less and less frequently—I learned to be cool and detached.

Determined to satisfy my own emotional needs—and create a home as tranquil as it could be in the midst of my eighteen-year-old daughter's acting out her own frustrations—I decided to focus on me, to fall in love with me. That's when I came up with a plan to write myself daily love letters.

A word of caution: I don't advocate doing this type of intense, soul-rumbling work alone. Even though I've done a lot of solo diving, it makes sense to have a trusted buddy along for the ride—someone who can be that extra set of eyes, ears, and all-important, loving arms.

If I'd had the courage to trust others—appropriate others—and confront the guard at my heart earlier on, I might have saved myself a lot of grief. But then again, this story wouldn't be unfolding the way it is, so perhaps—as I often reassure myself—everything is all right.

June 10, 2001 P.M.

Dearest Me, Sorry I have waited until the verge of sleep to honor my promise of twenty-eight daily letters to my best friend. I love you. May my dreams tonight show the honor of being myself, of being my best friend.

June 11, 2001 A.M.

Hi there, dear friend. How are you this fine day?

Oh, Debra, how I wish for you to see clearly, to feel clearly your own hopes and dreams and love. As I build my own heart, as I redefine my life, as I step into my power, my wholeness, I can once again venture into relationship outside of myself.

But for now, for these precious days, I am the one for whom my heart sings.

There once was a girl named Debra, who hid away in shadows and fear. She hoped desperately for love, yet pain was always her partner. First one, then another partner unable to love. Partners who also knew pain, yet professed deep commitment. Finally, young Debra broke free of her bonds. Finally, the truth of Debra's love broke free from its shadow hiding place. Finally, Debra had found someone worthy of her love. After many years of fruitless searching outside of herself, Debra turned her game inward, to her own heart, and found a wellspring of devotion, kindness, courage, gentleness, and greatest of all, forgiveness for all those who had crossed her path in their own search for love and fulfillment.

I'm sorry, Donald. May the love you have to give be given first to yourself. In this way we may both be free to thrive.

I'm sorry, Mark. May your anger show you the path homeward. May you rebuild the boundaries of your own inner fortress.

I'm sorry, Edward. So long ago we met. Two children seeking the truth in the fairy tale of love. May your life's path be gentle and wise.

To all the others—lovers, friends, unknown ships in the night—I release you. I thank you. And I honor you, as I honor the path of my life.

Unresolved anger, frustrations, and hurt no longer serve me. In this time I see my path as one of learning. For in taking the path of not-love, I have returned at last to love.

> *The fire of purity burns in my soul.*
> *The light of wisdom guides my path.*
> *The voice of my heart makes light my step.*
> *Rejoice. Today is a day of celebration.*

Today Debra has come home.
Welcome, friend. I honor your presence.
I cherish your being.

June 12, 2001 P.M.

Perhaps tomorrow I will remember sooner, and enjoy a more leisurely check-in with myself. I love you.

June 13, 2001 P.M.

I wonder why I wait until I'm so tired to write? I love you. You're in my heart.

June 14, 2001 A.M.

Woke up this morning feeling sad, lonely. Lying here, sifting through the thoughts, I realize sharing with a best friend is something I want but am afraid of. I'm afraid my neediness is too big. I'm afraid you'll turn away. I'm afraid you'll, I'll, be overwhelmed and not able to listen.

Dreams of smoking pot again. In the dream, I remember thinking, I didn't want to do this anymore, but I'd already started. In the dream, I wanted to continue, and that makes me even sadder.

I see how desperately I want to reach out for an understanding friend. I see how much I want to be accepted 100% by someone outside of me. Yet I'm still learning how to be my own 100%. This is how, why, I've twisted myself into so many faces, lives, lifestyles that aren't me. In my desperate attempts to be liked, accepted, and taken care of, I read others' discomfort, then twist around, removing the offending behavior from my actions. (That is, of course, unless I'm trying to piss them off.) Yet by denying a behavior, I'm denying part of myself. I'm literally telling myself all of me is not okay.

Oh, I think I've touched on something very big. I would very much like to share, discuss this with someone outside of myself. All this time I thought I wanted to be accepted, but I really wanted to be understood.

I'm tired of being on the outside. I wonder if I keep myself outside of me, too? Has this been part of my life struggle, the battle to get inside myself? To "stand under" or "stand in" myself.

What a bizarre concept. This is one of those light-breaking-through-the-clouds, aha moments.

Thank you, dear sweet Debra, for trusting your pain enough to follow the thread. I love you; I honor your willingness to explore and be seen.

Around this point, I purchased an audiotape series titled *Becoming an Empath*. And while, for me, it wasn't so much about *becoming* as it was about being aware of and managing my permeable edges, I loved the author's presentation style. After I'd listened diligently to the tapes' boundary-defining and aura-clearing meditations, their influence showed up in my letters to self.

June 15, 2001

Hello, dear friend. I know; I feel the sadness just below the surface. It's hard sometimes to know where it comes from. Is it mine, or does it come from people around me? Learning to define and defend my space is a tricky balance.

I'm so tired of feeling attacked, so tired of Amy's bitterness and pain attacking me. I continue to live with someone who treats me like shit. I know she's in a huge amount of pain. And I know she's unwilling—perhaps incapable—of working with it, but does that excuse her behavior?

I deserve respect. Am I willing to surround myself with it?

Why do I let her continue to throw psychic daggers at me? Am I secretly hoping she'll see that she's hurting me and feel bad enough to stop? Do I believe I failed her, so it's okay for me to be the brunt of her abusive ways?

Goddess, please help me. I feel so all alone; I need a friend. Yes, I'm glad I've got myself. And I'm extra glad that I've been staying clean. But I'm afraid to really be honest with myself about the steps I need to take. I want to be in integrity with myself, but it feels like it'll leave me even more alone with my anger and confusion.

June 16, 2001 P.M.

Sweet dreams, dear one. I love you. Thank you for remembering.

June 17, 2001

Dear me. Yes, I am dear to me and becoming more so as each day passes. I am my precious one. I have a beautiful child self inside, as well as a host of other aspects. We can all get along. We can all find agreement at mission control, if I am willing to simply listen. Listen to my own internal voice, that nurturing parent I'm building inside.

That's a trick in itself, being inside of me. It's actually a strange sensation to feel myself in my head. It's second nature to drift off, out. When I do focus on being in my body, in my head, and really seeing out of my eyes, I'm also aware of my second chakra in the lower belly. I've got a hole down there that energies escape from. Or perhaps that's the area I'm still looking for confirmation from others through: "Please tell me I'm okay."

Problem is, we're back to the fact that most people aren't okay with themselves and that's what I pick up. Back to that twisty-turning game of, "I'll be who you want and you be who I want"—and we'll both come up empty 'cuz we're still not who we want.

Yikes. It's so simple, so comical when I step out—or is that in?—and look. So now the new game: be in me.

I just took a few minutes to focus on my lower belly, to actually sit with my hands over the hole in my field, and it felt very nurturing, very safe being protected, covered.

As I watched the mind's eye image, I saw my aura being ripped open. A large hand reaching in, ripping a hole. If I use the analogy of my energy field and a garden, then someone came in and ripped off my ground cover, the tiny, green softness of Baby Tears, leaving a large expanse of rich, moist earth exposed to the elements.

Now it's time for me to replant this area. To protect and cover the ground once again. Allow the depth, the darkness to once again be undisturbed in my garden. Not the darkness of ignorance or something evil. Darkness as something cool, a complement to the light, a place of stillness, a place of gestation for my inner seeds of growth.

Thank you, dear Debra, for taking this time for our healing, for your healing, for my healing. I feel so connected to myself right now, so nurtured, so alive, so honored. Yes, mostly honored. I'm giving myself a place of regard in my life.

Taking this time to write, especially first thing in the morning, like now, shows me I am worth something to me. I'm not just a passing whim to remember to say "hey" to occasionally. I feel good. And strong. And whole. Thank you.

As I revisit these pages I'm touched by the willingness I had to dive within myself. What jumps out most is the image of my second chakra, my sexual center, being covered by the plant Baby Tears. Knowing what I know today, I see the irony. At the time, I simply saw it as an image of tender, green, grass-like growth.

June 18, 2001 P.M.
Dear me. I know. It's been a long day and I'm exhausted, overwhelmed. It's okay to be sad, too; sometimes that's just what's up. I love you, Debbie, Debra. Big hugs. Yes, big hugs. I love you so much.

June 19, 2001 P.M.
I love you, Debra. Enjoy a good sleep. XOXO me.

June 20, 2001 P.M.
Feeling annoyed with myself for promising to write for twenty-eight days. I'm tired. I want to read. I want to be lazy, and I'm feeling sad. It's hard to follow through with being my best friend when I'm feeling needy, feeling sad.
Sometimes I feel too needy, like now. This part of me calling for attention when another part wants to simply tune out and read. Books are one of the original ways I disconnected or sedated myself, though I'm not really sure why I can't feel sad, tired, and allow myself to read. There is no rule that says I have to be happy all the time or figure out why I'm sad. I just am.
It was a long, busy day. Lots of people, lots of activity, and lots of energies around me. Time for an energetic healing session with me.
As I close my eyes, I see an orange-filled bubble around me. Feels very rejuvenating . . . ahhh, thank you. I am going to hang out there for a bit. I love you.

June 21, 2001
Have been tossing and turning for an hour now. Sense a general uneasiness. Lots to do for work, but this is more internal; work will be a welcome distraction.
Lying here I feel my back surrounded in shadow. As though something needs to be released. Then comes the image of a dark cesspool-type hole, and babies.
Me at first, crawling up out of it, then others. Anna is one of them, too. The thought crossed my mind that these are the children my father molested.
The thought alone makes my head ache.
I really do want to heal and to release any psychic bonds, clear the slate, so to speak. Yet there's a sense I'm missing something; there's something yet to be resolved, a missing link.
In my mind I go and sit with these young ones in the shadow land. Let them crawl into my lap. I feel overwhelmed by their terror, their need to be taken care of. It

sparks and conflicts with my anger, my need to get away. I can't possibly handle all this sadness—though secretly I wonder if perhaps I can.

I tell myself I don't have to fix this. I simply have to—or can choose to—sit and hold them. Stroke their heads, their hands, their poor little abused, broken bodies.

It doesn't have to make sense. It's eons of sadness. These babies have crawled out of a huge pit of grief residing here on the planet. It's as though I've journeyed into the middle of the earth to find lost souls. And now, after sitting with the children, comforting them with my presence, I feel we're ready to walk out of the darkness, out of this cave of horrors.

Those who are ready follow me, or hold my hand, or hold each other's hands. We form a human chain, a love chain, a healing chain, helping each other out of the timeless realm.

I'm holding my two-year-old self, as we come to the end of the cave, and the sunshine shows many waiting for us, waiting for their lost innocence to be returned from the darkness. Again I repeat, I don't have a fix for this; I'm simply a guide.

Feeling calmer now, and at the same time I'm in touch with deep, core sadness. "The" sadness. An emotion reaching deep within the earth itself, Herself, raped, defiled, abandoned by so many.

Yet many are also in these human chains of recovery—women, men, girls, boys, winding their way out of the depths of the Earth's core, returning to the light of the outer world. United in assisting one another.

Form a bubble around myself again. There is a sense of a pale green light at my back, as the shadow lifts. The light becomes stronger, clearer, a beautiful swirl of blue green, like my chrysocolla crystal.

Then the light is gone. I'm surrounded again by darkness. And I hear the word "pot."

Is this what all my smoking has created? A dark, shadow residue?

Thankfully, the light returns, and I begin to move into a tunnel of golden light. Moving through the light, with the light, the dance continues.

And so it went. The ins, the outs, the good days, the grieving, fighting myself days, and the dealing—or not—with my daughter's moody days. Then there were the days I went back to my smoky lover, marijuana, blatantly ignoring the messages I'd received in my healing visions.

As before, I'd dance and play, letting my creative juices flow, though I'd never pick up the pen after smoking. I didn't want to hear what the stoner aspect had to say. But I can tell you this: it's hard being your abuser *and* your best friend.

40: Life Patterns

Even when self-soothing through a smoky haze, I remained diligent in my search for healing and tried on many a recovery method. Some of those explorations fell into the "rage" category. It felt empowering to stand with a semi-circle of women behind me, yelling, cursing, and hurling imaginary daggers at the invisible rapist we pinned to the wall. But I wonder if it might have done more harm than good; my nervous system certainly didn't feel tranquil after that session.

Physical, mental, emotional, spiritual—over the years I've tried practices offering a bit of each, ever vigilant to touch all bases in my quest for wholeness. Ironically, while I searched for wisdom during an out-of-body experience, my team of etheric helpers spoke clearly, "You are meant to be in-the-body. Put your attention there."

I first learned of Hemi-Sync technology and its brain-balancing frequencies—which many claim transport them into other realms—back in 1991, from a college professor who praised the tapes' content. The premise is simple: when the brain is synchronized, evenly active between left and right hemispheres, it's more receptive to enhanced mental, emotional, and physical states. It made perfect sense to me, so in that post-Bjorn, pre-launch-to-Northern-California search for bliss, I purchased three *Mind Food* tapes.

The first offered freedom from mental constraints, a tool I was definitely ready for as I created my life anew. The second laid a path toward connecting with one's true purpose in life, a question I'd wrestled with off and on for years. The third title opened the door to skillful, concise manifestation, something I figured would come in handy in my upcoming adventure into the unknown.

Daily listening to the cassettes—and diligently practicing each of the three distinct cues they taught—I quickly realized the technology's potency. I have no doubt using the tapes gave me the clarity, strength of purpose, and patience I needed to create my ideal home in a world where single women—especially those living in their driveways in VW campers—were looked on with suspicion by the good ol' boys.

I also credit the Hemi-Sync tapes with accelerating my dream life—something that had always been detailed and vivid—to the cosmic "E" ticket lane. One of those nighttime journeys introduced me to amazing, full-body ecstasy. A circa 1992 journal entry captures my maiden voyage:

It's dark and I'm walking down a clean, well-lit alley in a modest suburban neighborhood. I turn left down a narrow walkway that runs along the side of a nondescript stucco house. The outside wall of the house runs windowless along my left, while a thick green hedge appears to my right.

I reach the front gate, an ordinary metal chain link design, and as I lift up the latch, I hear a female voice.

"I must leave you here. Our time is complete."

I don't see anyone around me, but sense the voice is coming from one of my spirit helpers. The formless voice continues, "It is time for you to work with the Dark Goddess of Vietnam."

After stepping through the gate, my body's density shifts as though I am suddenly lighter. I look around, noticing I'm standing alongside a concrete driveway on a street lined with single-story tract houses.

I head across the empty driveway to a long bench that sits near the front door of the house. From this vantage point I can see pools of street light evenly spread down the otherwise deserted avenue.

The sounds of laughter reach my ears, and I see lots of people exiting what appears to be a stately high school. I guess an event has just finished, and everyone is now walking home. As groups of two or more pass by, no one seems to notice me sitting in front of the quiet house. They also don't notice the incredible light show beginning overhead. I stretch out on the bench to get a better view of the celestial festivities.

It's beyond anything I've seen at a fireworks show, as though the stars themselves are bursting into beautiful waves and patterns of spectacular color—a stunning display. As I'm watching this heavenly dance, the brilliance and majesty of the explosions move into my body, and I experience a star orgasm. Right there in that ordinary world, on that ordinary bench, in my—up to that moment—ordinary body.

That was my first experience of heavenly orgasm brought down into the flesh. Happily, that dream began a fabulous run. A few months later, while my waking hours were focused on decorating my newly completed home, I experienced another such sleep-time journey. By that time I had also become adept at dream flight, often lifting off and soaring like a large, graceful bird:

I'm gliding over what looks like a new neighborhood, as the streets and yards don't show any signs of life. I fly lower over the fresh new greenbelts that run between the houses and decide to take a peek inside, curious to see how the homes are decorated.

I land and open the sliding glass door at the back of one of the houses. I'm drawn to the color scheme and choice of tile in the kitchen across the room. Stepping inside, I walk across what I guess to be the family room, and head down the hall. The first door on the right is open and I'm surprised to see furnishings.

On the wall to my left is a mirrored dressing table, complete with intricately designed bottles of various sizes and shapes. I step over to the vanity to appreciate the articles more closely. After sitting down on the low-backed stool, I hear a sound behind me. Glancing at the mirror's reflection, I see there is also a small bed in the corner of the room. And in it, an old, frail man quietly moans as he pushes himself up to a sitting position.

The small, gray-haired man says nothing as he slowly stands and walks across the room, stopping directly behind my left shoulder. His garment, a worn-out robe, falls open, displaying his equally used-up manhood. Without words, I turn my head, ready to gently take his shriveled member into my mouth, when he suddenly disappears.

I turn back to the dressing table, and instead of antique perfume bottles, I find a beautiful stone carving of an erect penis—blue green stone, rough at the bottom, then rising up to a soft smooth erection. Clearly a sacred object, it begs for ceremony.

As I reach for the stone, music fills the room, intoxicating, resonant classical music. Leaning back on the cushioned stool, I slowly insert the sacred lingam, sending powerful waves up and down my spine. The rhythm of the invisible orchestra raises in intensity, matching the power rocking my body. Within moments, the roof of the house dissolves, and I am once again viewing the stars and their blaze of fiery ecstasy. As the music reaches a crescendo, so do I. And so do the stars, displaying my explosive delight in the night sky above.

I didn't have supernova orgasms while awake. Those spectacular nighttime visions introduced me to an element of sexuality I'd never suspected, let alone experienced. I'd climaxed before—alone, and on some occasions with men—but in my sleep adventures, I felt at one with the forces of Creation.

At various times since those introductions to cosmic ecstasy—typically periods when I've lived alone without the distraction of a man in my life—I've experienced sex as a recurring nighttime theme.

Occasionally the subject matter revolved around things in the everyday romantic world, like kissing, though it was common for that simple act to be distorted and clumsy. However, often as not, my nighttime consciousness took me into worlds unlike anything I had previously imagined. Like the morning I awoke from doing reconnaissance work on an alien planet.

In that dream I was a lab specimen, wired up and connected to a series of machines. Naked, I sat next to the technician, a surly woman with a lit cigarette hanging out the side of her pursed lips. Her eyes focused on the overhead display, a series of peaks and a few valleys, while her fingers adeptly held me at the height of orgasm. Her boredom with the project was evident as I quaked and shivered uncontrollably.

With the experiment complete and the monitoring equipment removed, I walked across an open expanse of grass, escorted back to my room by a young man. I knew he was aware of my spy status, and after switching off a small microphone hidden in my goatee (yeah, it kept getting odder), I said, "I'm so tired of all this. I want to go home." *Voila*, I woke up. Baffled and definitely grateful it had only been a dream, I had to wonder, *Where the hell did my psyche come up with these scripts?*

Much more pleasant to recall, though still out there, is what I've titled *The Priestess Lounge*. This dream, experienced in the post-Don era, remains vivid in its tactile details. Sensations I slip into every now and then:

I'm walking down a glistening white marble corridor. The walls and ceiling form a smooth arch, while my footsteps tread softly along the floor. Gentle warmth radiates from the slightly rough surface, soothing the soles of my bare feet.

At the end of the hall, a guard stands before two doors. I know the one directly ahead leads to an open courtyard and garden. The other, to the right, leads to the priestess lounge.

The bare-armed sentinel recognizes me. Bowing his head, he silently opens the heavy oaken door, allowing me admittance to the space I know only women are allowed to enter.

The warm air is thick with mist, and I notice that my sheer white, dotted-Swiss gown quickly clings to my otherwise naked form. As my eyes adjust to the soft light, I hear the hushed tones of women conversing.

Along the wall to my left are several large square baths, also built in white marble. The source of the mist, they are filled with hot, rejuvenating waters. Along the wall to my right, several ladies are stretched out on what appear to be a cross between a massage table, mattress, and chaise.

A woman with dark, soulful eyes and long ebony hair comes up to me and, after removing my shift, takes my hand, gently assisting me as I step over the edge and into one of the tubs. She follows and sits down behind me, inviting me to relax back onto her. Sighing a deep, contented breath, I slide down to rest my head on her full bosom as her arms enfold me.

Going back to that memory brings my body into a place of calm. I feel connected with ancient knowing, something that exists in a place deeper than my bones. There's honoring too, as I remember an aspect of myself that's been unconscious, a sacred aspect held in safekeeping. It felt good to have a glimpse into a time when healing, sacredness, and sexuality were one. In my waking life, they were still estranged.

LIFE PATTERNS

Another dream from around the same timeframe sparked further questions about who I truly am, at my core:

I'm looking out a large window of a building, down to the street at least four stories below. A procession of young women approaches. I know they're temple virgins. Not virgins as in chaste, hymen intact, but sacred healers who know the spiritual ways of sexuality. They're dressed in white flowing gowns and as they come nearer I can hear their laughter and see the light in their smiles and step. I turn to a man standing next to me and say, "I used to be one of them."

Taking me into his arms, he says, "You still are." While we embrace, I shape-shift into a large, powerful polar bear.

That dream left me melancholy and puzzled. A tiny part within—a hopeful aspect—felt connected to the priestesses, yet I also felt unworthy, shunned, and shamed as though my current life choices had forever tainted my sacred nature. Yet the purity of the snow white bear, not to mention its power, along with the man's complete knowing and supporting of my true nature nudged at something inside, something urging me to stay connected with my primal nature, despite the apparent detours and distractions of my path so far. That bond with a deeper, greater knowing—an essential self—prompted me to keep searching, keep healing, however slow and erratic my progress.

My waking life in the fall-in-love-with-myself phase revolved around work I did with Karla McLaren and the meditations in her book *Rebuilding the Garden: Healing the Spiritual Wounds of Childhood Sexual Assault*. Although now out of print, its pages offered me a way of seeing the myriad forms of abuse in relationship to their spiritual aspects, a connection I had, up to that point, never made. With my long-time interest in—and continued navigation of—the unseen realms, the book's visualizations brought tangible results in the process of clearing myself of the past.

A lot of my life's damage I can, did, and occasionally still do blame on others, though blame is a chameleon behavior that certainly hasn't helped me recover. I also accept responsibility for some of the abuse—

my own lack of care, honor, and self-respect—although I was simply living what I'd been taught in my broken family.

The definitive crack in my psyche—back in 1984 when the word Incest landed and attached itself to me—was certainly the first step on my path toward transformation, toward reclaiming my sacred feminine nature. That early awareness—even without distinct mental confirmation—also had a direct result on my physical body, allowing my digestion and elimination to move freely and, for the first time in my life, effortlessly.

In addition, in those early, tender days, I received a back-handed confirmation of my abuse, when I told Mom of my talk-show-induced suspicion.

"I don't want to believe such a thing happened to you," she said in her standard emotionless state, "but I know your father is completely capable."

From that one line, I made up a life scenario I held as reliable truth for over twenty years: on some deep level, Mom was aware of the abuse, and that's why she split from my father—to protect me. I needed her to be a good guy in the plot, my rescuer, despite our lack of emotional connection.

When I finally learned the truth behind my parents' divorce, I was shocked, but also had to laugh. . . .

We were sitting at the dining room table: Mom, me, and my by then young-adult daughter. Mom, who had started having her own cracks in the psyche, began giggling as she got up to pour herself another cup of coffee.

"What's so funny?" I asked.

"Oh, I probably shouldn't say," she murmured, repressing her laughter as she rejoined us.

"Well, now you have to," I said lightly, smiling as I glanced toward Amy. "You can't leave us hanging."

Looking up from her cup, and blushing a deep pink, Mom said, "I was thinking of Alden."

"Who?"

"Well, I really shouldn't say anything; you'll think I'm a slut."

"No, I won't. We won't," prompting my daughter to join the act as I shook my head.

"It's okay, Grandma. You can tell us."

After taking a sip of coffee and folding the newspaper into a nice, neat stack, perfectly aligned with the edge of the dark cherry wood table, my mom grinned mischievously, took a deep breath, and began.

"He was a musician—a jazz musician. He played the drums. His band played at a party I went to with your father. I spotted him from across the room and had an instant connection. He felt it too. I gushed all over him that night. I think your father may have even been jealous."

Clearly excited by her trip down Loose Lane, she continued, "I'd get Grandma to baby-sit you and your brother and take the bus downtown, telling everyone I was going shopping. But I'd spend the day with Alden. Oh, he was something else. He's the reason I divorced your father."

"Holy shit!" my startled response interrupted the flow. Turning to my daughter, who by then had had plenty of her own sexual escapades, my reaction changed to nervous laughter as I blurted out, "Well, I guess we come by it naturally!"

I tried to get more information from Mom, like what happened next. Did they continue seeing each other after the divorce? And what caused them to break up? But the bubble from deep within her do-not-touch-zone had burst. No further details could be recovered.

I felt as though a string of dominoes fell into place. I could almost hear them clicking across the table's wooden surface. Was it possible, I wondered, to have psychically picked up Mom's lust? Astonished, I watched as parallels with my own quest for love—and obsession with musicians—lined up.

Although I can't climb back in history, or into the mind of Mom's lover, I'm pretty confident Alden only wanted a fling, not a ready-made family. And while she didn't say he'd broken her heart, she had to have been devastated, and I'm willing to bet she blamed us kids for getting in the way. It also explains how she could stoically distance herself from me and my brother during her second marriage, her retake at a happy life.

Mom's secret affair also aligned with my own unraveled marriages, especially the one to Mark—except I let my babies go. And while the lover I coveted during that 1986 divorce worked in construction, all of the previous infidelities *had* involved musicians. It makes sickening sense. I made the decision to relinquish custody of my babies from my inner toddler's level of experience: children mess things up.

As thrilled as I am to have this understanding and a way to categorize a huge piece of information from my life's script, my heart also feels deep sorrow and, fortunately, compassion—not just for me, but for Mom, too.

She did the best she could. Damn it. I can hate her for her ignorant choices—and for a long time I did—but I can also see the child in her that is desperate for love. On some level, we're simply reflections—literally the next generation—of each other's yearning for completion.

41: Happy Fiftieth

As my mid-century birthday approached, I felt good about my life.

It had been four years since I'd untangled myself from Don, and during that time, I'd returned to living full time in my beautiful, serene, country home. I'd also traded the corporate world for self-employment.

My original get-out-of-accounting plan looped back to my dream of working with women, especially those who had a history of abuse. I was even offered a position as a program director for a local women's services organization, where I had studied to become a battered women's advocate. But in our financially restricted, rural community, the salary they offered would barely cover gas back and forth to the office, let alone my mortgage. I also decided against taking a volunteer position, despite the training I had completed, realizing I wasn't emotionally stable enough for middle-of-the-night intervention calls. Once again my dream of working with women was put on hold.

Instead, I went back to what I knew: implementing and training others on their accounting software. Fortunately, my exemplary reputation with the past employer was well known, and clients, once they found out I'd jumped the mother ship, came searching for my skills. Unfortunately, that put me back on the road, though with my sort-of shift in career, I was able to set my own hours and rates, allowing me time—at least in theory—to figure out what I *really* wanted to do with my life.

Still frazzled by the Don experience, I became a bit of a recluse, venturing out of my nurturing space for work but avoiding most social contact. I'm not saying I didn't leave the house; I did. For a time I drove over the mountain to Santa Rosa, where I took yoga and Pilates classes with my daughter, who had followed me north. Though still reluctant to take on country-girl status, she'd found her compromise in the relatively nearby city, where she—*we,* if you count exercise classes as higher education—attended junior college. Other than these mom-and-daughter-workout-followed-by-lunch dates, I spent most of my home time in solo rejuvenation.

As the summer of 2006 sped past in a blur of this town and that, a new client landed on my calendar for the week preceding my birthday. Since the company was located in Orange County, where most of my family still lived, I decided to shake off my reliable hermit lifestyle and plunge into celebration mode.

Thinking a pool party would be fun, I enlisted my sister's help. Well, not her *help*. I asked if I could use her Newport Beach backyard and swimming pool, assuring her I'd take care of everything: food, beverages, cake, and cleanup.

Since I've never been one of those people with dozens of friends, the guest list was easy. Other than blood and by-marriage relatives—mother, daughter, son, sister, two brothers, one sister-in-law, one brother-in-law, one nephew, and two nieces—the only guests were some friends from San Diego, a couple whose children were close in age to my sister's three kids. My son, who by then attended college back in Atlanta, declined the trip, but everyone else responded with a resounding "Yes."

All in all, I thought I had the perfect "big day" planned, and assured myself I'd be fine having almost everyone I cared about at one gathering.

It may sound odd, but in my world, parties equaled stress. Attending them was disquieting enough. Throwing one and making sure everything lined up just right and no one felt out of place—except perhaps me—was a daunting task.

Back in my cocaine days, I had been the quintessential hostess; nothing ruffled my high. But those coke-enhanced days were gone. Marijuana, however, continued to demand a presence on my social calendar. I realized my smoking had a direct relationship to my isolation tendencies, yet I justified the habit as well-deserved relaxation, telling myself I didn't need friends—other than my growers.

Determined to push myself into celebrating, I made mental lists of important things—*food: Thai and cake: German Chocolate*—preparations I'd finalize once I got down south. Since my daughter and I would be staying at Mom's house—my step-dad had passed on by then, so spending time with her had become a pleasant experience—I figured it would be easy to pull everything together in the evenings after spending days with my client. There was only one hitch: my sister hadn't returned my confirmation phone calls.

I told myself she was busy with her three young ones, but when I mentioned the upcoming party to Mom, as I settled into her den, she seemed surprised.

"Your sister's not having any party," she blurted, in one of her tactless, did-I-just-spill-the-bad-news, sort of ways.

Figuring Mom didn't know what she was talking about, I said, "Sure she is. We talked about it last month." To be on the safe side, I called and left another message—though an inner aspect, eager to cancel the whole ordeal, snapped to attention.

Later that night, as a result of my third call, I finally got to speak to my sister, and she—as Mom had foretold—broke the news: "You can't have your party here." Without even a lame excuse!

In response, I muttered something designed to help *her* not feel bad, then hung up the phone. Pissed, but determined not to let Mom see me cry, I pushed my devastation down and wondered if I was up to finding a Plan B.

Mom, a woman equally awkward about parties but sensing my disappointment, offered her backyard, but a pool party without a pool is obviously flawed, and I felt certain I needed a focus for my guests. Heaven forbid they should be left to talk among themselves—or gather around me—as a form of entertainment.

The next morning, still uncertain about how to solve the missing-body-of-water issue, I shifted myself into confident-businesswoman mode.

As I sat in my new client's conference room, detailing the four-day engagement and exactly what I would need to get started, it became obvious the staff wasn't quite prepared for my service. Ordinarily, I'd figure out some way to make good use of my time, especially since I'm paid by the hour, but that late summer morning I saw my out.

"No problem," I told them brightly. "Let's reschedule for next month."

Once free of their building, I grabbed my cell phone and dialed Mom's number, asking to speak with my daughter.

"Pack it up," I said excitedly, "we're heading home."

Initially stunned with the pronouncement, she quickly got on board with the alternate plan: bolt.

Less than two hours later, adrenaline continuing to pump, I made cancellation phone calls as we sped north on the 405. Yeah, people were disappointed. So was I, but I didn't let myself feel dejected—or *rejected*. Those reactions were stuffed down in the bottom of the luggage and stowed in the cargo hold.

I blamed my sister for the whole ordeal, dismissing the voice of wisdom who spoke the truth: I was running home to my lover, the one who would always be there for me, soothing me with wafting plumes as I inhaled deeply.

And so it came to be that I spent my fiftieth birthday in the comfort of my home, stoned out of my mind, too high to care that I couldn't pull it together enough to bake myself a cake.

42: World Traveler

After the birthday blues' smoky haze lifted, I realized being fifty felt pretty good. Suddenly liberated from society's constraints, I found myself stepping into an I-don't-give-a-damn-what-you-think-of-me attitude about life, an incredibly freeing mindset. I also decided to get busy and start doing the things and seeing the places I had dreamed of.

My first trip, to Scotland, was a garden variety vacation package, literally. Figuring it would be easiest to start what I hoped would become regular global travels with an English-speaking country, I signed on for a tour of gardens and castles, two subjects dear to my heart.

A grand exploration—complete with afternoon tea and biscuits—brought my bold and curious nature out of hiding. I even broke off from the tour with a pair of renegade sisters, landing in a haunted mansion for two nights before we rejoined the group.

With ten days of guided-tour-bus fun behind me, I stood in the Edinburgh train station saying fond fare-thee-wells to my traveling companions before boarding the first-class car for my next destination: Findhorn.

I'd first learned of the spiritual community tucked away in the northern region of the United Kingdom back in the '80s, when I'd read a book by one of its founders, Eileen Caddy. She had written about communicating with nature and plant spirits, and how, by following their advice, the community members had created a thriving garden despite the harsh environment.

I felt so civilized traveling by train, sipping my afternoon tea, and chatting with people who thought *I* was the one with a fun accent. By late afternoon, after a short taxi ride, I arrived at my lodging, a stunningly beautiful, waterfront retreat center just down the road from Findhorn.

Once I'd organized my things in my room, I set off to explore the grounds of my temporary home. I had known the lodging was owned and operated by practicing Buddhists, but I didn't realize the B&B was also the hub of ongoing activities for the area. When I poked my head into the main meditation room, I felt immediate peace. Drawn in by the floor-to-ceiling windows overlooking the placid bay, I was most captivated by the stunning array of Tibetan Buddhist art and holy items. Any doubts I'd had about joining the upcoming public meditation disappeared.

Settling down on a meditation pillow, or *zafu*, I welcomed the deep sense of calm that slid over my being as I attempted to join in the chanting of the Twenty-One Praises to Tara. However, after a few botched rounds, I simply allowed the hypnotic rhythms to penetrate my grateful being. Thirty minutes later, I left the room blissfully content.

Ironically, the reason for my visit, the Findhorn community itself, turned out to be a bit of a disappointment. I found the site interesting, in a socially evolved, eco-village, college-campus sort of way, but I didn't feel drawn to explore its inner workings or attend any of its offerings. Instead, I wanted more of the Buddhist retreat center and its praises to Tara, the Great Goddess.

I found the other guests and our discourse around the large dining room table fascinating. There was the nun from South America and the mother-daughter-granddaughter trio from Atlanta, Georgia, as well as the owners themselves, who shared mealtimes of marvelous vegetarian cuisine with their guests. That conversation-stimulating dining room also led me to meet the healers from Australia.

These three women had traveled across multiple time zones to arrive late for dinner on Thursday night. I'd seen a flyer posted on the bulletin board in the main hallway, advertising their weekend workshop on energetic healing, but had dismissed the notion of extending my visit in order to attend.

It's not that the subject matter didn't intrigue me; it did, but I also found myself a little envious when I read the bio of the primary teacher, Kim, a previously successful attorney who had walked away from her corporate world into that of a spiritual mentor and healer.

As dinner dishes were replaced with cups of hot tea, the random conversation shifted to specifics about the type of work our Aussie companions did. One of the women from Atlanta offered me as a guinea pig, since, she reasoned, I would be leaving before their session began and wouldn't want to miss an opportunity to "get a taste of their gifts." In truth, I'd hinted at the idea, and my newfound, southern gal pal did a great job of selling it.

Kim came around to my side of the table, where I had pushed back my chair to allow her full access to the space around me. After asking my permission and offering a silent prayer, she began the first stage of their work, an energy scan.

The process itself wasn't new to me, as I'd studied energetic healing with a number of gifted practitioners, but always curious to explore—and experience—a new "touch," I opened myself to the reading. With her hands systematically feeling the space about two feet out from my body, she gently swept and patted the air around me from top to bottom before stating her diagnosis: "You could use a clearing."

Obviously road-weary, she continued, "But I'm really feeling the effects of travel and need to go to bed. Let me see if one of the other women can help."

So that's how I came to be sitting in a dining room in northern Scotland getting an energy body clearing from an Australian woman named Jo. Curious about the process themselves, the ladies from Atlanta asked if I minded their presence. I told them they were welcome to stay, though as we rearranged the chairs for everyone's comfort, I wondered what I'd gotten myself into.

Jo, a gifted healer in her own right whose smile and good nature put me instantly at ease, began her work on my subtle body.

"You have a lot of energy moving through your crown chakra," she said as she moved her hands over the seemingly empty space at the top of my head.

The information was nothing new. I'd started feeling "fizzies," as I call them, about twenty years earlier while studying yoga and meditation with a teacher from the Hindu traditions. Although I had moved on from the Southern California teacher, I'd continued feeling the soda-pop head in a variety of settings. I'd also been chanting and meditating with the Buddhists at every opportunity over the past two days, honing my connection to the higher realms.

One by one, Jo worked her way down my energy body centers, noting colors and movement with each one. Third eye, throat, heart were all open, light and vibrant. Then she got to my solar plexus, the third chakra, the center of the will.

"You're corded to someone here. Do you know who it is?"

Immediately, my daughter came to mind. Although she had moved into her own space years earlier, we continued to be deeply involved in each other's lives.

I'd first heard of cording—energy tendrils between people—when reading the book *The Celestine Prophecy*. And certainly the disconnecting I had done while clearing Don out of both my home and body had expanded my knowledge of the subject. So although a part of me was okay with being connected to my daughter, I wondered if an energy cord might be detrimental for both of us.

After I voiced my concern, Jo offered a helpful alternative. "Let's help your daughter connect to another source of nurturing."

"How about a dolphin?" I asked.

I'd used dolphins in healing before and knew my daughter also felt a resonance with these amazing sea mammals, so with Jo's guidance, I imagined a sparkly pink dolphin swimming around my daughter, a nurturing image that gladly held the cord I released from my belly. I added a shimmering gold dolphin to my own energetic field for good measure.

As Jo continued down to the second chakra, the seat of emotions and sexual energies, I braced myself for darkness.

"You have a lot of excess energy here," she said. "You're holding onto a lot that isn't yours."

Yep, that made sense, as much as working with invisible—at least to me—energies could make sense. Despite years of self-improvement study, I still experienced sexual confusion and shame. I also knew the area we had reached, the center of sexuality, related to my father. But in the nearly twenty-five years since I'd stumbled into the incest-survivor classification, I still didn't have clear details of what had happened to me as a child. And Jo didn't offer insight as to specifics of what she saw or felt. Instead, I sensed she was walking a fine line between healing and awakening trauma.

After a check-in with the base, or root, chakra, the next stage involved clearing out layer upon layer of energetic refuse. In a seemingly timeless process, each go-round went deeper than the next, until I felt light and buoyant.

Mindful of the fact that my healing angel had been doing this after more than twenty hours of travel—something I was about to embark on as well—I gratefully offered thanks as she brought our unplanned session to a close. Writing down some tips Jo suggested on keeping my subtle body tuned, I also requested her contact information, making a mental note to send a generous donation once I returned home. After stacking our empty tea cups in the dirty-dish bin, we shared good-nights—and in my case, good-byes—all around.

After I slipped past the Buddhas lining the main entrance hall, and before I stepped into the pre-dawn mist, I sent blessings and prayers of gratitude to the diverse group of travelers whose paths had crossed mine. Heading back to the train station light and full of grace, I felt as though I could fly home without a plane—on my very own angel wings.

The following year my gift-to-self travels took me to Bali.

On that adventure—a tour of sacred temples and participation in traditional ceremonies—I knew in advance the package would include a visit with a native healer. What I didn't know was what an appointment with a medicine man, also known as a white magician, would entail.

His home and office were in the typical Balinese style: a series of thatched roof buildings, many open to the thick, moist air, with lush native plants growing throughout the small compound. While four of us got comfortable sitting cross-legged on the examining hut's woven grass floor, a friendly dog made his way to each in search of attention.

Another client, a young local boy escorted by his parents, received his treatment directly in front of us. Because I had joined a small contingent from our group earlier in the week, I was familiar with the procedure: lots of pressing and poking, mainly on the energy meridians running throughout the body. As I watched the child squirm and cry, it was obvious his treatment wasn't any less painful than the ones I had witnessed previously.

Soon it was my turn.

The session started with me sitting on a mat in the center of the ten-by-ten, open-air structure. Our healer, renowned for his gifts far beyond the community, had kind yet piercing eyes that studied me from his heavily grooved face. He then began gently pressing his fingers into various spots on my head: ears, throat, forehead, temples, eye sockets, cheeks, nose, jaw, and skull.

With each, he asked about pain, which we found in the area above my ears. "Just a little," I reported to our group leader and translator, who stood behind our native doctor.

With the body check continuing, I reported pain at the base of my neck, my right arm and my right shoulder. The left side revealed more pain in the region of the neck. Then the translator, who now sat beside me, announced a diagnosis, "Your lymph is dry; stress causes the block. You're not in harmony."

By that time I was crying gently from all the poking into sore spots, but that didn't stop him from continuing the examination. After a few rounds—up and down, right then left—and a discussion I didn't understand, the translator announced, "He opened it up, so the blockage is gone."

Oops. Not so fast. With another pass, we discovered my right shoulder still held pain. So the healer pressed his palms firmly on the top of my head. As tears continued rolling down my cheeks, I was told he unblocked my aura.

Next I was directed to lie down on my back and breathe deeply, which I did. Closing my eyes, I focused on the inhale and exhale instead of the throbbing that continued in my shoulder. My attention was distracted by the scent of incense, and I opened my eyes to see its smoke wafting around my body. That's when I saw the medicine man pick up his little pokey tool, the blunt stick he used to test the meridians on the feet.

As he poked the middle toe on my left foot, I announced, "Yes," forgetting about the pain in my shoulder.

In choppy English, he explained, "Lung, memory, tension, stress, taste; all in pain." Continuing with the baby toe he stated, "Kidney, liver—okay. Pancreas—okay."

Finally, I thought, *something's okay.*

"Organs good," he announced.

Just as I'm thinking I'm out of the woods, I felt the most searing pain of my life. I screamed and instinctively tried to pull my foot away, wondering if he'd switched the pokey stick for a red-hot coal, but the frail-looking elder was stronger than he appeared and kept a tight grip as he spoke.

"Past memories of long ago. They make stress. Nature of the memories block your senses, your sight to see."

By that time I was sobbing in reaction to the nearly unbearable pain. Internally I prayed, *Please make it stop.*

As time slowed to a merciless crawl, the translator held my hand, encouraging me to breathe while the healer stood over me—well, on me, as his toes kept my feet pinned—waving the incense stick in the air.

"He's writing mudras on her body to connect the energy together," our guide told my traveling companions.

Once the designs were completed, the healer once again picked up the dreaded pokey stick, though thankfully there was less pain in my lungs, memory, tension, and stress points. And the dreaded hot poker toe had relaxed to merely an intense stinging sensation.

Not yet satisfied, he returned to the smoke drawings, only that time he lifted my shirt and traced the symbols gently on my belly with the non-burning end of the incense.

Still somewhat in shock from the pain, I watched as our host stepped off the raised platform of his office and into his pharmacy, also known as the garden, plucking a few leaves from a single plant I didn't recognize.

He placed one in my bellybutton. He told me to chew the second—it tasted slightly bitter—and the last he used as a brush, once again inscribing symbols in the air.

Another toe check later, things still weren't quite as he wanted, though fortunately the sensation of fiery, stinging pain had subsided. For the next course of treatment, he placed a small glass bottle upside down between my big toe and its neighbor as instructions were translated.

"Breathe out tension. Blow out tension into bottle."

With the bottle held firmly against my foot, he once again pressed into my body's "check points" before returning to my feet with the dreaded pokey stick. As I held my breath, I was amazed—not to mention incredibly relieved—to find myself pain free.

"Finish," he announced, though I came to understand he spoke to the issues causing the pain, not the visit itself.

Rolling over, I was helped into "child's pose," a yoga posture that's similar to the fetal position with knees tucked up and under the belly. With my back facing up, I was once again poked for lingering pain points. From that position I heard an inner voice speak.

Connect and give back to the Mother.

Along with the words came the sense of a wave connecting me through the generations, a thread of pain and trauma. I not only felt the link between me and my mother, but also to her mother, as well as to my daughter. In pondering the moment, I realized a hundred years are covered in those multiple generations. I also realized the egg that became me originated in my grandma's womb, in my mom's ovaries—a most intriguing thought.

For one final check, I was once again instructed to roll over on my back as the stick made one last pass over what had previously been a raw nerve. Thankfully, I remained pain free.

"Okay," brought my session to a close.

The healer explained through the translator that there had been toxins in my past story stored in the body as gas. It was their memory I'd released into the bottle. The plant leaves helped me to balance myself.

In the hours and days that followed my healing session, I continued to ponder the connections, the lineage of wounding, as well as the potential for healing, passed from mother to daughter. Again the image of a cord presented itself to me, along with a physical space ceremony that could be done between my daughter and me, a recreation of the energetic counterpart I'd experienced the previous year in Scotland.

I saw a thin, cotton rope, like the ones I've used in countless home-decorating projects over the years, connecting the two of us while we sat in sacred space, anchored with prayers, reverence, and mutual respect. When ready, with both of us holding the scissors, we cut the cord.

The ritual is a gift-giving ceremony, to celebrate my daughter's step into her authentic place of power, unencumbered with any remnants of abuse I've wrestled with. It's a fine balance to see the act with love, as a step into self reliance, and not as a form of disconnecting or abandonment, a wound my daughter already carries deep in her soul.

To date, this rite of passage lives only in my imagination, though I hope it—like my own reclamation—will come to pass.

43: A Gift of Heart

In addition to world travels celebrating my post-fifty, freedom-loving self, I went to the Monroe Institute for a weeklong workshop based on Hemi-Sync technology, the same brain balancing frequencies that had upped my dream imagery to miraculous. I'd been to the Virginia-based Institute several times over the past fifteen years, and each time I had returned home with a renewed sense of purpose. In fact, my September 2000 visit gave me the determination I needed when telling Don it was time to move on.

I'd learned of the August 2007 workshop—focused on self-love, self-respect, and connecting with heart—a few years earlier but hadn't felt ready for the depth of exploration I knew the program would offer.

As summer reached its hottest days, I grew excited to once again gaze over the beautiful vistas of the Blue Ridge Mountains, taking some much-deserved time off from my busy world of clients and computers. However, I also came face to face with that smoky-haze aspect of myself who would have preferred a week off with her trusty mind- and heart-numbing pipe. In fact, the stoner part of me fought so hard to gain control, I smoked myself as high as the plane I was about to board before entering the airport.

A GIFT OF HEART

I told myself it was simply pre-workshop jitters, a pattern I had come to recognize anytime I stepped out of my ordinary routine, but that trip I was particularly panicked. While watching the tiny mountains and fields pass below me, I convinced myself I needed to escape. Once on the ground, I actually looked into turning around and flying home; however, all outgoing options from the small, rural airport were fully booked. Classifying the workshop as meant-to-be, I took another dose of Rescue Remedy and climbed into the familiar shuttle van.

Once I was settled in my room—and past the withdrawal/fear attack—the days fell into an easy, familiar routine: brain-balancing and consciousness-expanding audio sessions, fascinating debriefing discussions, and yummy southern-style food.

Although I didn't have any expectations of what softening into my heart might look like, I wasn't surprised when my father's image came to mind. How could it not? Since the Incest TV show had cracked my psyche open, all explorations eventually led back to the core question, *What happened to me as a child?*

But it wasn't me as a child who showed up in the heart-centric workshop; instead I saw my father, the troubled little boy called Channy. Amazed at the compassion, as well as the bigger-than-me forgiveness I felt toward him, I figured my heart was ready for a change. Only later, when reconnecting with a fellow workshop participant, did I learn that Christ had appeared to him, requesting his assistance in a healing session directed toward me—an attunement with the vibration of pure love.

However it came about, I left the workshop a new woman: light, joyful, and full of life. The radiant, welcome change still enveloped me a week later when business took me once again to Southern California and into The Family Zone.

I had no intention of calling my father—it had been over ten years since we'd spoken—but when I finished up early with my client, inner guidance spoke clearly: *"Call your father."*

Not sure the voice of wisdom knew what it was talking about, I questioned its advice. *"Really?"*

"Yes, really. Call him."

So that's how I ended up outside his apartment, pressing the security buzzer. I knew he lived alone, having lost Liesl to cancer and a divorce back when we still talked. Once again, I'll let my journal tell the story....

"Wow, you look good! You really look good."

His words still ring in my ears. Yes, it had been almost a decade since I'd seen him, but the surprise in his voice haunts me. Did he expect me to look old and haggard, as he looks to me, or did he forget my being blessed with good looks? Another option that occurs to me now, as I reflect on the visit, is that I have changed. I've grown into a graceful, elegant woman, one who radiates a peaceful confidence that comes from a full heart. The suspicious voice in me, the one who felt the slight twist in the gut, wonders if his compliment had an ulterior motive. The reaction tells me I still don't feel completely safe around this man, despite his gaunt body and thin white hair.

As I walked into his compact one-bedroom apartment next to the high-voltage electrical towers, I was immediately hit with the stench of cat urine. How is it possible he doesn't notice this smell? I took one final breath of the hot North Hollywood afternoon and closed the door. The room looked much the way I would have expected. The tired and worn sofa an afterthought—does he ever have guests?—as the room is primarily occupied by the 50" TV and his oversized desk, jam-packed with electronic gear ranging from his copious ham radio equipment, to a new Mac, to items so old their plastic covers have yellowed. After the initial niceties—"Can I offer you something to drink?" "No, thank you, my water is fine."—he says, "I want you to look at this."

He started pulling papers out of a file and presented me with his will and statements from two bank accounts. Wow ... I didn't expect this, though honestly, I don't know what I expected. If someone had told me even ten days ago that I'd be having an afternoon visit with my father, and that I had initiated it, I would have told them they were nuts. I had fully expected this man to die without my ever seeing him again.

As I looked over the brief and to-the-point legal documents, I was struck with a mixture of emotions. A part of me felt so sad for this lonely old man, while the flip side said, "Good, you got what you deserve." When he tells me he's got several thousand dollars in his estate for me and my brother to split, I think, "Wow, he really is doing his best to make good by us; in his own way he's trying to make restitution." Yet again I hear the inner rumblings of the angry daughter who wants to lash out and attack. She would laugh bitterly and say, "I don't need your stinking money." But the good daughter, the nice girl simply says, "Thank you." It is this aspect of self that knows needing the money is irrelevant; money is simply a form of energy, in this case energy in the form of a peace offering.

Then he asks if he can pass along my contact information to a ham radio friend, the same friend I am to call when it comes time to clear out all his electronic gizmos. He points to the organ against the back wall, something I hadn't noticed until that moment and says, "You can have the organ." In retrospect I am struck by the play on words of his statement. Even as I write these words I feel the lingering energy imprint of his "organ" in my throat; the first of many inappropriate sexual encounters in my life. Yet again I realize that in the duality of this visit, the organ is one of his prized possessions. I'm reminded of mini-performances I sat through during past visits with him, visits where I felt more like the mother witnessing a child desperate for approval than a daughter attempting to make sense of her life.

I'm amazed that despite the lingering fragments of sexual abuse and trauma, I am able to open my heart to this man. During the visit I was actually able to look into his eyes and feel compassion, as well as see remnants of the sweet little boy that had appeared to me in one of the Heartline exercises only days before. Even more incredible, when he confronted me with one of his sociopath comments, I was able to speak up for myself in a calm, forthright manner.

We'd been fiddling around on his computer, where he showed me some of his favorite video clips. I held my breath as each new file opened, fearing I would be assaulted by porn, but surprisingly they were all lightly humorous, including one hilarious collection of cat antics. How liberating it was to sit and laugh with joy and innocence in this man's presence. These moments proved amazingly healing while at the same time they touched a deep chord of grief. On some level I believe our souls agreed to the path this life has taken, and from that awareness I have profound honor and appreciation for the soul who brought me such dark lessons.

The sense that this visit was somehow a clearing for him, too, continued as he pulled out the old picture albums to send home with me. Sitting on the couch, we reviewed his prized collection of personalized, autographed head shots of actors he had worked with over the years, a few pictures of me and my brother growing up, and the most fascinating: images from his own childhood. The only photos he didn't pass on to me were those stuck to the refrigerator in plastic frames: snapshots of me and my *children—all close to twenty years old. I was definitely struck by a wave of guilt as I realized I'd stopped sending pictures, so he had simply kept the circa 1990 ones prominently displayed. I made a mental note to gather some current family photos once I returned home and mail them to him.*

As the afternoon wore on, my comfort level lessened. Despite breathing into my heart to find a place of inner peace, I reached my limit of fiddling to fill time. I was gathering the will power to say good-bye when he looked at me and said, "I'm sorry about what happened when we were on location." I was stunned. To hear "I'm sorry" come out of his mouth, even if the occasion he chose to be sorry about was one of the lowest in my traumatic life-event chronology, was a miracle. I had been more affected by the "Incest is best" comment made by the logistics director back in 1974 as we checked into the shared hotel room than I was by walking in on him and her later in the movie shoot.

However, he quickly negated his apology, as directly behind it came, "But you were in that drug thing." Here is where I did the heretofore unimaginable. I didn't shut down and pout, but I didn't bite on to victim status either. I very calmly said, "There wasn't any drug thing. I have done drugs, but there wasn't any drug thing." What he was referring to is a complete figment of his damaged imagination. It's the story he invented after I confronted him about the incest twenty years before. His daughter was a drug addict who had concocted the whole abuse scenario to hurt him. He was in the clear. It's a story he's held on to. But I had no need to argue with him today. His apology, however buffered by his fantasy coping mechanism, was a miracle I was willing to accept.

Will I see him again? Who knows . . . He would certainly like that; he's called me twice in the twenty-four hours since my visit with seemingly insignificant questions. What I do know is that I have a new level of internal freedom when I look at the picture of the eleven-year-old boy I have placed on my altar. Even with the strain I see in his eyes—or perhaps as a result of it—I feel a deep love and connection beyond anything I would have imagined possible. The victim self that held tightly to the estrangement and justified resentment has loosened her hold, and today I can truly feel love in my healing heart. I have come one step closer to feeling complete and at home within my soul, at peace with my life's journey.

44: Merry Christmas to Me

Although we rarely spoke outside the requisite birthday and holiday schedule, I enjoyed the renewed contact with my father. We'd even begun speaking of things a bit deeper than "What did you eat for lunch today, how is the cat, and what's the weather like down there?" And, thankfully, a subject my father had touched on numerous times throughout my life—that he wanted a girlfriend just like me—had slipped out of the rotation.

Dabbling at the fringes of letting him get to know me, I attempted to tell him about my adventures as a computer consultant and some of the places I'd visited. But generally, when I'd bring up my life, he'd interrupt with his classic line, "Well, I don't want to run up your phone bill. Thanks again for calling, sweetheart." Of course, he was the one who had called—unless it was his birthday—but even then he'd toss out his "I'm done" signal. It was part of the script, part of the delicately awkward dance of dutiful dad and caring daughter.

I thought about calling him on Christmas morning, but I wanted to meditate first. Best to be grounded and focused before stepping into father realm, however comfortable it had become.

I'll let my journal detail the cheery holiday's events. . . .

December 25, 2007 Merry Christmas

    A good day.

    Yes. I affirm today is a good day, filled with love and joyful hearts overflowing. This is true, and yet there is also the aspect inside that cries, the one who just got thrown into chaos by a phone call from Father. It seemed innocent enough; but then it always does. Moments that shake up my core never start big.

    I was in the midst of my morning meditation when the phone rang. Straight up 8 a.m. I knew in an instant it would be him. For a moment I questioned answering it, interrupting my prayerful space, but decided to take that sacred energy into the call.

    "Merry Christmas!"

    Never wanting to be outdone, he began singing the Happy Birthday tune, changing the appropriate lyrics. Dear old Dad, some things will never change.

    He updated me on his health and most recent doctor's visit, then surprised me by asking what I had going on that made me happy. I stopped for a moment and dismissed telling him about a work project. This was an opportunity to be real, to come from a deeper place, so I answered with the first thoughts I'd had this morning.

    "Actually, I am happy to be breathing the crisp, cool air."

    It felt good to respond in such a simple manner, especially when it really was the first thought I'd had in the early minutes of the day. I'd been searching the landscape of my mind, trying to find something to be grateful for on this Christmas morning, and the cool air passing through my nostrils was all I could initially find.

    Of course, I didn't bother telling him the back story. I know his attention span on someone other than himself is limited, and sure enough, he quickly returned the conversation to his health.

    It's like a tennis match. He volleys a self-focused concern; I send it back wrapped in a positive light. One such return was "At least you've got good health insurance. Think of all the people who would be devastated with the prospect of surgery."

    After he bragged about his great coverage, I once again responded, "Well, I'm self-employed. So my insurance premiums can get expensive." Here I was, guard down, foolishly expecting sympathy. I'd gotten careless in negotiating the minefield of our conversations. So, bam, his reply struck a clean blow, right in the gut, "You can marry me and get on my insurance."

    My mind went blank, momentarily stunned. *Quick, come up with a response*, my inner voice screamed as my gut wrenched. I'd been lulled into a sense of fatherly comfort these past few months, yet here once again was the reality of the horror this man can still invoke in me. I gently brushed his comment aside. "Ah, I don't think so."

His childlike, gleeful response "I thought that would get a chuckle out of you" ignited suppressed fury.

Chuckle? Scream maybe. Jaw clenched in long-held rage, definitely. But chuckle?

Shaking my head in disbelief, I chose a logical route. "I don't think that's legal." To which he responded, "It is in Utah."

Help! I'm sinking in quicksand; how do I get myself out of this living hell?

My mind was so split between staying calm and lighthearted on the one hand, while finding and holding onto the child/teen who has been down this road far too many times on the other. I have to find the frightened part of me and tell her it's okay. "I am doing my best to take care of you. I promise this man won't abuse you anymore." It's as though danger, warning flares are going off in my psyche. I don't even remember the last couple of minutes of the conversation, just the usual sign off of him saying, "Well, I don't want to run up your bill. Oh, that's right, I called you." And my polite, "Thank you for calling. Enjoy the rest of your day."

I didn't even consider adding in "I love you," something I had managed to say on a few of our recent talks. But not today. Today I'm reeling. Anger. Confusion. Sadness. Bewilderment. Questioning. Oh, the questioning.

Is this a test to see how far I've come in healing, to see if I can keep my heart open in hell? Or was it a test to see if I'd stand up for myself?

I find myself running through the mental list. Who can I call and rant to of this injustice? But will that solve anything? Ease the troubled voice that cries out for mercy? Then the tape replays again, our conversation, stuck in seemingly endless loops feeding the discontent.

What about the voice of power, the voice that puts an end to that make-nice game? I could have said, "You know that kind of comment makes me feel yucky."

"Yucky? What are you, five?" sasses a judgmental inner critic.

Yes, on some level I am five. It's the five-year-old who wants so desperately to be Daddy's little princess. It's the five-year-old who cries in confusion with the chaos rumbling around inside.

So it's the five-year-old I call to my side as I stand up and ask God to help me ease the pain, to help me release the victim status. I call on God; no, I demand God to return me to a sense of calm, a sense of inner beauty and light, knowing that all good comes to me.

As I stand in this place of light and power, I feel my guts settling down, my jaw relaxing. The battle cry of "I've been wronged" fades in the distance. I can almost laugh at the absurdity of the phone call. I choose not to go towards pity. Sending pity to this man is far too close to seeing myself as victim. Labeling this situation as any one thing seems inappropriate, as any one response is limiting. This is a huge conglomeration of emotions, reactions, fears, wishes, many of which have been deeply ingrained, deeply buried throughout my life.

So perhaps my gift this Christmas day is a step towards self-love, self-reliance, self-acceptance. I am here for me, even when things get rocky. I am here for me. Today I sense the Christ light shine a little brighter in the heart and soul of Debra. Thank you.

And so it was. The open-heart policy with my father went back for reassessment, while I kept a clear, empowering connection with myself—which, by the way, felt wonderful.

45: A Different Kind of Bath

It's February 2009 and I'm sitting in the jungle of Belize, Central America; well, incredibly diverse, lush foliage is outside. I and about twenty others from across the globe are getting comfortable throughout the colorfully decorated living room of Rosita Arvigo, a renowned herbalist and healer.

Restless for the workshop to begin, I watch as smoke from burning copal resin billows into the warm, moist air, gently swirling through the space. Each of us has had the sacred smoke whisked around our bodies, front and back, top to bottom. This "smudging" is a definitive first step for creating a clear space. I find the scent intoxicating, one that calls me to remember wisdom older than my bones. Although I have no idea what to expect, I feel the familiar pull of destiny urging me to fully immerse myself in the experience.

"For the next six days we'll be studying Mayan spiritual healing," begins the dark-haired woman I guess to be around sixty.

Knowing my teacher has spent over ten years as an apprentice with one of the most revered shamans in Belize, I experience a clumsy combination of feeling both honored and unworthy to be in her presence.

I'd stumbled onto the jungle healer and her work by coincidence, though I've come to look at such things as a gentle nudge from spirit. Once again, the Internet and Google search results played a deciding role.

After looking up cures for a tipped uterus and related bladder problems, I came across Maya Abdominal Massage and Dr. Arvigo's website. Immediately intrigued by the variety of courses offered by both Rosita and her certified practitioners, I decided to start with a gentle—and somewhat local—weekend workshop, where I learned self-care massage techniques.

With my belly much happier as a result of the loving attention and my inner voice offering a simple *Yes,* I decided to step into the larger commitment: the weeklong training in Belize.

I hadn't really thought about the connection before, but my womb most definitely directed me toward that next step in healing—or "whole-ing"—myself.

Although neither of my other gift-to-self holidays—Scotland when I was 50, and Bali at 51—had been intentionally focused on healing, both had provided just that, so I was cautiously optimistic about what I'd discover in the jungle with the shaman's apprentice.

To say Rosita had trained in the Maya healing traditions is an understatement. She'd been immersed and infused in them, and is considered by many to be *the* authority on medicinal plants, so I paid close attention to her outline of the week's key points.

"There are a variety of spiritual diseases. They are universal conditions, and we'll be looking into the causes and, more important, the cures for them."

Rosita continued, telling of *susto* and *pesar,* which translate to "fright or trauma" and "grief or loss." As she explained the potential causes of these maladies, I could hear my inner voices keeping track of the hits.

Late birth, afraid to come out; sexual abuse; incest; unable to trust, stay in relationship; perfectionism; self-criticism.

The laundry list of issues continued: sadness, depression, anger, all related to spiritual diseases. I settled in, knowing I was in the right place.

A DIFFERENT KIND OF BATH

As Rosita spoke of these diseases and working in the subtle energy realms, I recognized a similarity with some the healing methods I'd previously explored. From the breath worker who recognized the hitchhiker being escorted off with Jesus, to the Balinese healer and his pokey stick, to the Aussie woman working with my chakras, each had addressed these unseen—at least by my physical eyes—aspects of life. With each of those methods, I'd come away feeling healthier, more aligned with a core self, and empowered—for a while. Tired of my erratic path of healing, I hoped the Maya tools would offer a more lasting cure.

"You'll be doing spiritual baths," Rosita continued, "on yourself and on others. We'll try to get a bath a day."

A bath a day sounds reasonable enough. But a spiritual bath isn't anything like filling the tub, tossing in some bubbles and splashing about or lying back and luxuriating.

Preparation for this kind of cleansing calls for focused prayer and clear, heart-felt intention, as each bath contains a unique blend of sacred, medicinal plants and flowers. And those plants can't be mindlessly plucked from the roadside, though all of the healing gems we used did grow throughout the rainforest and along the hillside trails surrounding Rosita's home.

For effective transformation, the spirit of the living plants must be honored, respected, and asked if they are appropriate for the bath. The reason is obvious: it would be a most unpleasant ritual if a poisonous plant were included. So herbal knowledge or an ability to listen to the plant devas, also known as nature spirits, themselves is important. Fortunately, Rosita included a guided tour of the thriving tropical growth, pointing out plant after plant and its unique healing properties.

For my initial bath I selected four prayed-over jungle beauties, including what turned out to be my personal plant ally, Rue. She's a powerful healer, as well as a strong protector, and I'm fortunate to live in an area where she likes to grow. Since returning from that trip, I've planted several wonderfully thriving bushes around my home, keeping Rue readily available for ongoing baths.

But let's get back to Belize.

With Rue and her sisters in a bucket of water—yes, bucket; this wasn't your ordinary bath—I began the mashing stage. That, too, was blessed with prayer and wafting copal smoke.

I prayed more in that week than I had in years. Meditation had been a familiar—albeit off and on—component of my spiritual practice for a long time, but prayer simply wasn't part of my upbringing. No grace at meals and no kneeling by the side of the bed before sleep, except for our brief period of Catholicism before Mom married my step-father, another non-church-going guy.

I was a pray-in-the-heat-of-the-moment kind of girl, though I did appreciate the Serenity Prayer I learned and recited in the twelve-step programs. So I found it odd when the prayers we learned that week brought a sense of joy and contentment, as well as a way to commune with Spirit from a deep, heartfelt place.

Although, now that I think about it, my journals include a great deal of prayer. The difference appears to be in speaking the words aloud. Something about hearing myself and others and following the resonance through my body allowed me to embrace a practice that continues to offer a profound sense of solace.

Once the ingredients in our buckets were blessed and mashed and prettied up with flower blossoms, they sat resting in the sun, absorbing both heat and—at least in my mind—good vibes from the Sun God "Ra."

After lunch and more lecture, we began the first ritual, again surrounded by a cloud of copal smoke. While repeating specific prayers to the Nine Maya Spirits and any deities of our choice—I included Christ—we sprinkled, splashed, and downright threw our sacred waters around our bodies.

Remember, this was a spiritual bath, and the spirit lives not only *in* the body, but *around* the body, so best to cleanse a good arm's length all around.

Finally, I stuck my feet in the bucket, allowing the last bit of plant-infused waters to draw away any lingering impurities.

Ahh . . . I felt light and fresh as I gazed out across the densely forested green hills. Overall, I thought my first time went pretty well—except for the growling.

It was a brief, but palpable sensation of aggression. Something in, on, or around me, didn't like the bath.

When I mentioned the experience later, as we gathered back in the living room, Rosita asked for volunteers to pray with me at night, before bed. Three women rose to the task, and each became a cherished friend long past our training in Belize. To this day, one remains a steadfast sister. I have no doubt we've been connected in previous lives.

Because I'd opted out of the campground accommodations and had arranged for a fabulous stand-alone cottage in the resort adjacent to Rosita's, each and every night the ladies walked a quarter-mile jungle trail to fulfill their promise. What an experience, being encircled with prayer and devotional songs we'd learned from class. Our voices blended beautifully, swirling around, then upward through the thatched roof, a chorus lifting to the heavens.

If only it had helped with the growling.

It probably did lessen the tension. In the past, antagonizing my inner demons like that would have prompted extreme fear, like the straight-up-cat-hair, electric-jolts-in-the-back period of my life. So being infused with powerful prayers and invoking the healing presence of Christ, as well as having the Maya spirits to assist me, must have had an effect, as every night I gratefully fell into a deep, rejuvenating sleep.

Yet each time I received a bath—after that first day we practiced on one another—I felt a lingering sense of unease, like something was stuck on my back, there, in the middle, behind my heart. I told myself I didn't want to be a burden, and as a result, chose not to share the nagging sensation with Rosita or my bedtime singing sisters. I just figured I'd deal with whatever "it" was by myself, once again stepping into familiar—and comfortable—solo mode.

It's not that I didn't appreciate the tools and assistance I was offered during the week. I simply didn't want to stick out as the problem child, the especially broken one who would overwhelm the gathering with the complexity and dark stickiness of her story.

Better to stay quiet, my inner voice of shame whispered. *Baby steps are good enough; don't reach for anything more.*

46: Lily and the Rose

On our third morning in Belize, lively conversation—along with the smoke of copal resin—filled the air surrounding the group of by-then-bonded-in-friendship spiritual bathers. After we defined sacred space with several rounds of a song honoring the four elements of nature—earth, water, air, and fire—the morning lecture began. Soon the topic focused on the subject of unemployed spirits.

"If your clients are dealing with unemployed spirits, they may experience night terrors or hear voices."

Having personal dealings with both, I perked up immediately.

"They may feel as though they are being beaten up if these voices are critical," Rosita continued. "However, these may be ancestral spirits, in which case they can't leave, so you'd best give them a job."

Hmm. My thoughts rapidly scanned for crossed-over relatives who might be hanging around. Not coming from a large family, I quickly came to rest on Grandma and Grandpa Hawley, who had died a couple of years after my Thanksgiving visit. Although I hadn't had any recent beyond-the-grave contact with them, I'd been told these paternal relatives attended my spiritualism classes back in the late 1980s. It also made perfect sense they could be tied to me in a karmic way since the sexual abuse wove itself along my paternal line.

The longer I sat with the concept of an ongoing connection to my grandparents, the more distraught I became. I wanted the lineage of incest out of my thoughts—and the perpetrators out of my energy field. The notion of being tied to those barely known relatives and needing to employ them was too much. With some effort, I returned my focus to Rosita's lecture.

"A key question is: are they there to do you harm? If they were healers, you can assign them something. Remember, they are beings of light and want to help you love and care for others. Their aggression can be due to boredom."

Throughout the morning, my incessant thoughts played on, interrupted only by a familiar and chronic pain in my ass—literally.

The tail-bone ache, which that day was more of an ongoing throb, had started two years earlier, right about the time I returned from Scotland. I'd never connected the two before, but the relationship between the clearing of lower chakra (root energy) clutter—performed by the Aussie healer in the Buddhist B&B—and getting down to the root cause of my life's healing appear obvious to me now.

In Belize, hoping to alleviate some of my pain, I had signed up for a bodywork session, a pampering gift to self that typically brought peace and inner quiet. However, as my appointment grew near, I felt anything but peaceful. It was clear that the morning's topic had opened an inner beehive—and a righteously pissed off colony at that.

Before the massage began, Eva, a workshop assistant and skilled practitioner, asked when the pain first started. I explained it had begun about two years prior, around the same time I began writing my life's secrets. I offered a quick recap: sexually abused as child, but so far no clear memories of the incest itself; TV talk show twenty-five years ago prompted what recall I did have; confronted my father approximately five years after that, when he told me his father had abused his sister, triggering an abrupt end to my conversation with him.

Eva's next question threw a wrench—or a key—into my psyche.

"Was your grandfather alive at the time you spoke to your father?"

Then, as it does today, the answer remains unclear. My brain simply refuses to lock in and do the math, resulting in a vague "I'm not sure" response. What did unfold as my body received deep, nurturing touch were a series of "knowings" regarding my grandmother, Lillian.

With emotions from intense rage to horror to disbelief, I "listened" to her tale, and finally landed in a moment of peaceful grace and forgiveness. With that welcome release came the image of a rose. I could even smell its heady scent, though roses were nowhere to be seen in the native Belize foliage.

At the end of the ninety-minute roller coaster, a.k.a. massage, I clearly heard dual titles for the story: *Lily and the Rose* or *The Story of the Ass*.

I tried to recount the mental journey in Belize while my thoughts were fresh, but time—and willingness to revisit the subject matter—eluded me. However, within a few days of getting home, somewhat comfortably seated on my red tweed sofa, I once again braved the subject, reaching back for a connection with my little-known grandma.

February 15, 2009

The ass. It has caused me great embarrassment. [Em-bare-ass-ment]

"Bare ass!" A youthful voice inside me giggles as she speaks, to which a stoic voice responds, "Okay. Ha Ha. Funny, funny. Can we go on now?"

So I could go in two different directions at this point: the story of the shame or the story that says, "Lighten up." The former feels dark and morose. The latter, although it speaks of lightening up, is a distraction, a detour. It comes from the part of me unwilling to hear the story.

It's that part that giggles or blushes or says, "Nice girls don't use that word, let alone talk about their bottoms. But then again . . ." Okay, got it; but—butt. Are you happy to be acknowledged with your silliness . . . now where was I?

Another part of me protests, "You can't write a story about your grandmother; you barely knew her. How can you possibly know what went on in her head? You're just making things up. You don't even have clear memories from your own childhood; how dare you?"

Ah, distractions—fear.

"Don't look. Stop digging into the past. Just live your life."

This is the counsel that comes from a part of me that would rather live a surface existence. Watch TV. Rearrange the furniture. "Oh, I know! Let's go shopping."

Another part says, "Please, I must travel this road. I must tell the story of the thoughts, the connections that presented themselves on the massage table thousands of miles away. I must give voice to the story that lives hidden in my body, hidden in my cellular makeup."

Perhaps there is a darkness that hangs on secrets, that feeds on shame. Perhaps by telling the story, perhaps by stepping back into the skin of the grandmother I barely knew, yet who also lives on in me, I can find some release, some peace, some freedom. Perhaps the physical pain that clutches at my ass can be released by speaking up, by saying, "What if?"

And so I ask the spirit of Lillian Chandler Hawley to come forward. I see you as my ancestor spirit and I recognize you as a spirit ally.

The mind resists yet again. I feel my jaw clench and my throat tighten. Fear and anger skirt the periphery of my awareness, so I pray for assistance.

God the Mother, God the Father, God the Holy Spirit, please guide this pen. Please help me to clear a space for the words of truth. Thank you. Amen and Blessed Be.

So, Grandma Hawley, I barely knew you and this makes me sad. You always seemed so thin and frail. What memories I do have are of you in that cold, dark kitchen making hot apple cider. And I can hear your kind voice, though it too lacked power, lacked presence. Then I think of you being raped there on that same kitchen floor. Eighty-five years old, and Grandpa tied up next to you enduring his own torture. At the time it happened, I was so distant from you and from myself, I could only think about karma and how it comes around to catch up in the most horrendous ways.

I saw you a couple of times after that, bedridden and, if possible, even more fragile than before. Was there ever a time in your life when you were bold and full of vitality? Was there ever a time when you were light and happy? Did marrying my grandfather put out your spark, or were you already hurt?

So many questions I'd like to ask. So many stories I can dream up. Yet only one seems to be pressing, waiting not-so-patiently to be told—The Story of the Ass.

In Belize, so many visions, so many seeming truths passed through my mind, all related to anal sex. And I have to wonder, did this back door to sexuality bring pleasure, or was it forced upon you by Grandpa?

Again my mind resists, refuses to wrap around the story line. Thoughts either race by too quickly to sort through, or consciousness simply shuts down, my eyes drifting from the page to the steady rain outside.

So let's try the facts I do know:

1. Grandfather had sex with his daughters. The oldest admitted this to my father.

2. My father's first sex was with his sister, or so he told my mother. And what about the fact that he was taken into his mother's bed when his father went away? (This information was passed along through my step-mother around the time I confronted my father about the incest.)

3. Father instructed my brother, "The ass is best. It keeps the women you're cheating with from getting pregnant." (I am still somewhat shocked and uncomfortable with this tidbit gifted by my brother.)

So how do the dominoes line up?

"Let's make them nice and neat. Can't go to all the trouble of telling/making up a story if we don't have a consistent and congruent story line."

Argh! This is ridiculous. How many parts of me are going to chime in? Again I hear a voice inside scream, "You could be making all this up!" I wonder why this voice is so afraid?

"Because you make fact out of your wild stories; you add labels; you…"

No. Not you, I. I want . . . I want what?

Why do I once again come to a roadblock? It's as though I keep circling around the subject, like a pack of wild animals, slowly, intentionally closing in.

Oh, stop it. All of you. Let me tell the story. Let me tell the secret. The darkness. The pain. The confusion. Remember there is light in this too. There is a space of loving compassion. At this point, I feel like there has been such a buildup for a terrible insight, when in reality, we simply have confused, hurt people looking for a partner to connect with.

Yes, a part of me wants to hold onto the anger I feel at Grandfather Hawley for having sex with his daughters. And yes, another part of me is disgusted and outraged that my father had sex with his sister. And yes, father sleeping with his mother is also an outrage. Did he have sex with her? Does it matter? Did she teach him the secrecy of the back door? Or is this something he learned from his dear old dad? Is this the way grandfather passed along his sex play to his daughters, so they offered the ass to brother?

It's all story. It's all conjecture.

Sure, I could ask my father if any of this happened, if any of my ranting is real, but would it matter? Would he even be able to hold the truth? And what is truth anyway? Is it true that on the massage table, I felt Grandma Hawley's anger, felt her shame about the family's secrets and sexual connections?

Yes. On the table, the energies were real. The shame. The disgust. The pleasure. The guilt. The confusion. The secret of the ass—the men I've had up mine, and the men I've explored; they all came back as I lay on the table.

And yet what also presented itself while I lay prone in that wild paradise—tears and snot running freely to the ground beneath me—was a bit of peace, a bit of release, a bit of forgiveness. God knows, I am not perfect. God knows I am doing my best to heal, to release, to transform the energies of fear and darkness, anger and shame. God knows I use these words to sort through the confusion that pulls me this way and that.

Please help me to transform. Please help me to be cleansed. Please help me to move into a space of love, a space of forgiveness for myself, for my ancestors, for my ass, for my heart.

It was my heart I saw as a rose there on the massage table. An open rose. And it is such a rose I offer to my Grandma Lily. An offer of peace. An offer of strength. An offer of purity.

Let's clear the dynamic of shame and anger that has been passed down through the father side of the family. Let's you and I together stand up and say, "No more." Let's ask light, love, and the power of the rose—with her intoxicating essence and her power of beauty—to hold us. But beware those who disrespect, those who wish to abuse, for they will learn by way of her thorns.

And so it is that I invoked my grandmother's spirit to assist me along the path of healing.

47: Grandpa's Key

My thoughts naturally shift to Grandpa Hawley after focusing so intently on Grandma. They belong together. And though I never saw one without the other while visiting their perpetually chilly house, they seemed to live in rarely intersecting orbits.

Real, waking life memories of Grandpa are limited and a bit fleeting, but his influence on my dreamtime has deeply ingrained permanence. This dream from over fifteen years ago is a good example:

I'm standing on the side of a deep gorge. I can't see the bottom, though I can see across to the other side about fifty feet away. The land is rich and moist, and the smell of the forest fills my nostrils. There are trees, tall trees, like mighty old pines or spruces, but their branches don't start until quite high up, so my view is mainly that of thickly barked trunks.

My step-niece Anna is there with me. I sense we aren't far from Grandpa Hawley's house. I tell her to be careful, not to slip over the edge. Then I see one of the trees from our side of the gulch has fallen down, stretching across to the other side. It lies in such a way that it has dug a deep horizontal wound into the exposed earth on the other side. The wind blows and causes the downed tree to continue etching its way into the soft moist earth. The sound of the tree's creaking movement sounds like screaming.

I drop my purse. As I'm picking up my belongings, I see Anna is perilously close to the slippery edge. I call out to her just as she disappears from sight, down into the ravine. I scream out, but it's too late. She's been swallowed up. Devastated, I wake up sobbing.

Later that same night, my dreams offered another clear message:

I'm in Grandpa's house, sitting at an old wooden desk. The main drawer is locked, but I have a cigar-box-sized, wooden puzzle in front of me. I sense if I can figure out this box, I'll find a key inside. I sit, sliding panels this way and that, slowly unlocking layer after layer of the tricky box, until I come to a small, gold skeleton key. I open the desk drawer to find a screwdriver inside.

It was this dream—experienced in my late thirties—that led me to suspect my grandfather had had a direct hand in my sexual abuse. While I also held my father accountable, especially with the clear memories of teenage improprieties, the signs from my nighttime psyche were too obvious to ignore.

Shortly after those dreams—during another visit to the Monroe Institute in Virginia—I received additional waking clues as to the mysterious yet haunting details of my abuse.

Initially, the scene was so theatrical I dismissed the chance of its having any literal correlation . . . .

February 1995: Lifelines workshop
We've finished debriefing from one of our journeys into the subtle realms; the focus was to look for wayward souls that needed assistance crossing over. Several of the workshop participants found entities they ushered across. I, however, seemed to be finding pieces of myself, and it was causing me quite a lot of grief.

One of the skilled and nurturing workshop leaders, Karen, offered me some private one-on-one time to delve more deeply into the scene.

I'm sitting with a toddler-aged me. She is—I am—about three years old. My collarbone-length, dark blond hair looks shiny and soft, and I have straight-cut bangs covering my forehead. I'm wearing a white, ruffled pinafore over a short, puffy-sleeved dress. The dress itself is navy blue. I look cute, like a doll. But there is something wrong with my eyes. They are hollow, vacant, as though I'm not there. The child me's whole body seems empty, robotic, as the adult me takes her hand. We begin walking along a cave-like corridor.

At the end of this rocky passage is a well-worn, wooden staircase. We climb the creaking steps to a massive, deeply carved, wooden door. The image of a dragon with wings extended rises from its surface. At this point, I realize I'm once again alone, as I was in the group journey. The child me has led me to the door and vanished. I take a deep breath, afraid of what I'll see inside but knowing I must face the vision. Karen reassures me she is there with me. Nothing inside can hurt me; I have the power to confront whatever lies on the other side.

I push back the heavy door to see a cavern lit by the flickering light of candles and a large fire in the center. It is approximately twenty feet in diameter. There are old men in the room, speaking in hushed tones. They don't notice me, as they have their backs to the entrance. They are focused on what is going on at the altar across the room.

Here is where I see my grandfather. He is holding the wrist of the child me with his left hand, while his right hand waves symbols in the air. She turns to look over her shoulder and I see terror in her eyes.

I burst into the room, a wild woman, displacing the chairs and low-lying benches that get in my way. I reach my grandfather in a few furious strides and grab up my child self. Holding her close, I feel rage, which sends out a wave of power that is picked up by the flames, and they gather in strength. The men in the room reel in stunned disbelief.

With words that cause the fires to burn even hotter, I speak a curse, damning these men for taking my innocence. I then calmly and intentionally turn and walk back across the building inferno, holding little Debbie close to my heart. As I make my way back down the rickety stairs and stone corridor, I hear my captors' screams as they are burned in hell. It seems to me that justice has been served and I feel satisfied.

Stepping from the dark shadows of the earth into a sun-drenched meadow, I sit down on the lush green grass and continue to hold my child self close to my heart. I am crying deeply. Karen asks if there is someone there to help in the care and nurturing of little Debbie. I see a wise, old, grandmotherly being. I know that little Debbie will be tended well by this angel who glows with love.

After that fiery vision, I told myself I had an overly active imagination, but the story line refused to fade away. Instead, over the years of this healing workshop and that spiritual practice, the image of my grandfather and the circle of men sat patiently, whispering, *What if?*

48: Flushing Puppies

With the new tool of spiritual baths tucked into my ever-expanding healer's treasure box, I continued to delve into my psyche's inner workings through my writing.

A lot of self love and gratitude flowed through my beloved journal's pages, but after Belize, there was also a distinct shift toward addressing the ever-present self-hatred.

February 16, 2009

. . . As I write the word fear, my right thigh stings in recognition. This is where fear resides in my body. This is where anger resides in my body.

My hope is that I can do my prayers and spiritual baths and sacred ceremonies to be clear of this darkness once and for all, but part of me resists. I hear the wicked witch cackle in my head, "You're mine, sweet pretty; all mine. You'll never be free of me."

It's like an addiction. I know this voice causes only tension, and yet somehow I feel tethered to it. It says, "You're not good enough," or "You'll never amount to anything." It's an old, tired tape, and perhaps it will be with me always.

For a moment, I consider hand-to-hand combat—the angels of darkness and light doing battle—but that seems to be a waste of energy.

I'm reminded of a dream I had while in Belize:

I was leading a group of women and we came to an organized line, like those at Disneyland. The group was afraid to enter into the queue because a crazy man stood at the turnaround point. I went in to show them it was okay, prompting the man to jump on top of me and throw flailing punches. I thought about fighting back but instead allowed my energy to be contained within myself, building and strengthening instead of draining. Once he tired himself out, I threw him off and began punching him in the chest. I woke up at that point. I didn't want to kill him, but I did want him to be disarmed.

So the lesson in this moment: focus on my power, my light, love, and gratitude? Or am I on the wrong track completely? Was the dream showing me that I don't have it together as much as I think? That when confronted with obstacles on my path, the key is to ask for assistance, ask God/Goddess, my angels, my guides—call out the troops—instead of going it alone?

So please, healing deities, guides, angels, spirits, help me . . .

I didn't leave my quest for inner understanding to my dreamtime insights. This next entry details a waking vision.

February 19, 2009

A bit of blue peeks through the morning fog. Soft air inside too, as copal smoke fills the house. I've added prayers to the nine Maya spirits to my morning ritual, prayers of love and light which leave my heart fulfilled.

During meditation, I saw a child standing before me: a wild, unkempt stranger. She looked as though she had been forgotten for many years. A crazed look to her with matted hair and torn clothes. She seemed unable—or perhaps unwilling—to speak. I imagine the only sound she knows is a haunting, lonely wail. Like the call of a wolf at the full moon, though her cry would bring tears to the eyes of any who hear it.

Yet she wasn't alone. Beside her I saw a twin. A healthy, happy, well-loved child. This bright and beautiful one reached out a hand to her wild-animal companion and the two morphed into one. Both girls live within me. Just as I have so many other parts of self that make up the greater whole.

I am a combination of many selves. As I recognize and welcome home those that have been lost or split off—wandering the darkness of hell—I come to a new place of compassion. Compassion not only for me, but for others who may be running on single cylinders, unaware that their spark, vitality, and loving selves have simply gotten sidetracked, pulled off the main highway.

Everyone deserves love. Everyone deserves integration. Everyone deserves a second chance.

I open my heart to the healing aspect of self, and so it is. Slowly but surely, the children are coming home. The lost, disowned, misunderstood, disrespected aspects are coming home. And peace fills the land.

Peace didn't fill the land for long.

Sunday, March 1, 2009

A string of intense dreams during a busy, out-of-town work week.

I had infiltrated the Italian mafia, pretending to be loyal, but I was also some type of police or government informant, so I had to bide my time to escape without injury. I was afraid my cover had been blown.

The next night I was in the Middle East with a friend. She was claiming her inheritance of antiquities. A war went on around us—fire, explosions, gunshots—then I was alone in the battle, alone on an open platform. A man came up and shot me, first in the left shoulder, then in the head. I remember thinking it odd that I didn't feel any pain.

And then last night.

The preparation was very detailed, with fancy braided hair and elaborate gowns. A strong storybook setting, like being a lady-in-waiting for a priestess, but I was also a protector. I had to keep the space clear for an upcoming healing ritual.

A large black and white cat with black boots appeared. It looked wild and kind of glowed, so I told it to get away. Then it turned into a man with curly black hair and very white skin. He told me his name was Don something (Don as in "Mr." in Spanish). I repeated his name and he corrected me on the pronunciation. I told him he wasn't welcome. He was charming, cunning, but also dangerous, black magic. He told me he would find a way in. He also said something about knowing I liked the ass, which I denied.

As I thought about the dream after waking, I could see this as another layer of healing the darkness and the shame, and admitting that I have sometimes enjoyed anal explorations—though memories continue to be laced with anger.

Thursday, March 5, 2009 11 P.M.
Long day, long week; fucking exhausted.
So why am I staying up to write? I guess I'm looking for some elusive peace or nurturing.

The evil one, the part that downright hates me, hit hard the past couple of days. Perhaps it was prompted by the rawness I felt on Monday evening as I reviewed my life and considered writing this story. It was certainly exaggerated by the speeding ticket I got while hurrying to the airport. The speeding ticket I wouldn't have gotten if I'd listened to my intuition.

"Be careful . . . a cop is around."

But no, not me. I was feeling invincible. Big shot. "Big dummy" is more like it.

Then tonight: coming home again, got to the airport in plenty of time for the earlier flight, but did I change my ticket? No. That would have been too easy, too logical. It's like a part of me is intentionally tripping me up, causing me to fail, pushing the idiot button.

I spiraled down in intense rage as the earlier flight boarded, then filled up without my name being called from the standby list. There hasn't been that much self-directed viciousness in a long, long time.

The dark thunder cloud descends. Bang.

The sound echoes as the dungeon door slams shut. An eerie, altered sense creeps over my psyche and I go somewhat numb. I try not to listen to the voice that berates, the one that flushes puppies down the toilet. An image from a dream last night provides the perfect analogy:

A clean, white toilet, and—depending on the stage of the dream—one or two puppies swim around the bowl. Adorable little golden retriever pups who are so sweet, so trusting. With horror, I watch my hand reach out and flush the handle.

Part of me hopes the puppies will flush, will disappear, but another larger or perhaps stronger part, silently cheers the swirling puppies on. This latter me is terrified of what will happen within, what dark, self-loathing rage will come and overtake me if the former succeeds in making the puppies disappear. Fortunately, it doesn't happen. The puppies circle around and slip halfway down, but they never disappear.

Just before waking up, I ask myself how many puppies are living in the toilet, and about five or six come up from the drain. They all look healthy enough, but why I have them in the toilet doesn't make sense.

Upon awakening I asked myself why I didn't take the puppies out. The answer: They were safe there.

I'm still chilled by the hand controlling the flush. Is this the evil one who has commanded the hand of self-abuse? Each of those times I gouged at my skin, I felt so very split, horrified, yet unable to do anything about the actions, unable to stop the atrocity. Kind of like the imploding that happened tonight at the airport, though thankfully the attack stayed hidden in my mind.

I tried to find positive suggestions while waiting for the next ninety minutes to pass.

"You've wanted time to catch up on reading."

But it was too late; I'd already flipped the switch—or flushed the handle, as the case may be. So round and round the sweet, innocent, trusting Debra went, pulled deeper and deeper into the swirling vortex, until the cycle finished and the emotional waters once again became still.

It scares me to go this deeply into self-hatred. And it exhausts me. I don't know, what . . . what don't I know?

Well, lots.

So what do I know?

I know to pray, to ask for help from Spirit.

But the self-loathing can come on so forcefully it crowds out any cry for help. It bullies its way into the forefront and tells me I don't deserve any better.

"Don't bother asking for help. Don't even bother thinking about asking."

Asking for help leads to a whole lecture on how needy I am. How I suck the life out of any attempts at friendship.

"You deserve to be alone. No one wants to be around such a wet blanket."

I even overheard a conversation on the plane, a woman behind me saying how she likes to surround herself with positive people, to stay away from "downer Debbies."

Ironic and funny in a sick-humor sort of way how even unwitting airline passengers got in a good jab.

Okay, enough of this. I have to get some sleep.

God/Goddess, Ix Chel, Angels, guides . . . I was going to say, "Take pity on me," but perhaps I'd rather have you take pity from me. Help me to heal, to be gentle on myself, to be care-full of the puppies.

Maybe it would be okay to take the puppies out of the bowl and roll around on the floor playing with them. Though that brings a sense of fear, fear that the angry jailer would find out and take revenge. Perhaps it's best they stay put.

Previously, I would have taken a dive into the soft and fuzzy world of drugs after such a vicious inner attack. But that year, as the sun peeked through winter's darkness, I chose a new direction—and began writing this book.

49: A Shaman's Vision

Gong.
My heart awakens.
Is it time?
Almost.
Prepare the Masters.
Sense it may not make,
The words you hear in your head,
Yet the heart knows and remembers
A call to arms.
(No, silly, not armor and guns—arms that wrap around your chest. Reaching out in love, in knowing compassion. These are the arms called into service now.)

Let us say, no more.
No more will I knowingly inflict pain or hardship on another.
No more will I reach out in fear.
No more will I close down in hate,
for hate simply closes me off to myself, and self is where the healing begins.

With myself I offer space.
With myself I offer compassion.

With myself I offer peace.
With myself I open to joy.

Just a little at first, if that is all one can bear.
A small grin of knowing, a whisper of ahh, a gentle tug of happiness.
These I will recognize.
These I will say thank you for.
These I do say thank you to.

Thank you for awareness.
Thank you for tears.
Thank you for guidance.
Thank you for holding my hand, my heart, my uncertainty.
Thank you for saying, "It's okay, we'll hold you in the dark."
And thank you for helping me to know you'll be there along with that ray of hope.

I trust in your presence, as I am beginning to trust in mine.
Thank you, dear angels; thank you for being mine.

Those words were written just a few days before the Spring Equinox, a time of equal light and dark. Since I'd returned from Belize five weeks earlier, the questions regarding my father—and the what-ifs regarding my grandfather—had crowded my brain. In that time of balance, I asked a friend—a gifted psychic and shaman—for assistance. With her help, I felt ready to uncover what had happened nearly fifty years earlier.

"I invoke the inner God and Goddess," began Sage Runningbear, "and ask for the blessings of the Archangels. We honor the nature beings, spirit guides, teachers, and helpers who join us here today."

She and her assistant, Christine, sat across my sturdy oak dining table on a bright, sunny afternoon while my dog and cat—happily, I was no longer allergic—snoozed nearby. I listened with a combination of gratitude and trepidation for wisdom from spiritual guides and teachers who pressed themselves to the front of the etheric queue.

The ladies passed along items of interest, but with a digital recorder capturing their words, I allowed my mind to drift in and out. Between picking up threads about the teachings I'm meant to share with women and the shamanic manner in which I work, my mind kept returning to the primary question: how would I touch on the subject of childhood incest? Instead, when an opportunity for a question came up, I asked about my draw toward smoking pot, even though I hadn't imbibed since returning from Belize. Sage responded first.

"The energy coming in that is making you feel like you want to get high, this isn't you; it doesn't belong to you. It comes in because it really wants to steer you away from being centered, grounded in your physical body, and moving forward."

Picking up the thread, Christine continued, "Any time we want to move forward with our power, something wants to get inside and make us feel as if we're crazy. Marijuana is an easy way to go out of our body, into the cosmos, and to let something jump in. I'm actually seeing it as a spirit that lives here on the land with you. It's a spirit who's been with you for many years. It actually moved here with you."

Her words made perfect sense. I'd often noticed the correlation between making progress toward a goal and then slamming into a period of heavy smoking. It was during those sometimes month-long "wake-and-bake" periods that I fell into the habitual self-loathing and contempt.

Sage continued, "This is a spirit that doesn't want you to be healed. It especially doesn't want you to heal any aspect of your abuse. The reason why it doesn't want you to heal comes from another lifetime. It all makes so much sense. . . .

"You actually worked with Isis in an Egyptian lifetime. You worked with what they call the sexual magic. Isis taught many of her disciples about the rising of kundalini energy. Women had the capability—if they could unleash it—not only to heal themselves, but to heal others.

"They would raise the energy from their second chakra, and it would come up and shoot out their heart chakra. Anybody they were around while they were practicing this would be instantaneously healed, so they were very careful. . . .

"Some of her students were the Mother Mary and Mary Magdalen. Mother Mary taught Jesus. And then Jesus and Magdalen brought this up in their union as a way of sending prayer and healing out to the world. It's like an intense blue vibration shooting out.

"This energy, people were afraid of it, thought it was witchcraft. It was something to be contained, trapped. A group of men—sorcerers—wanted to get a hold of it, to use it for bad. That's how they got their power: robbing these beautiful women of second chakra energies. It had to be hidden, taken under ground, so it wasn't completely eliminated. . . .

"You remember this. It's in your DNA, your cellular memory."

As I sat with her statements, I remembered a message I'd received from my own internal guidance at a recent Monroe Institute workshop, "You came in on the orange ray." Orange is the color of the second chakra, the center of sexuality.

The correlation between my "entrance" vibration and the reading with Sage and Christine reinforced the inner calling to accept the reality of my roots—and my role as a sacred priestess.

As I think about sexual energies and running them through my body, I am reminded of a past lover, Rick, a man who has circled through my life on several occasions. . . .

Our first go round took place primarily in Hollywood, a perfect match of rock 'n' roll musician and dedicated groupie. That chapter included lots of drugs and backstage passes plus the requisite post-show sex.

A year or so later, when his band passed through Houston, we hooked up again—almost. In a lukewarm attempt at being faithful to Ed, I graciously accepted a free ticket to Rick's concert, and I definitely enjoyed my night of party-girl VIP access, but when it came time to pay up—in the form of sex—I said no. He slammed the hotel door in my face, yelling a few not-so-kind words.

Twenty years later our paths crossed again at a San Francisco party, though at first I couldn't place him.

"I know that name," I told my friend as we walked away from the guy who didn't look familiar, but caused my gut to tighten. "Why the hell do I know that name?"

"He works at the music store here in town," she supplied. "I just bought a guitar from him."

Perplexed, I started searching my sketchy past, looking for a clue. About an hour later, the dots connected, bringing a mixture of excitement and dread. Nervous, but trusting that time smoothed out any lingering animosity, I searched out Rick in the lively gathering.

"We've met before," I told him, "a long time ago." Taking a large swig of beer to calm my anxiety, I continued, "Actually, we used to know each other quite well."

He was clueless, at least at first.

There had been plenty of women, so he guessed we'd been lovers. But who I was—or had been—was a blank. And I don't blame him. He'd traveled all over the world getting it on with hundreds of willing partners. I was simply part of the fast-lane parade, despite our repeat performances.

When he finally did remember—with a few hints from me in my game of please-confirm-I'm-memorable—he was most apologetic about his parting behavior.

"I was a real jerk back then," he said calmly. "I'm truly sorry."

And so began our chapter two. No rock 'n' roll, just sex and drugs. Well, drug singular, my buddy—and his—marijuana.

Although we occasionally went out for a meal, for the most part we'd simply smoke and then fuck like the bunnies encircling his set of erotic coffee mugs. During one particularly intense ride of ecstatic bliss, Rick encouraged me to open my eyes and gaze into his. But I couldn't. I was afraid of what I'd see there, or perhaps of what he'd see in me. Besides, I had far too much fun exploring the inner realms our sexual energies sparked. . . .

I'm lying on a narrow strip of soft golden sand with the waves gently lapping at my back. I don't generally lie with my back to the open sea, but today I feel safe. Today I know there are others keeping watch. I lazily open my eyes and gaze up the beach to my cave's opening. As I scan the rocky cliff that reaches up several hundred feet, I feel calm, content, and gently warmed by the rays of the noon sun.

Rick approaches on the beach, bearing a large woven tray piled high with colorful fruits. This he places next to my relaxed snout. He has no need to fear the powerful dragon lying before him. We are united, man and beast, confidants in a mystical land outside of time.

One of the last times Rick and I got together—by then I'd learned he was in a committed, though open, relationship—I experienced the electric, orgasmic vibration Sage talked about. Though I didn't raise the high-powered energy up to my heart, I did offer it to him. . . .

Placing my fully charged hand about twelve inches above my lover's naked belly, I innocently asked, "Do you feel this?"
"Yes!" he shouted, pulling back as though I had offered him a blowtorch.

So I've known that I sometimes build tangible energy. However, finding partners I felt comfortable sharing it with—either verbally or otherwise—was almost impossible. The level of vibrancy that literally flowed from my pores had been reserved for me. Back then I'd smoke pot, slide down into my body, and draw the energies from my deeply anchored roots up into my swaying hips. Continuing to pulse the intensity in time with one of a few select songs, I'd direct it into my hands, where it would flow as ribbons of light. Wrapping myself in these rainbow tones, I would dance myself into an earth-quaking, star-blazing orgasm.

The only witnesses to those performances were the unseen spirit guests I welcomed into my small country home.

So pot and sex—and shame about what I considered my too-intense passion—were all tied up together. Their union became clearer as my psychic reading continued.

"The energy trying to prevent you from moving forward doesn't want you to heal. Because once you heal your second chakra, you'll remember your knowing and your ability to work with sexual magic. And it doesn't want that. The energy that has followed you from Southern California to here is actually part of that group from centuries ago that wanted to squash the practice."

The connection between the anti-healing energy and my family lineage was too obvious. I had to ask.

"How is my grandfather Hawley involved in all of this?"

"When this being came forth, it actually showed itself as a father figure," Christine answered. "It might be a father or grandfather."

To bring the ladies up to date, I explained that while I had limited memory of the actual events from when I was two or three, I had recently begun having a sense that my father offered me to his father, a self-made expert in the Asian warrior arts. I suspected my father and grandfather weren't alone in the abuse, that there was a small group led by Grandpa—The Order of the Dragon—and I was an initiation gift.

Sage spoke her vision first. "I want to say witchcraft, but that isn't quite the word. They were dabbling in something they shouldn't have. It had to do with money and influence, evoking powers they felt would bring them abundance, wealth, control.

"But it kind of backfired because they weren't doing it in a respectful way. They sent out negative energies and as a result had a curse—an unconscious curse—placed on them. Your grandfather's life work, his collection of Asian art, samurai armor, and swords were not taken with integrity. They invoked the powers of darkness, though unknowingly."

I hungrily absorbed each thought-provoking key as Sage continued.

"When you were a child, your father was very afraid of you, afraid of your light.

"We all carry light in different parts of our beings, and you carried yours in your second chakra. You came in with a strong theme and determination to reclaim the ancient sexual magic. That's where you held your power. And that really frightened your father. . . .

"To him, the word sexuality has such a negative connotation. It is kind of a dirty thing—especially for a child to carry such a powerful sexual energy and vibration—it made him feel uncomfortable, as it did your grandfather."

Christine added, "I'm seeing that your grandfather may have been sexually abused as a child, but it was unspoken."

"It was destined," Sage began again, "there was going to be a child in your family who would carry an immense energy in her second chakra. And that energy had the potential not only to heal her, but to heal her family and to heal other people, and as a result heal part of the world.

"Any time there is such a prophecy, energy comes in wanting to destroy the child, even though they're not really sure when that child is going to be born or who that child is. Sometimes they start attacking all the female lineage, whether it be your grandmother, your mother, or yourself—it's kind of like an annihilation—to make sure they hit all females in the family and destroy the energy before it becomes anything."

As I once again listen to the words of Sage and Christine, the scene plays like a fantastical Hollywood script and not the reality of a simple family growing up in the hills overlooking the land of make-believe. However, it reminds me of another reading, from a spiritual counselor I saw a year or so after the incest memories surfaced.

"I see you surrounded in a cocoon: a concrete shell. It's been placed around you for protection. But it is beginning to crack."

Although my counselor didn't say specifically what I was being protected from, I sensed I held a treasure within. Though, as I've shared throughout this story, at twenty-eight I didn't yet recognize the precious nature of my essential being.

After a few moments of silence, Sage confirmed my fears: "There *was* abuse with your father and grandfather.

"There are bits and pieces—I'm seeing this metaphorically . . .

"I'm seeing this basket with gold coins in it, and it sits in your second chakra. It's not only wealth for you, it's wealth for your community—the potential of great healing. By committing this act of violence, they actually took some of those coins: they took some of your spirit.

"What needs to happen is a spirit retrieval—a soul retrieval—so that piece can come back to you. Once it does, then you can go on to the next phase. That's why you're feeling like there's a big part of the puzzle missing, because there is."

"Soul retrieval" wasn't a new term to me. I'd read many books on the subject and had even attended workshops, learning the skills required to navigate the shamanic realms. I knew enough to be both relieved and unsettled by what would come next.

"There is also energy there; I'm not sure where it comes from, but it's kind of lingering around you about writing your book, about telling your story, because it definitely will affect other people. Just hearing the story resonates as a healing."

"Do you know where that energy comes from?" Sage asked Christine. "The blockage?"

"I'm hearing she has to get her last piece back before she can finish writing."

"It feels like it has to do with anger, or rage."

"It's this big black box. I'm seeing it right here," Christine said as she looked at me and placed her hands over her heart. "And there's something like a lock on your second chakra."

I knew the lock was rage and voiced my concern about tapping into the power of the emotion without turning it against myself.

"You need to have a ritual," Sage said. "Your guides are telling me: one, it needs to be in a place where you feel safe; and two, it needs to be with people strong enough to hold the circle for you. These may be other women who have been sexually abused themselves. Because not only is it going to be healing for you, it's going to be healing for these other women.

"I'm seeing this . . . A circle of women—I'm one of them—around a fire. We're guiding you, helping you. . . .

"But first the anger must be released into the flames, as though you're vomiting, expelling the rage into the fire that burns it, absorbs it, so it doesn't affect the others in the circle or go out into the universe. It needs to come out of you.

"We're drumming and chanting, building up the power, holding sacred space while you're letting it go. Once you let it go, we can help you bring those bits and pieces back. Bits and pieces, especially your second chakra.

"It wasn't just one person who took your power. It was several. . . ."

Interrupting, I shared my parallel vision: that my father had presented me as an offering to my grandfather, hoping that by bringing me, he would be allowed access to the small group led by Grandpa.

"The soul retrieval is an unraveling. It's a de-possession. It's definitely traveling to the other dimension and getting back your essence and making you whole again. . . Because what you're feeling, what you're sensing is very real. What you think happened to you, did happen to you.

"But there's a part of your logical mind saying, 'This is a little far out there. How could they do that to a child?'

"Doing the ritual with a group of individuals who can hold sacred space is important. This isn't work to be done alone. So when you're ready. . . ."

Ah yes, ready. Though I felt anxious, I also felt thankful. After all the years of both unconscious and conscious sabotaging behavior—along with entertaining tireless what-ifs—I finally had a clear vision and a next step.

50: Setting the Stage

Not wanting to lose the momentum inspired by my reading with Sage and Christine, I looked at the calendar to determine a good night for my ritual—I never once considered daytime. A new moon was to occur the following week, and while I felt drawn to work in the dark lunar phase, part of me protested acting so quickly. Choosing to ignore that voice, I set about calling a few friends—women I knew shared an incestuous past. Each invitation presented me with a test of courage: reaching out and asking for help.

I opened each call directly, "Hi. I've got a question for you. And please, only say yes if it feels one hundred percent okay for you to do so."

After explaining the purpose of the gathering—a soul retrieval to reclaim my little girl—I asked each woman, "Will you stand and hold sacred space for me?" Each of the three, without hesitation, said, "Yes, of course." Their collective response left me awed and fueled for the next step: finding a place to hold the shamanic gathering.

Remembering a ritual I'd attended years before, I searched out the phone number for another powerful female healer from my rural community, Leslie. Encouraged by inner guidance that said, *Yes, this is good*, I again stretched into the discomfort of asking for assistance.

I explained the connection I'd felt with her land during the previous ceremony and how I felt it would hold us well for a fire circle under the moonless night. Not only did Leslie agree to let us use an area she had designated for sacred work, she offered to hold space for the ritual itself, as a gatekeeper between the realms. Once again, I felt completely supported and satisfied. However, like all good plans, it had to be adjusted to meet with everyone's schedule. And as I do so well, I found meaning in the B version: a gathering three days after the new moon. Since I'd been born at that same "smiley-faced" moon phase, I took it as an auspicious sign.

Although Sage had warned me about delving deeper alone, my journal reveals my continuing quest for answers.

Monday, March 23, 2009
Sadness wells up. Sadness for the little girl still trapped in the bad man's arms.

"Don't worry," I hear inside. "We know you are preparing. We know you will be whole soon. We're here to assist, to support."

And yet I feel so tired, so inadequate, so inept. An angry voice accuses, "Why did it take you so long?"

It sounds like the condemning voice of Mom, the "perfect" mother inside, always ready to jump at a chance to attack; so much for perfection.

A truly perfect mother is kind and nurturing. She would simply rejoice that a long-lost child is coming home. The perfect mother takes up her battle with those who are the child's captors—those who would do harm. . . .

I'm so sorry, little Debbie, precious little three-year-old Debbie.

Part of me wants to call my father and yell at him. "What the fuck is the matter with you? How could you even think that offering your daughter—your princess—how could you think that was okay? Are you really that sick in the head?"

Another part says, "It's okay, he was abused as well."

To which I scream, "Not now! I'm not ready to forgive. Now I need my rage. I need my power. I want to nail him to the cross. I want to see pain in his eyes. I want him to see the pain in mine."

How could I have held this so deeply for all these years? What happened that night so long ago to send this part of me underground? And, more important, is it safe to bring her back?

Ah ha. Just remembered something. She—well, I—didn't split off; they took a part of me.

"Did I give it willingly?" *I hear something inside ask.*

Willingly or not, I reclaim my innocence, my light, my heart.

You can't play off a three-year-old's love of her daddy that way; it's pure evil. You're pure evil, Father. Or perhaps you're pure stupidity. For that I have pity.

Oh yes, that nagging part of me wants to return to "All is good in love and light."

Yeah, yeah; but let's cut that bullshit right now. This is time for rage, this is time for action. Though I know the action needs to come from the heart, with the light, the guidance of Christ, and the angels by my side. . . .

How many men?

"Three," *I hear,* "Grandfather and two others; Father was a weak bystander."

What did you do to me?

I could dial the phone. I could demand an answer from him. Would I get one?

Does it matter? It's the power that comes from demanding that's the key. I must reclaim my voice; his is inconsequential—his voice lies.

Argh. That nagging do-good voice sneaks in again.

"Perhaps you are doing his soul a service by speaking the truth. Perhaps you can offer his soul release by forgiving a sick man and his actions. Are you really so cold and bitter you would curse an old, weak man?"

To which I reply, "Are you really so kind and forgiving you would forgive and . . ."

Another voice steps in before I can finish the sentence. "Who said anything about forgetting?"

Yikes… Stop! This is so frustrating.

Voices here and there all clamoring for a nice neat package to wrap this up in. A clean-cut, organized cubby; a way to move past, move through, move on.

"What if there is never an end? What if I pull back a long dark chain of ugly events that set me up to forever deal with darkness?"

That's the fear talking. That's the voice that has run the show for so many years. To this fear I say, "It's okay, I see you. I acknowledge your presence and I ask you to call on the Archangels and the Christ Light for protection.*

"I have to do this. I can no longer live without my whole being. I must reclaim the energies that were taken from me, permission given or not. A three-year-old is in no position to be placed in a ritual where her light is . . . is what?"

Again I look for details. I want to know exactly what occurred that night.

SETTING THE STAGE

How do I know it was night?

I just do. I let my imagination run free . . .

I'm holding Daddy's hand. I look up and he smiles at me.

"It's okay, Princess."

I see love in his eyes, yet they are also glazed over, the familiar haze of alcohol and that stupid alcohol grin.

"We are going to play a game. You're going to climb up in the lap of each man here. You're going to lower your head."

I hear a warning from within: "Careful. You are dangerously close. Don't do this alone. Don't look in their eyes."

But did I? Did I see the evil in each one of those men? Did they see the light in me? Did they see the power my soul carries? Did I lay a quiet curse on each of those men that night? Or did I enter willingly? Did my soul bless? Did my soul open in light and love, innocence and purity, as only a child knows to do?

Perhaps.

It's the fifty-two-year-old woman who knows the rage. It's the woman of today who reaches back forty-nine years. Is this a cycle of seven sevens? Connecting me back to when I was three. Somehow that feels right. I like the power of sevens. The number of Ix Chel, the number of my birthday. Lucky seven. Seven chakras. Seven notes in the scale, do re mi fa sol la ti. Again I look to the world I know, the world of numbers, to find comfort as I venture into the unknown.

Part of me wants to go back to the vision, the eyes of the abusers. And yet another part says, "Wait, you've found your doorway."

Seven days are available for gaining wisdom, for gaining insight. Seven times seven. It is this power I invoke. It is this power I choose to bring with me to the ritual. Seven women. In seven days.

I'll allow the process to build its power, its honor, its glory. I'll allow the process to be blessed by God, Goddess, Holy Spirit. And so it is.

Amen and Blessed Be.

And so the week began. Fortunately, it was a busy work week, including out-of-town travel, so I didn't have a lot of time to obsess over the upcoming ceremony. Instead, my thoughts revolved around another topic from my reading: sexual magic, especially as it related to Jesus and his hotly contested union.

For several months I'd felt called to learn more about Mary Magdalen, and while I've since found many fabulously juicy, easy-to-read resources, back then my search had turned up only scholarly texts, interpretations of her words that left me bone dry.

I've also turned up ongoing debates around whether or not she was a prostitute. I don't really care. What brings me satisfaction is reaching out to a lady who resonates deeply with my soul. Who, when I call her name and invoke her presence, brings a sense of loving grace and "rightness" throughout my being, as though somehow everything I've done in my past—layered heavily with shame and guilt, judgment and remorse—can be seen through a lens of perfection, even the time I worked as a call girl.

In my reading with Sage, she too had touched on my dirty little secret that now isn't. "When you think about a prostitute selling her sex, it's not all in a negative connotation. In a sense—in a roundabout way—she is actually using some of that sex magic herself, unknowingly."

I felt comforted—even redeemed—by the thought that my time as a hooker ran deeper than simply money and carnal pleasure. On some level I was a conduit to the divine—a holy vessel—who has blessed many.

At the end of the week, on my evening walk, I was graced with a winged messenger. I realize it's an oxymoron to say that birds ground me, but they do, especially the one I now refer to as "Magic Bird," who made his first appearance during my sunset stroll. The sighting was important enough to be recorded in my journal.

This bird was incredible. For perhaps three seconds my eyes were riveted on its sleek passage through the air. A slow, steady, yet powerful beat, beat, beat. Legs and feet tucked back in the perfect aerodynamic point. While its long, bomber-gray body moved silently in a solid, straight line of focus and determination. I felt that bird in my bones. Its power and grace shot through me head to toe. "Wow" slipped through my lips as I followed its all-too-brief passage. I hope to see this majestic messenger again. For now, I simply remember and once again feel the gift it bestowed. Thank you, magic bird.

I've since learned the magic bird is a blue heron, who, according to several Native American traditions, brings messages of self-reliance and self-reflection. For me, when this majestic bird appears overhead—something he does now fairly often—I am riveted to the spot, instantly one-hundred-percent present. During these moments, my heart swells, sending an electric pulse of pleasure throughout my system, a sensation that settles fully in my hips. It's a luscious response, one I can now slip into at will by simply closing my eyes and remembering.

And then it was Sunday: ritual day—well, ritual night. At moonset we would light a fire, journey, sing, and dance. But first I'd have to make it through the day. That morning's journal once again reveals my mood. It's fun to note it was a seven day: (3+29+2009=25, 2+5=7).

Sunday, March 29, 2009
Scared. Apprehensive. Agitated.
Just glanced at the bookshelf and misread a book title as There Is No Place To Hide.
Part of me wants desperately to run and hide, but I realize I've been hiding all my life. I want to do tonight's ritual. I have to reclaim my child aspect; that I know, that I want to do. And yet a shadow of this child lives in me, and she is terrified of reliving what happened all those years ago. She has been sworn to silence.
I feel it in my throat. There, with the growling rage. I see hands too. Dark hands. Evil hands. They reach around my neck.
"Don't tell," he whispers in my ear, "ever."
And I'm about to break the silence.
"Nonsense," a part of me says. She sounds like my mother. "You have no idea what happened to you. Stop making up stories."
The next voice sounds like a jealous sister. "You're always trying to get attention with drama. Cut it out."
Part of me wants to crawl into the corner. Like a wounded dog, whimpering, licking my wounds. Please, just leave me alone. Let me just curl up in a ball. I'll be okay. Maybe, like I used to imagine as a child, Superman will come and rescue me. . . .
I'm sad. So sad.

"Then be sad," I hear from inner wisdom. "Curl up. Cry."

Oh, but I'm afraid if I start, I won't be able to stop. There is such evil in this world. If I stop to look and acknowledge, I may be washed away by a river of tears.

Yet oddly, simply admitting this brings a ray of hope to my heart. Simply saying, "Yes, I see pain," opens a door to feeling love and compassion. It's as though when I open my heart, the light of Jesus Christ shines through, and that allows me to take a deep breath and relax.

Yes, I am still scared, but I'm not alone. I see Jesus and the Magdalen.

"Yes, dear one," I hear. "We are with you. We see and support the work you are doing. You are not alone."

And then there is the voice that says, "Call him. You must call and confront him. He is directly responsible. Part of reclaiming your soul is to confront the man who is the vehicle to abuse. Whether he denies or confirms is irrelevant. You must speak up. You must allow your voice to break the silence. It is imperative. Now or later today, but the call must be made."

I did make that call. It was early afternoon as I pressed the numbers on the keypad. Ordinarily I memorize important digits. His I've always had to look up. It gives me a bit more time to shore up my inner state before diving into the precarious waters.

After the standard "Hi, how are you," I got to the point. "I need to ask you something."

"Okay," though he sounded tentative.

"Do you remember taking me to Grandpa's house when I was two or three years old, after the divorce? It was just me. Jimmy wasn't along."

"That's a long time ago. Why?"

"I believe you took me there as an offering to Grandpa. To him and a group of men that called themselves 'The Order of the Dragon.' I believe I was sexually abused that night."

"Oh, sweetheart. Your brother just recently accused me of telling him that anal sex was best. And now you say this. I don't know what to say."

After a moment's awkward silence, he continued.

"It wasn't me."

"I've had memories come back," I said. "I'm seeing things."

"I wouldn't let it bother me. It was a long time ago. Put it out of your mind and forget it."

Yep, good old fatherly advice. His words were so poignant. The "I" statement blatantly stood out, flashing neon in my mind before he continued.

"Well, I've got a Happy Meal waiting here for me, so I'm going to say good-bye now."

It's hard to say which caused my heart more sadness, his statement, "I wouldn't let it bother me," or the image of him sitting alone with his denial and cheeseburger.

On the other hand, I hung up the phone exuberant. I'd faced the first demon. I'd made the call. That in itself was a huge step.

51: Soul Retrieval

As the day drew to a close, I gathered my ceremonial arsenal: cedar and sage smudge stick to both bless and clear the space, firewood, water, drum, and—not to be forgotten—Rescue Remedy, the flower essence formula designed for calming nerves.

The drive to my friend's property itself turned out to be the first hurdle. Trying not only the ability of my non-four-wheel-drive vehicle, the steep and deeply rutted road also tested my fortitude. Thankfully, I made it, though any hopes I'd had of arriving fresh and relaxed were left back at the first pothole.

I'd imagined welcoming my guests in a calm, confident manner. We would gather in reverence, share hugs, connect to the earth, and give thanks before forming a procession to the area designated for the fire circle, each woman in deep, thoughtful prayer.

Instead, I stepped from the car to find a gaggle of nervous women chattering. Fortunately, they owned vehicles better equipped for rocky country roads, thus arriving a little less haggard, but nonetheless they all gratefully accepted my offer of Rescue Remedy. Since the drive had scared—well, nearly shaken—the piss out of me, I asked directions for the bathroom, where, after relieving myself, I shared a little one-on-self pep talk with my reflection.

"You can do this; I know you can. It's okay to be scared. You're not alone. These ladies care about you; they're all here supporting you."

When I stepped back outside to rejoin the group, I found them still gabbing excitedly amongst themselves. I so wanted to call them to attention: *Ladies, thank you for coming. I'd like to request we leave this everyday world behind for a while and enter sacred space.* However, since speaking up has never been my strong point, I simply took a deep breath as I gathered up the supplies and told myself to trust that all was perfect.

Hiking up the moderate incline with Leslie guiding the way, I too got into the conversation and recaps of the latest news. Heck, I had invited women who didn't see each other often. What did I expect?

Seven of us made the trek up the slightly damp path, the air filling our nostrils with its rich scent. It wasn't the configuration I had planned. Due to illness, one of the women had to cancel, so instead we were six females and a lone male—Leslie's cat.

When we reached the pasture and a ring of rocks, clearly the fire pit and its charred remains, we set about building a new blaze. While I helped tend the fire with wood from my own land, our four-legged participant made his way around to the guests, checking in and receiving a good rub behind the ears from each. Leslie told us he was a protector kitty, who attended all of her rituals.

With healthy flames throwing sparks into the growing darkness, five women and a feline stood in a circle while Leslie took her place at the top of the path about twenty feet away.

Feeling a bit intimidated, I looked at each of the daring friends who had come to my aid: Sage, Christine, and two women I'd gotten to know over the last few years: one from yoga class, the other from a spiritual studies group. I'd managed to arrange getting us there; what lay beyond remained a mystery.

I figured Sage would take the lead on drumming—setting a hypnotic rhythm the others would follow—plus speak the words to open and close the ceremony, but after that? Well, I trusted spirit and intuition to guide me.

"We call in the spirits of the four directions," began Sage.

I've always hated calling in the directions. I can never remember what goes with what, and the perfectionist in me hates to be wrong. I know different traditions have different systems, so there really isn't a wrong way, but still. East, south, west, north; air, fire, water, earth; yellow, red, black, white; relation spirits, nature spirits, archangels, angels, spirit teachers, guides, and of course Jesus Christ; they all got invited and invoked with gratitude and respect. That much I can say for sure. By the time the smiling-Cheshire-Cat moon slipped behind the horizon, I was ready to see what lay hidden behind my mind's thinning veil.

It's good to point out that even now, as I recall the events of that evening, I give thanks to my angels and guides for their presence. I'm also reminded to ground myself—to connect to the earth's core—and to surround my body with a protective vibration. Spiritual journeying is not to be done with a flimsy aura. Doing so creates more trouble than it solves. This is sacred work and it demands respect.

After dancing around the fire, my companions and I sat directly on the naked earth. I knew my anger needed to be released, but at first I felt self-conscious, locked in a mental debate of questioning. Could I break the stubborn silence? Then, growling softly at first, the emotion I had wrestled with for so many years burst forth.

Spewing rage into the fire, I began to wail incomprehensibly, thrashing about and pounding my fists on the earth with increasing fury. At the same time, a part of me stayed fully cognizant—a witness self—making sure I stayed a safe distance from the open flames.

With the bulk of my energy spent, I sat and stared at the mesmerizing blaze. My thoughts revolved around the scene I'd written in my journal: my trusting hand held by Daddy, as tears continued to slide down my cheeks.

"It's okay, Debra," Sage said confidently. "I'm right there with you. Tell us what you see."

I'm with my father. I'm about three. We're climbing all the steps up to Grandma and Grandpa Hawley's house. It's a lot, and I get tired before we reach the house. So my father picks me up and carries me to the front door.

"I can do it," I say, as I push myself away from him to climb the remaining flight to the living room above.

"That you, Willie?" I hear Grandma's voice from the kitchen. "They're waiting for you upstairs."

The adult me wonders, does Grandma know I'm there? Does she intentionally stay in the back of the house? Is she aware on some level of what's about to happen? Maybe she's looked the other way while cousins of mine have been brought as offerings, though I doubt my aunts would be willing to sacrifice their daughters this way.

Of course, none of that goes through the mind of the child. She's just happy to be alone with Daddy. She doesn't get to see him much since the divorce and his remarriage. Now she's the lady of the hour.

Once again my father takes my hand and we cross the living room before he helps me up the tall wooden staircase. At the top of the stairs, we stop outside the first door on the right—the same door the adult me opened at Thanksgiving over twenty years ago. But now I'm in the eyes of a toddler.

My father is knocking on the door. "Enter," I hear from inside.

Daddy bends down and I can smell the familiar scent of his drinks. The ones I pretend to taste each afternoon during the cocktail hour—it's our little game. I can feel the burn of scotch in my nose.

"It's okay, Debbie. Grandpa has a special treat for you. You go inside and be a good girl. I'm waiting out here."

The door opens to a small circle of men. I see four of them, including my grandfather to my right.

"Come here, Debbie." My grandfather reaches out for me. "We've got a game for you."

He lifts me up to his lap and sits me down.

"You have to be a good girl. And if you play our game, you'll make your Daddy very happy. You want to make your Daddy happy, right?"

I'm nodding yes, but wonder why he is taking off my dress. He also slides off my underwear. I like my underwear. Mommy tells me I'm a big girl because I wear underwear and not diapers like my baby brother.

"Now stand in the middle of the circle, Debbie. Stand there and let us all get a good look at you." I notice the men are beginning to take their clothes off too; they're undoing their belts. I've seen Daddy do this. This is part of Daddy's secret game. The one he comes to play with me at night, after Mommy is asleep. He comes to the edge of my bed and slips the sleeping dragon between the bars of my crib.

"Kiss the sleeping dragon good night," he says.

But the dragon never stays asleep. The dragon always wakes up and starts to twitch. Just like the dragons I see around me that night.

"Okay, Debbie. Now it is time for you to kiss the dragons. Go on, be a good girl. Start there." I see my grandfather is pointing to the man closest to the door who has a funny grin on his face. He's holding his dragon in his hand and says, "Come here. Kiss it."

I do as I'm told. Again and again. In turn, each man in the circle gets his dragon kissed and licked. I don't like this game. These men are rough, hitting me in the face with their hard sticks. The last man grabs my mouth and sticks the solid flesh deep into my throat.

"Here, take it," he demands as I'm choking and trying not to cry. I want to be quiet, just like I am with Daddy. I know the rules of this game.

"Stop," Grandfather says. "That's enough." And he pulls me back to himself. He picks me up and stands me on his lap. I'm looking directly into his eyes.

"Are you ready?" he asks.

I don't know what I'm supposed to be ready for, but I nod yes. Grandfather takes his finger, licks it, and smiles as he reaches down between my legs. Suddenly I feel a searing pain. My bottom screams as my knees buckle. But Grandfather has a strong hold on me. He turns me around to face the other men, then slides me down onto his stick. Nothing's ever hurt so bad. I stop feeling anything.

The grown-up me watches in horror as the child me is pinned on my grandfather. His hips are thrust forward to the edge of the chair. I'm mounted on his cock like the carved figure on the front of a ship. His trophy. There for the others to see.

And while I'm stuck there, he tells them to step forward.

"Come, pleasure yourselves some more."

Once again the men in the circle push smelly penises around my whimpering mouth. No wonder I've blocked this memory. It is truly a living hell.

"Willie!" my grandfather commands. "Now. Come in and take your place."

I'm totally lifeless at this point. The child me is gone. My body is a shell, a puppet. Do with me as you like. You can't hurt me anymore.

I continue watching as my father enters the room. He sees me there, an appendage protruding from grandfather, but he doesn't respond with alarm or attempt to rescue me. He too has been replaced. He's just another one of the men, pushing an eager dick into my face.

Sage calls my attention back to the circle.

"Debra. It's time. You must face each one of these men and demand your spirit back. It's time to refill your basket."

The words I've been speaking and the visions I've seen leave me stunned. Part of me doesn't want to accept what's been playing in my mind's eye as reality and can't believe I'm telling the others. I feel deeply shamed. I wonder why I ever agreed to this night. What can I possibly hope to gain from reliving this hell?

And yet I know I've gotten this far. I can't turn back now. I close my eyes and return to the scene from that house in the Hollywood Hills. . . .

I step into the room as the adult me. In my hands, I find a beautifully woven golden basket. I'm uncertain of what to do, though I know I am being supported by my sister allies drumming and rattling around the fire.

My three-year-old self is gone, though I know she is safe within. She's done the hardest part: providing the memory, the elusive key.

My father is the first man I turn to. He glares at me, trying to intimidate.

"No!" I state firmly, raising my hand to a stop position. "You hold no power over me. Return what you have taken. Now!"

As I speak the words, his gaze drops and he lowers his head while a sparkling orange light appears at the level of his lower belly. About the size of a basketball, it moves towards me, then, like thick syrup, flows into the outstretched basket.

Turning around, I face the man next to my grandfather. He is older, with a gray beard. I see shame and fear in his eyes.

"You have daughters of your own. How dare you come into this room and rape a child? Do you think this crime is any less of a curse on your soul? Look at me! You are a weak fool. You are haunted. You have lost your spirit to others who play off your weakness."

Stepping directly in front of him and locking my eyes on his, I continue, "Stand up and face the effects of your action. Reconcile your life. God have mercy on your soul."

And so, one by one, I confront each man present, demanding he release the energy he has taken from me before it is placed into the basket. Finally, I turn to my grandfather.

His face reveals amazement before he bows his head. Yet I detect a flicker of a smirk. As though he is thinking, "Okay, you got me this time, but I'm not finished."

> "You. Now!" *I speak firmly, with confidence.* "Return that which you have taken from me. I demand it. Return the innocence, the purity, the power of trusting love. I end this curse of connection to you once and forevermore."
>
> *With the powerful words spoken aloud, I see a spiral of blue and gold light exit my grandfather's belly, swirl around his back, come up to the top of his head, and then swoop down into the basket I hold tightly in my hands.*

Opening my eyes, I looked around the circle to the faces of my friends. All stared at me through tearful eyes glistening in the firelight.

Continuing to hold the drum beat steady, Sage spoke once again. "Now take that golden basket and all that has been returned to it. Hold it high over your head as it is blessed by all the goodness and light that is present here tonight."

I followed her instruction, lifting up my hands and the etheric container they held into the clear, dark night.

"Now open your crown chakra and pour your essence back into your being."

Ah. A tangible vibration flowed into the top of my head and down my spine before filling every cell of my body, bringing with it a sense of aliveness, wholeness, and most-important closure. Except for one small detail, that faint sense of a shadow looming on my back—in the center, behind my heart.

I wanted to whisk my hands behind me, to throw off any lingering demons, but one of my friends had come around to rub my back, and I didn't want to punch her in the face. Besides, everyone was so elated that I didn't want to rock the celebratory boat.

As I once again revisit that pivotal 1959 reality, questions race through my mind.

How did my father explain my bloodied state? Did he clean me up by himself?

No, that doesn't feel right.

So who was his accomplice, his mother?

No, there's no bodily sensation of truth in that either. My grandmother was a participant by omission. It's my step-mother, Liesl, who comes to mind.

Her first husband had been an officer in the German army during the Holocaust. So it's not a reach to believe she was well versed in the art of silence.

And what about my mother? Didn't she notice any damage when I came home from that first post-divorce overnight visit?

As a matter of fact, she did, though she never sought the root of why a perfectly potty trained three-year-old would start wetting the bed. Mom just put me back in diapers—a routine that brought deep shame until I was ten years old. That's when my new step-father's ridicule and cure—forcing me to drink large quantities of water while denying me access to the toilet—solved the behavior. It wasn't until I watched the Incest TV show, prompting me to enlist Mom in the search for clues, that I myself made the connection. And while she has never confirmed the sexual abuse, she came close by her statement, "I know your father is capable of such a thing."

As I reflect back on—and cuddle with—my precious younger self, another key is presented, passed on by my beloved dolly: Matilda. She disappeared that terrible night. For years Matilda was presumed lost, never to be seen again. But when I was about seven, Liesl made the miraculous find, returning my favorite doll with a simple, "Look who I found."

Pondering these memories and questions, Matilda is the one who steps forward to show me how she got "lost" in the first place, back when I was three.

I see Liesl tucking my beloved friend into her purse. "There," she says to my father. "We'll just tell Debbie's mother she's upset about losing her dolly."

52: A Clean Spring

Refusing to listen to the voice within that said, *Stop*, I told myself I was a savvy twenty-first century shaman who could easily balance deep inner work with out-in-the-world life requirements. And so, less than twelve hours after the soul retrieval ceremony, I climbed into my car and drove nearly two hours to a client's office, once again swept up in a busy week. A few days later, I offered myself a first glimpse of post-ritual self-reflection.

Thursday, April 2, 2009
   "You're avoiding me."
   I hear these words in my head as I ponder picking up the pen.
   "You're avoiding my wisdom, my insights, my guidance. You're running scared. Amped up on caffeine, overdoing, and avoiding the heart, avoiding the breath."
   Yes, you are right. I am running on high speed overdrive to the point of exhaustion. I'm overcommitted. If I keep myself busy enough, then I don't need to acknowledge all the voices that thought change was coming.
   Oops . . . look at the time. Gotta run.

On the weekend, I allowed myself additional time:

Saturday, April 4, 2009

Exhaustion has caught up. Could be my waking up early all week, but this feels much deeper, as though years of running have caught up with me. This is deeper; this is bone level, soul level. Pushing myself to the edge—then a little bit more. Perhaps it's me trying to outrun the devil.

And now I've stopped running. I can't do it anymore. So much on the plate, this project and that, yet right now even holding the pen seems to require a huge amount of effort.

If I recount the past eight weeks—the time I've been back from Belize and spiritual healing—it's no wonder I'm spent. Uncovering the anger; The Story of the Ass with Grandma Hawley; listening to the voices that got stirred up, awakened, each clamoring for attention. Then Esalen and more writing, more delving into the abuse and trauma, back to the roots, along with all the stories of coping, or not, as the case may be. Then last weekend, the retrieval, the confrontation, the memories. . . .

"Or story?" questions a doubting voice inside.

Reality is a tricky place. Bottom line, (sorry, no room for humor here) that was unconscionable abuse. The three-year-old child within me had no choice but to retreat, to shut down. This is not just a simple game of hide and seek, let's go see where baby Debbie is hiding.

Oh goody, found her, all bloodied and mangled. Let's toss her in the back with the rest. Call on the angels and spirit guides—they'll take care of her while we continue racing through life looking for answers.

Ouch.

No wonder I'm exhausted. I've been on a healing binge. Quick, let's push through it—get to the other side—so we can be better.

But what the fuck is better?

Am I afraid to slow down? To nurture, to listen? What will I hear if I stop and pay attention to the child?

"Thank you." Plain and simple. "Thank you."

All she wants right now is to be held. To be loved. To be safe. She is indeed grateful that I brought others to witness the atrocities she endured, and she understands that a part of me still doesn't want to believe it is true.

But that doesn't matter right now. She just wants to be held. She needs to curl up and relax—fully relax—something I've perhaps not been able to do for fifty years. That's why I feel soul exhaustion.

Part of me is uncomfortable with simply being, with not doing. And to this part I say, "It's okay." This pause will pass, and the creative flow will take up again. Yet for now, in this moment, please savor the wait, the stillness, the space between.

As I sat with the inner wisdom that flowed into my journal, actually reading the words aloud to absorb them fully, the frenzy of my life became glaringly obvious. The cycle of hiding out in drugs may have come to an end, but the workaholic and her just-a-little-more belief system remained. So—as I had done with pot and self-medicating—I took a firm stand.

It required several practice runs inside my head, but a few days later I gathered the courage to call the next client on my calendar.

"I know I'm leaving you stranded, but I've hit a wall, so I'm taking the month off."

Although disappointed, my client understood. I hung up the phone elated. For one of the first times in my career, I had put myself first. What an amazing sensation of personal empowerment, followed by a deep, full-body exhale of blissful freedom.

With renewed vibrancy, I turned my attention to writing this book, and the annual springtime garden.

Sun's up, I'd hear before my eyes had time to adjust to the morning light. *Come on, let's get those hands in the dirt!*

Part of me loves the brilliant, blue-sky mornings of spring. Another part prefers the gray, wet ones; those are the days I give myself permission to stay inside, to watch movies and eat popcorn. Once the sun comes out, the gardener starts to push.

I recognize her voice, the one who loves to rip out the dead of winter and fill its void with the yet-to-be-defined colors of summer. But with the invitation of nature came the call of habit.

Ah, it's a beautiful morning. How about a little smoke, a little inspiration before heading outside?

Oh, the offer was tempting. Especially that first "clean" spring when even writing about my old lover awakened the craving.

Just a little. It'll be fun. Come on. It's part of the springtime routine. Smoke and garden. They go together like hand and spade.

But I recognized the trap, grabbed my will power, and said, *No!*

Then I noticed something curious.

There seemed to be parts of the garden that called for me to get stoned, as though there were actual pockets of smoking energy I would pass through while I worked from bed to bed. The yearning made sense at the back porch, where I'd spent many an hour sitting and staring at the garden oasis from a contented fog. But what of the other vortices that whispered to me?

With a bit of a shock, I realized I had stepped into the vibration of spirit beings who hung out on the land, the very presence Sage and Christine had pointed out during the psychic reading a few weeks earlier.

Enticing like the old friends they thought they were, the disincarnate beings were persistent.

Come on, Debra, you'd enjoy a smoke.

Would I? I wondered. Or had I simply been feeding the desires—and addictions—of earth-bound spirits who had taken up residence? Although disturbing, the scenario explained a lot about the plethora of voices ever present in my head.

53: Tenderness

As the spring days grew in length, so too did the pages of this manuscript, accompanied by my ever-vigilant inner dialog and its quest for answers.
Can I really tell this story?
Each time I checked inside, the wisdom I attribute to my spiritual cheerleaders offered a resounding, *Yes!*
But another aspect of my tired-to-the-brain-cell psyche wondered what I hoped for, digging up these bones from the past. She questioned what good could come from reliving—not to mention writing about—my life's hell. And yet, as I gave myself permission to dive deeply, to sit with and acknowledge what presented itself on the video screen inside my head, miracles occurred. Space showed up, understanding stepped in, and most important, grace filled my previously hardened heart. But it didn't happen alone. During that time of energetic unraveling I returned to my old friends: flower essences.
For over twenty years, during times of turmoil, I had called on trusted companions like Crab Apple or Walnut, two of the thirty-eight Bach flower remedies, and I was certainly never without my trusted Rescue Remedy. But that spring—thanks to a recommendation from Rosita Arvigo in Belize—I came to discover another producer of botanical

healing support, one with a vastly expanded list of flower, plant, and herbal remedies.

Browsing the Flower Essence Society website, I felt like the proverbial kid in a candy store. Viewing blossom after blossom, I let my inner compass guide me through the plethora of vibrational tuning options.

Before long I landed on Magenta Self-Healer, a pre-blended "foundational remedy in any wellness program." Perfect. Especially since I was all about hot pink that season; not only the seeds I'd been planting for summer blooms, but my daily attire also revolved around the vibrant shade. In fact, if I could have found magenta food, I would have eaten the lively color as well. I made do with strawberries and beets.

In the past I had always relied on my intellect—and the positive or negative indications related to each remedy—to choose the ingredients for a blend. But when my new magenta spray bottle was empty, I decided to get creative for my next formula's mixture. Since I'm also a big fan of divination systems—Tarot, Runes, and Medicine Cards are just a few in my collection—I used that same select-at-random method with a deck of Bach *Affirm a Flower* cards.

After praying for guidance as to which flowers and herbs would serve me best, I picked five. I suppose I shouldn't have been surprised when the first three selections dealt with ever-increasing levels of fatigue.

From "being weary" to "struggling on" to "mental and physical exhaustion, sapped vitality with no reserve," each card revealed its diagnosis. Was it true? Part of me, the one that perseveres and pushes, said, *Nah, I can't be that tired.*

Setting the comment aside, I continued the "reading," turning up a flower for "those who have surrendered to the struggle of life." At first I didn't get it. I hadn't given up the fight, I was anything but resigned. Then it clicked. I had surrendered to the process of struggling. In some respects, I actually fed on strife.

For my final selection, I picked a card for those "quick in thought and action, who require all things be done without delay."

Combining the wisdom of the five—Hornbeam, Oak, Olive, Wild Rose, and Impatiens—I reccived their message: it's okay to slow down and rest—really rest—and allow the elusive state of serenity the time *it* needs to find me.

I knew from experience that a new formula can exacerbate symptoms, so in the weeks to come, I simply gave in and let myself sleep—many nights more than ten hours—something unheard of in my adult life.

As my rejuvenation time sank in, I continued a promise I'd made back in Belize: ongoing spiritual baths. Not only had Rosita encouraged us to take the subtle body cleansing practice home and incorporate it into our lifestyles, the Maya Spirits had assigned me a schedule, *"Nine times nine."* A fan of numerology, I took the message to mean I needed to prepare a bucket when the day added up to nine, to complete the healing process begun in Central America. For example, April 30, 2009 was a nine day (4+30+2009=2043, 2+4+3=9); in fact, that date was my last nine day, though I didn't retire the routine.

With the onset of May's warmer weather, the process of clearing my energetic field with blessed water became a pleasant experience, one I thoroughly enjoyed. Although I relished the aftereffects, convincing myself to do the spirit-care ritual inevitably touched into a host of reasons "why-not." However, I didn't let procrastination get the better of me, assigning Sunday as "bath" day, in spite of continuing reluctance from the inner brood.

Despite the cleanliness of my aura, I still experienced frequent attacks of painful ear cramping. My first memories of the intense ache came during the biker incident, back when I lived with Margie and Suzanne. I also suffered chronic earaches while married to Mark, though fortunately a diagnosis of TMJ—temporo-mandibular joint disorder—prompted me to become aware of a previously unconscious behavior: clenching my teeth. Dismissing the dentist's suggestion of braces, I instead focused on relaxing my shoulders, neck, and jaw—a practice that helped immensely.

Many years later, in the midst of a rebirthing session at Esalen, the throbbing pinch again kicked in, and with it came the clear image of a steel-toed boot, aimed at my head. That's when I made the connection between birth and forceps, the cold-metal "welcome" my body still remembers.

While I was married to Don, the ear pain started up again. Its pattern took some time to detect, but soon the correlation between a throbbing ache and listening to Don's lies was obvious. So I came to a place where I thanked the pain. For offering me a reminder to both check in regarding physical stress levels and clear any subtle interference that might be hovering in my "field"—or living under my roof.

In the spring of 2009, my friend Sage suggested another alternative, one whose results I captured in my journal.

Tuesday, May 26, 2009

"I have to be strong. I have to hold you up."

These are the words I hear as I focus on my third eye. My attention expands around to my right ear, the ear that has been cramping off and on lately. My throat is swollen as well. I'm reminded that Sage suggests I check in with the third eye to "see" what's up with the pain.

As I shift my focus back to the point between the brows, I see Christ standing before me. The brilliant golden light surrounding him fills my heart with joy. Then I feel my ear and an expansion of the energies around it as I see the little boy who spoke. He's about twelve. He's been trying for so long to hold me up. I tell him he's been doing a great job, before he continues.

"Someone has to care for you. You think you can do it yourself, but the world is a tough place. I hold you up. I love you. I care for you."

I feel resistance as I look toward the ear a second time. There's an angry voice, a hardened voice, and a tightening in my jaw.

"I don't need looking after. Leave me alone. I'm tough. I'm streetwise."

As fast as I see a glimpse of her, she's gone. . . .

It wasn't the first time I'd had children appear during morning meditation, innocent ones who opened a gateway of truth. A journal entry from a few months earlier—when I actively engaged the voices within—is especially poignant.

Sunday, December 13, 2008

What needs to be spoken today?

What aspect desires a voice?

The little girl. The lost, or lonely, little girl. She's been patient, watching the others come forth. Yet she holds back.

She is actually a keeper of many lost souls. She gathers them up and comforts those she finds wandering in the realms, which helps to explain the sense of wayward souls hanging around the house and garden. . . .

So, little girl, keeper of the selves, why are you lonely if you have all these aspects keeping you company?

Of course, even as I write the question the answer is clear. Loneliness doesn't stem from being alone. Loneliness is a symptom of not being seen for who you are; it comes from lack of recognition.

Well, I recognize you. I love you. In fact I cherish the strength of your heart. You are indeed a very strong and powerful little girl. I honor that you recognize and have gathered a small arsenal of wounded children, children who don't understand, who don't have your wisdom. Children who are waiting to be reclaimed by their . . . by their what . . . their true self, their adult selves?

"We simply ask for recognition. We simply want to be acknowledged. We carry fear, anxiety, self-doubt; and often we carry love and compassion, joy and tenderness. We carry the aspects that cannot be expressed, we carry the aspects that would cause harm; so we dive deep into the psyche, deep into the unconscious, deep into the realms that few have knowledge of, and of those that do, many are afraid.

"They think we carry disease and disruption. Yet in reality, ignoring us, believing you are whole and complete without us, is the true cause of disease, disharmony, and ultimately death.

"Physical death is different from psychological death. There are many walking dead among you. As there are their opposite or complement: those who do not possess a physical body and yet fully embrace all remaining aspects of their beings. These are who you call Masters. They are the guides who help teach and nurture those of us who have slipped beneath conscious memory.

"Oh yes, learning continues for those of us who are split off, detached, temporarily out of phase with our true nature, our personality. And as said—and as you well know—it can be a temporary disconnection.

"Ultimately all return to the light. All will be blessed with a homecoming. A reunion. A filling of the heart and psyche. A reclaiming of the soul fragments. A reweaving of the tapestry. All are good analogies; simply pick the image that is soothing to you.

"And yes, there has been a shift in your power and presence as these words have been written. This is the work of recognition, the gift of awareness. Thank you for paying attention. Thank you for listening. Thank you for honoring this path of reclamation, rebirth, and remembering. Your willingness allows those on this side to witness integration. Your process gives others hope, gives others encouragement, that they too will be recognized and cherished and loved. Thank you for allowing me to speak."

This process continues to amaze me. From hesitancy to pick up the pen, to pearls of wisdom that flow across the page. I am truly blessed and grateful for this gift. Amen and blessed be.

The entry that morning was so profound that I read it out loud, letting the words soothe my core, before making one final entry for the day.

Reading this aloud touches me deeply. Especially the line about tenderness splitting off because it wasn't safe. I can see the ten-year-old, a sweet loving child within. The one whose love was mocked by mother. Is it safe now for this vulnerable, gentle aspect to return to my conscious awareness?

Yes. Welcome, sweet child. Welcome. You are indeed loved.

Who were these children who appeared in my mind's eye? Were they aspects of me, my psyche, split off due to the trauma? Or were they hitchhikers, lost souls, simply hanging on to help out or hold up as the little boy said? It's hard to say which option brought greater uneasiness. Both seem fantastic to the logical part of my brain, the accountant self who likes things neat and orderly. She preferred to focus on numbers, computers, and client's budgets. But she was on hiatus, so the inquisitive, book reading, we'll-solve-this-mystery, self-healer aspect continued to delve.

54: Moving Into the Light

I drew comfort from the idea that healing and integration occurred both in my physical, waking consciousness and—in conjunction with my willingness to gaze within—the subtle realms. It took some of the pressure off of my brain. Maybe I didn't need to figure it all out. Yet the everyday me, the one who lived with the bombardment of inner debate, wanted answers. Who were those voices, the ones that didn't quite fit? I saw them as the square-peg—or the whatever-the-heck-wasn't-me—parts of my psyche.

For answers, I turned to my towering to-be-read book pile. Scanning the stack that offered knowledge on topics ranging from health to spirituality and from economics to sacred relationships, one title clearly jumped out and yelled, *Read Me!*

The book, *The Unquiet Dead*, had been recommended by Rosita Arvigo for advanced spiritual healing, so I'd purchased it immediately upon returning from Belize. The subtitle, *A Psychologist Treats Spirit Possession*, brought mixed results from the inner gang, especially when I reviewed the list of the ten most common signs of possession. As I ticked a mental agreement with signs one and two—"Low energy level" and "Character shifts or mood swings"—number three really grabbed my attention: "Inner voices speaking to you."

MOVING INTO THE LIGHT

Excited to see confirmation right there in black and white, I continued down the list, recognizing varying degrees of the remaining signs. I also became aware of growing anger and a clenched jaw, not to mention a prominent voice in my head stating, *This is hogwash*. As I read sign number ten—"Emotional and/or physical reactions to reading *The Unquiet Dead*"—I vowed not to listen to the familiar, doubting voice, the one who had derailed me so often in the past.

Shifting my question from "Who?" to "How do I send them packing?" I dove into Dr. Fiore's work. Engaged by her style of presenting individual "possessed" patient stories, I found it easy to neutralize any fear surrounding the topic—a reaction that crept around the edges of my psyche, most likely held by those attempting to waylay the impending eviction.

Possession itself wasn't a new concept for me. That first hitchhiker, who brought the scared Halloween-kitty shocks up my spine, had been escorted off by Jesus Christ more than twenty years ago. Yet naïvely—or perhaps in a finely honed ploy by the next generation of residents—as the years slipped past, I never bothered to consider I may have once again taken on a guest. Unless I was stoned.

When high, I didn't care. I'd swing those psychic doors open wide in a come-on-in, party's-in-Debra's-body sort of neighborhood social. It simply didn't occur to me that once the pot wore off, I might have more to clean up than stinky bong water.

While reading the variety of case studies, I actually felt comforted and began to see myself as closer to normal—certainly less in need of a padded room and soft food. However, I didn't feel safe enough to talk about the process to anyone. It was just too damned intimate. I felt ashamed. Not to mention that my diagnosis of spiritual illness remained pretty "out-there" for a lot of folks.

So once again I chose to negotiate the path of healing on my own, calling on my support team of etheric helpers and the variety of tools I had collected over the years....

Thursday, June 18, 2009

During meditation this morning, I asked for assistance to clear the energies, the haziness there on my back, from my field.

I saw a young girl of about seven years old. She had long blond hair. It felt like she'd been here a long time. Then a grandmother stepped up and said she'd been caring for the girl. I talked with them both, explaining as I have learned in the book that they are dead, that they need to cross over into the light. I know they love me and feel this is their home, but they have loved ones waiting for them on the other side.

For the little girl, I created a beautiful golden carriage. I even turned a mouse into the coachman and a lizard into her footman. She was happy with the princess theme. As she left, I agreed we'd see each other again in the spirit realm. For a flash, I saw her as her true self, a beautiful young woman, and it filled my heart with joy. Back in the carriage scene, I spotted Christ hanging onto the back of the coach, escorting her across.

Next up was the young boy. He was jealous of the time the grandmother had spent with the girl but wanted to be tough about it. Again we talked about life on the other side and what might be in store for him if he agreed to cross over, as well as who would be there to greet him.

I could tell he was beginning to consider the transition when his mother showed up. She had a powerful light around her. As she wrapped her arms around her son, she nodded a thank-you to me and they were gone.

I didn't bother to ask why these spirits had been with me or how they had died. That wasn't important. What was important was that they were moving out and moving into the light.

With the children absent, the grandma stepped over willingly, met by her exuberant husband. He looked old at first, then they both de-aged to a vibrant middle-aged couple. Again, my heart fills and tears spill down my face as I recall witnessing their loving enthusiasm for being.

Once more I focused on the body, breathing in and out of my heart chakra.

A craggy old face—a woman's—appeared before me. I know she is me, maybe me to come, maybe me from the past. Along with that recognition is an agreement to step into my wisdom and honor my knowing—my being. I ask God, Goddess, Holy Spirit, as well as the nine Maya Spirits to assist me in holding this space.

With that, it felt like a door opened behind me at the level of the left shoulder blade. Through it began passing wayward souls. Some felt like they'd been associated with people I knew, so they'd seen me before, like a young boy I first glimpsed about fifteen years ago hanging around the guy I dated at the time. About six or so entities passed through the opening, then stepped across into the light realm, the spirit realm. The last was an old, disoriented, very round woman.

I wasn't sure who she was, but she was going the opposite direction from those who had passed previously, as though she was willing to step out of me, but had no intention of stepping into the light. I also realized there was something odd about her hunched-over stature, like it was an act. So I immediately called on Jesus and Archangel Michael while surrounding her image with a golden bubble. I then plunked it out of my shoulder, placed it in a white rose, and with love and light, exploded it.

After the spirit procession, I did a thorough cleansing of my aura, using a spirit vacuum to suck up any energetic remnants from my back. I let the vacuum empty straight down my grounding tube, leaving me feeling bright, shiny, and crystal clear. Then I put up an arbor of protection roses, healthy red and white ones, being particularly mindful of my shoulder area.

It was an interesting meditation.

Thank you, God, Goddess, Holy Spirit, and nine Maya Spirits. Thank you as well to the archangels and my personal angels. I am very grateful for your presence.

So there I was, feeling light and bright and spirit-free—well, somewhat spirit-free. In dealing with the easily accessible and willing-to-move-along tenants, I'd simply pissed off the firmly entrenched energy that clung to my back, the same ache I'd been trying to brush off since Belize. Nasty and dark, this formless entity wasn't about to be cajoled into passing over into the realm of light and love.

Its thick, life-sucking goo felt ancient, as though it had been clogging my flow for a long time. I knew it as the voice of the abuser, the one who relentlessly proclaimed my unworthiness, the energy that wanted to flush puppies down the toilet or have me slide into oblivion with pot. But I didn't bite—or light up. I'd gotten a taste of personal dominion and liked it, despite its foreign nature. I recognized my next step in clearing would require assistance and once again called on Sage Runningbear and her prowess in the spirit realms. However, feeling embarrassed about my faulty personal boundaries, I kept my diagnosis of "possessed" to myself.

The following week, we met in the park: Sage, Christine, and I. Surrounded by a variety of grand old trees, I felt aligned with the Earth Herself, held in the loving grace of the grandmother spirits. My friends knew that Christ had recently appeared to me as a healing ally. They also knew the vision had left me with a sense of profound unworthiness. From this vantage point—fear of being forever shamed—the session began....

"May this healing be of the highest vibration of love and light." Sage spoke softly as crows gathered, adding their "caw" to the invocation. *"We ask that this healing be divinely guided, as we open now . . ."*

With the spiritual stage reverently set, Christine said, "I see a big ball of energy and feel it in my chest."

Sage picked up the description, "Like a big hair ball, stuck in the drain."

"This energy isn't yours," Christine continued. *"It was thrown onto you. The being that put it there is no longer alive, but the entity's duty is to stop you from living and working with your higher vibration. To stop you from working with Jesus Christ."*

Sage picked up immediately where Christine left off. "This being was attached to your grandfather and your father, as well as many others you've been in relationship with. It is targeting you."

"How long have you been targeting Debra?"

The answer passed along by Christine, "Your eighty-six most recent lifetimes," explained my soul's core exhaustion.

"And yet," she continued, *"its energy goes back to the beginning of time."*

As the women explained how the entity appeared to them—cloaked in black with only eyes staring out—the disruption on my back grew stronger, more chaotic. Wishing I could twist around and extract the turmoil, I suppressed a scream, telling myself to breathe deeply and stay focused on softening my heart.

In agreement that they needed to look deeper, my shamanic guides called for information relating to how and why this being had attached itself to me. Selecting the most prominent past life—which appeared to them as bright rings running along my life's root—they began.

"We are in the time of Jesus, before the crucifixion. You and Jesus knew each other. There is a celebration going on. This being you have the contract with is stepping forward. You and he were in relationship; you were partners.

"You are female in this lifetime, dressed in flowing attire like a belly dancer would wear, very Goddess like. You have grace and freedom with your sensuality, with your body. Your second chakra energy is very vibrant; you really worked the sexual magic. This individual has such a strong cord, such a strong hold on you from your second chakra. There's so much fear you can't be without him, can't live without him."

"When he first came forward, I asked him why he was so angry, why he wanted to prevent your affinity with Jesus. He said because he was not allowed to have the same connection with Jesus that you had, that you actually trained with him. And because, he is telling me, he had betrayed Jesus' trust. The fact that you were trusted really pissed him off."

"This being was into sorcery. He never had his own power. He took it from women, especially powerful women. He knew how much divine feminine power you had, and, through sorcery, he had control over you.

"So that's your connection with the entity from that lifetime, in your second and third chakras."

Returning to their cosmic source, Sage and Christine opened another ring, brighter than the first.

Sage spoke first. *"There's an eye with flames all around it. I don't know what it is."*

"This lifetime is when you first started working with herbs and healing people. You're showing me your little hand-made hut. People came to you for their doctoring. But there was a lot of charge around this. It wasn't okay for anyone to have power, let alone a woman."

"Now I understand what I'm looking at. This is actually the entity itself, but it did not have a host this particular lifetime. It kind of reminds me of Oz—all knowing, all seeing—keeping an eye on you. It worked through other people, but it didn't have enough of a following to manifest a body. It always watched, manipulated those around you. So you had to be very secretive about your healing work. People had to come to you in the middle of the night. You were known as the old woman who lived up on the hill. No one really knew much about you; they just knew you had a capacity to heal.

"So you had to hide the power of your fifth and sixth chakras in that lifetime."

After explaining we had to look at these lifetimes to get a sense of how my agreements with the entity were started, Sage and Christine returned to my life rings one last time.

"This one is the strongest of all the rings. This is when Jesus was crucified. You felt that you couldn't survive without him. And he had promised to teach you more, so there is this huge feeling of unfinished business between the two of you.

"You almost wanted to scream at him and say, 'How could you leave me, how could you not help me to remember?' There is so much anger, and yet there is also guilt, questioning, 'Why would I be angry with my messiah?'"

"There is a feeling of betrayal."

"You have to go back to that portion of that lifetime and rewrite your contract with him. I'm hearing that it's not necessarily a curse that you put on yourself, as much as you told yourself, 'If he's going to abandon me, then I'm going to abandon him. I obviously am not worthy, so I give up.'"

After a momentary silence, Sage spoke again.

"It goes even deeper. I need to invite the Christ force into this sacred circle, because this has to do with an agreement the two of you had from before the time he came into the Earth plane as Christ."

With this statement, the crows—previously silent as though they too were hanging on every word—broke into excited chatter.

After graciously invoking the electric blue, loving presence of Christ, Sage asked for assistance in helping us to go back, to reveal the original agreement, the one I had made with the dark entity.

"It makes sense that this goes deeper," Christine clarified. "Christ has shown me an image of you and he growing up together as children."

"We need to go back—to the origins of time." *Sage drew a deep breath before continuing.*

"He's telling me he was a winged one and that you were his brother back at the beginning. You were his younger brother and he loved you dearly. You had a very gentle, kind nature, almost like the essence of sweet pea or lilac.

"We're talking about being in existence before there were oceans. It's hard to explain in earthly terms." *Sage paused.* "There was light and there was darkness, and then there was the abyss. There were the Pleiades and there were the stars, the stars and galaxies and planets. We're talking about Creation, the time of the Gods and Goddesses . . . all overseen by the Winged Ones. This is the place we need to work."

The rational portion of my brain, the accountant who lives in the world of standards and rules, treads cautiously as I recall these visions of soaring through universes. *Really?* she questions. *Come on now.*

Yes, reasons a core knowing within me, *Come on. Trust in realms beyond your five senses. Believe in what you see within your mind's eye. Explore dimensions outside your current form of skin and bones.*

Traveling in a manner that can only be understood through experience, I continued my inward—or was it outward—journey, effortlessly connecting with and transforming into my original form: my winged self. As that essential being, accompanied by a fellow winged one, I flew to a familiar, majestic world of spiritual beings. Although Sage continued to speak of what appeared before us, I too knew the way: I had explored this land of The Masters before.

After I stopped at a purification pool to cleanse and prepare for entrance to the sacred temple, my companion and I approached the temple guard, an extremely tall, muscular, loving being.

His words, "We've been waiting," rang directly in my mind as he allowed our passage.

Towering walls of white marble emanating a soft golden light drew us deeper into the noble structure and then down a grand hallway lined with images of ascended Masters, some of whom I recognized, such as Merlin and Kwan Yin.

At the end of the hallway, we turned right, stopping at the entrance to an immense room; I knew we had reached the Council chambers, our destination.

As we entered the space—furnished with a massive, round table surrounded by stately chairs—I felt a combination of excitement and trepidation. In this etheric realm, I convened with my sacred council—the group of twelve I call the Council of Elders. I'd met them once before, nearly twenty years earlier.

At our first meeting, my primary male guide expressed annoyance over my method of spiritual travel—drugs—and seemed reluctant to work with me. However, he acquiesced after his female equivalent compassionately argued, "Yes, but she's here, so let's work with her."

That day in the park, with my friends acting as skillful guides into the realms of Creation, I was respectfully welcomed. . . .

"This is your sacred council; they have known you for hundreds of lifetimes. They love you beyond human capacity . . . Notice on the table in front of you is a book—your book. I'd like you to open it, to read your sacred agreement."

At first I was reluctant, afraid of what I would see there; yet Sage calmly encouraged me, asking me where I felt the essence of the words within my body.

"I feel it in my heart," I said softly. "Love. Believe. Trust in your heart, your soul's agreements. Let go of the darkness."

"So that is your agreement with the highest loving vibration. It is on one side of the page. On the other side is the agreement they want you to face. Can you see writing?"

"I see an image, a padlock. And I feel it up around my right ear, an old, black padlock."

"So what your sacred council would like, with your permission, is to assist you in clearing this agreement that you have held for many, many lifetimes."

"Yes, thank you," I said.

"Notice to your right, a dim light has come into the room. Notice that this light is starting to take on form. Your council would like to remind you that they are there, that they are very, very strong and very powerful, and they will not allow anything to harm you. They will not allow any level of fear to penetrate into your space.

"Your council would like you to ask this entity: What do you want, what do you want from me?"

Pain in my physical body, a throbbing sensation in my back, distracted me, yet I heard and repeated the entity's clear answer, "Your soul."

"Why does it think it can have your soul?" Sage asked. "And when did this agreement take place?"

"It says I gave it to him. In exchange for leaving someone else alone."

"Is this someone else your winged brother, the one who sits next to you?"

I nodded a silent yes.

Although I was—and continue to be—reluctant to speak aloud the scene which unfolded before me, it appeared clearly. I had stepped into the contract—was tricked into the agreement—to protect my beloved brother. Take me instead: an archetypal story line.

Stating this vision as truth once again prompts the disbeliever within who treads lightly with such proclamations. She believes it is blasphemous to claim a relationship with so pure a being. And yet, to not honor this knowledge is an act of betrayal, both toward myself, and my beloved winged brother. From a place of deep peace, and a heart overflowing with loving grace, I return to the story in the park. . . .

Sage spoke the instructions clearly. "Tell the entity you are ready to end this agreement, that it no longer serves your purpose. Tell it whatever is in your heart, even if it means having forceful, angry words; even if it means bringing it up from the pit of your stomach. Just let it out."

After a deep sigh, I meekly said, "Leave me alone." Gathering force, I continued, "Get out of my space . . . I was wrong to believe you . . . You tricked me . . . Get out! . . . I don't deserve you . . . or any of the bad things that have happened . . . I'm not a bad person . . . I'm not broken."

For a moment no one spoke. I choked on a sob.

"Next," Sage said, "I'd like you to gather all these feelings . . . place your hands over your heart and gather all the guilt, all the negativity, all the pain, all the hurt, all the anger, all the resentment; I want you to gather it up, pull it up with your hands . . . from anywhere it lives in your body."

It took a while, but I cleared both front and back—energy from all lifetimes—and made it into a ball. At first this container was huge, as large as the park in which we sat, but somehow, in the manner of spiritual healing, it was easily compacted down to a very dense form that I returned to the entity.

"I give this ball back to you. It was never mine."

Although I'd been crying heavily, my words were calm, strong, and definite. With that release, I was given an opportunity to rewrite my sacred contract. It went something like this:

"From this day forward, I have ended any and all agreements with this entity. On this day, I return to my original essence: a winged one. I am worthy of the sacred love of my council. I am worthy of the love from all that is good, from what is above and below and all around me."

With my revised contract signed and witnessed, it came time to release the being itself. For this critical step, Sage called on the archangels, "Raphael, Uriel, Michael..."

Before I returned to everyday reality, each of my council members offered a gift: an energetic attunement with their unique vibration and the reminder I could reconnect with them at any time.

And so it was. A fresh start unlike anything I could have imagined—even *with* all my wild dreams.

55: First Communion

The world appeared lighter—to both my eyes and my heart—in the days following my healing session with Sage and Christine. Even the color of summer's dry vegetation, seen nightly as my dog and I walked, took on a fresh aliveness, a glowing brilliance: I saw creation through the eyes of Grace.

My life's activity also picked up, bringing new clients, financial freedom, and new acquaintances who led to opportune conversations. When it felt appropriate to do so, I'd mention this ever-growing manuscript—and its working title *Reclaiming the Sacred Whore*. A frequent response, "Oh, you have to read . . . ," often involved Mary Magdalen.

I'd already purchased several books about the controversial biblical figure and had even started reading one of them, but its scholarly approach left me slightly bored. Before long, it was moved to the come-back-to-someday pile. Yet her name continued to show up.

"I found a church dedicated to Mary Magdalen," a friend, also named Mary, said into the phone. "I was guided by Spirit. 'Turn here; now turn here.' We should meet there and meditate."

After hanging up, I decided to do a Google search for the church; however, instead of finding the Marin county house of worship, I turned up the website for a sanctuary further south, in Mountain View. As inner guidance so often directs, I heard a succinct, *Read!*

And read I did, about the Church of Gnosis and its founder Rosamonde Miller. The eloquent text, especially the pages about the Shrine of Mary Magdalen, began to quench a thirst I hadn't previously recognized. Even the founder's name, Rosamonde—same as my dear sweet maternal Grandma—filled my heart with joy.

The link, *Admission to the holy order of Mary Magdalen,* confirmed my hunch that I had stumbled onto something life altering:

"On the day we celebrate the Feast of Miriam of Magdala, which we always do on the Sunday closest to the 22nd of July, I usually admit into the communion of the tradition of M.M. those that feel a strong resonance with the feminine principle in any of the many names by which she has been perceived, especially that of Mary Magdalen."

Checking the calendar, I realized the annual celebration would occur in four days. Destiny had once again presented itself via the Internet. After calculating the time it would require to make the trip—three hours each way—I decided to add a night of fun in San Francisco and a luxury hotel to my adventure.

With preparations in place, my mind continued to ponder my relationship with the Magdalen—and her life with Jesus. Most claim the stories of her being a prostitute are false, and that makes me sad. I like the idea of having someone schooled in the ways of sacred prostitution as my divine guide. It validates my existence—or at least my earlier career choice—though I recognize being schooled in the ways of sexual magic and becoming a prostitute are not mutually inclusive. That belief is a remnant from growing up in this unseeing society.

However, the fact remains: I was a prostitute, and I feel an affinity—a kinship if you will—with those who have also called themselves "Ho."

Nearly six years ago I heard the call. Clear inner guidance that first said, *Sell the condo and move back north.* The detailed advice—dates, dollar amounts, all laid out—all came to fruition.

The next part of the message was equally clear: *You're to work with prostitutes.*

Okay, having dabbled in the world of sex workers, I could see the connection, but from what vantage point did I have anything to offer? I'm not a "get-out-or-you'll-be-doomed" believer: "Repent your sins, return to your Mamas and Daddies." I'm not a health-care professional either, and prevention of spreading disease isn't my forte; I've got herpes and occasionally deal with my own outbreaks. Tips on how to be a better lover? Hardly. I've been living like a celibate monk these last eight years. Even my faithful vibrator has grown dusty under the bed. So what then?

To continue the inquiry, I return to my journal.

Saturday, July 18, 2009
... The voice inside is loud and clear.

"It is sacredness. That you know. Perhaps there haven't been many conscious encounters of this lifetime, but you carry this ancient wisdom in your blood, in your bones, in your very cellular makeup.

"As horrendous as your path has been, you carry the light to hold it. You carry the light that dispels darkness and confusion, pain and suffering.

"You need only pray. You need only look. Gently.

"Ask your heart to remember. Allow your soul to turn unto itself. You are a child of the light. You have been trained in the ancient mystery schools of Isis herself. Trust your bones. Guidance you hear is sacred. Those whose lives you touch are blessed if you let them be. Stop holding back.

"You are being called once again. The time is here. Do not focus on what cannot be done, on who cannot be shown. And do not focus on fear, for that is not what you wish to manifest, is it?

"Instead, trust that those who read these words do so because they too are being called. They too are being asked to reclaim their light. To shed, to heal, to focus on the heart and its vast capacity for grace.

"Gaze into the eyes of the Master, whatever the body may look like. The form is irrelevant. The Christ light can be seen everywhere, if you are willing to look, to see.

"Ask to be guided to those who also hold the light, those who also remember the sacred sight. They will recognize you, as they always have, as they always will. The time has come. Your birth is imminent. Celebrate. Dance. Sing praises to the Divine. Fill your heart with joy and wonder. And in the quiet stillness, give thanks."

As I sit with the stillness, I recognize song lyrics in my head, "I don't know how to love him..." from Jesus Christ Superstar.

And it fits. I don't know how to love Him.

Part of me loves him as a man, a flesh-and-blood man, to which I hear, "Harlot, whore, how dare you look upon the Master in this way!"

What I hear next takes me by surprise.

"Stop. Do not allow these hurtful, biting words to fill your mind."

I know at once I clearly hear the voice of Jesus within. And yet I stop their flow. I question, doubt. Not their source, for that I know is pure. What I doubt is my ability to hear, to hold, to deserve the level of love and one-hundred-percent acceptance I am about to receive.

Inside, logically, I know this has been given. I feel it. But to hear the words spoken aloud, from that I still shy away. I question my ability to respond. No, I question my willingness to respond. To dive so deeply into the heart of my being, that communion with the Christ light—co-union with the Christ light—well... that type of connection is huge. It's paramount. And at its core, it is what this—life, living, being, doing, receiving, giving, all of it—is about. It's my core. It's my calling. It's my ideal.

With that, I again come to the lyrics in my head, "I don't know how to love him..."

"Yes, you do. Look into my eyes and remember. Allow the love of our companionship to flow over and through you. Allow it to wash away any talk of sin or sinner, as well as any foolishness about saint. Release the judgments, the labels, the highs, the lows...."

"Stop. Be. Become as one. Hold this knowing."

Morning journaling sessions such as this leave me humbled—grateful beyond words. I feel their imprint in my body as an expansive resonance of purity.

The next day, the morning of my solo visit to the Church of Gnosis, my journal entry is brief....

Sunday, July 19, 2009 Mountain View, California

These two phrases rang in my head during meditation:

I am loved. I am holy.

These simple phrases—mantras—helped to offset my nervous energy, my uncertainty about attending the church services. This apprehension is also evident in a dream I noted:

I'm in a training class with a dozen or so other women. Several times I realized I was naked and they weren't, and I felt ashamed. I kept going to my room to get dressed, only to end up naked again. The last time I felt frustrated and couldn't find the right thing to wear; I ended up with a bright yellow flowered print dress over a turquoise garment. I was still annoyed as I rejoined the group, feeling overdressed.

Our assignment was to learn a new dance step. I watched the choreographed moves, only to get frustrated again. I wanted to do my own dance. Irritated with the male teacher's routine, I went back to my room to pack and sneak out of the class, as the instructor had warned some people might do. I felt conflicted: pleased I was taking care of myself but ashamed of quitting.

I arrived about fifteen minutes early to the small, unassuming church tucked into a block otherwise filled with apartments. A line had already formed, and as we slowly made our way up the brick walkway, I overheard some women in front of me laugh over the idea that their sanctuary was becoming a mega-church.

Once inside the building, I felt transported, as though I had stepped into a temple somewhere in the Middle East, or perhaps Egypt. Amazingly intricate and colorfully designed silks—fabrics I envisioned wrapping around myself in flowing waves—hung draped from the ceiling. Abundant fresh flowers, candles, and various artifacts surrounded the dark wood pulpit. Resisting the urge to explore the setting more closely, I settled into one of the simple folding chairs to read the service literature.

A hum of excited chatter filled the room as at least a hundred women, men, and children took the remaining seats and more that were quickly added to the back of the room.

Silence and a palpable sense of respect fell over the congregation as Rosamonde Miller, wearing a deep blue robe, began the service. A charismatic leader, and beautiful in every sense of the word, she welcomed those who had gathered, before she began a typical Sunday service.

Fascinated by every word she spoke—both the message of the sermon and her distinct French accent—I was surprised how quickly the time passed.

Although I had reviewed the *Ritual of the Bridal Chamber: The Gnostic Mystery of the Eucharist* program, still I stumbled over its call and response style. Often lost as to what I should be saying and glancing at my neighbors to see what page I was supposed to be on, I remained open to the experience. Logistics aside, I was enraptured. When it came time to take holy communion and ask for admittance into the holy order of Mary Magdalen—both optional aspects of the service—I stood and joined the queue without giving it a second thought. With my bare feet on the church's wooden floor—I wanted to be as close to the earth as possible—I sang the repeating lyrics of a lively chant while diligently watching the action at the pulpit. Heaven forbid I should make a mistake.

Taking the sacrament passed in an instant. Bread, wine—no, thank you; grape juice, please. Then kneeling before Rosamonde. After I stated my name, she placed her veil over my head and whispered in my ear—what she said remains a mystery. As I stood, allowing the next supplicant to take my place, a bit of honey was dripped on the back of my right hand. Bringing it to my lips, I savored its sweetness as I walked—glided—back to my seat.

A few minutes later, as my mind replayed all that had occurred, it dawned on me—I had taken my first communion.

56: Welcome Home

As I drove from the church, still relishing all that had just transpired, She spoke to me: "You have caused harm to your men."

My first response was habitual. "Yes, but I had good reason." Ouch. My body, previously jubilant, contracted. Knowing that reason will always have an answer, debate, or rebuttal, I caught myself and chose a new approach.

"Yes, I have. And for that I ask atonement. My ways have been hurtful. As your daughter, as your sister, I have sinned. I have caused pain and for that I am sorry."

After settling in at home, I picked up the dialogue with Mary Magdalen in my journal.

July 19, 2009 9 P.M.

I ask your assistance, oh, great lady of the light. I have known you in so many lifetimes. I once again take up the path. I am once again willing to listen, to remember, to dance, to dive deeply into the void, the mystery. Naked I come. And naked I shall go. Bare of beliefs, following the light of my heart. And yes, if it is your will, your way . . .

Ah, thank you, for I began to put you above me. I acknowledge this is a path of balance, of equality.

"Each must go within and find her own way of the light. Each has a unique vibration, frequency, tone. It would be a sin to follow another's footsteps as your own. Do not ask permission to be. Ask for guidance: to see, to hear, to remember, to honor, to know—your song, your step, your dance.

"It is not time for you to lead others to your song, but time for you to be an example of listening, of communing, of caring for self within the greater good; the Greatest Good. The Holy I AM. For you are. We are. Thus sacred sisterhood. Thus sacred brotherhood. The way of the Christ union, Logos and Sophia as spoken today. Alpha and Omega, coming together as one. Not opposites. A blending, a being, a welcoming home. To be what Is. What has always been.

"Rejoice. We rejoice with you. Hear the angel's trumpets. They sound in celebration of you. Welcome home, dear sweet Debra. Take up your rightful place in Heaven, as your feet still grace the earth with your presence. Allow the Light, the Love, the Grace of Heaven to flow through you. Express these things here on the Earth plane. This planet needs your loving support. She feeds on the loving vibrations that you—and millions who too are remembering their song—are able to impart to her. Remember, and each step is blessed. Remember, and each step a curse is forgiven. Bless, and be blessed. Honor, and be honored. Care, and be cared for—care-full.

"Yes, your time has come. Reveal yourself, sacred sister. Reveal your true ways. Hear your call to arms . . . Yes, two arms that reach out and hold, and caress, and touch gently.

"Kind eyes, gentle heart, sweet touch. Or mix them up as you will. Kind touch, sweet heart, and gentle eyes. Each offers you a world of gems: the diamonds, rubies, and sapphires of your soul, your being.

"Sisters are remembering. Sisters are coming to light. They, as you, are awakening, some from a deep slumber. Awakening, remembering, re-joy-ening; as well as rejoining, finding each other. The vibrations magnetize, harmonize.

"Simply be. Know. Believe."

As I once again allow these words to fill my being, I drink deeply of their wisdom. A single tear runs down my cheek. I recognize the sacred vessel. I am the Sacred Whore *and* the Blessed Virgin. This I honor and hold.

Amen and blessed be.

Epilogue

In a matter-of-fact tone, my brother relayed the news: "Bill's dead. He fell and hit his head."

After listening to Jim's voice mail message—and unwitting rhyme regarding the death of our father—I found myself hyper-aware of two things: the crisp, cold, Virginia night air passing in and out of my nostrils and my feet firmly planted on the driveway's solid, though bumpy, black asphalt. In disbelief—of both the content and the delivery method—I stood in the dimly lit parking lot of the Monroe Institute, letting the words sink in.

Amazingly calm, I savored the moment, and its stillness. Several minutes passed before I felt the need for a sympathetic conversation. I tried my brother first, but continued the game of phone tag. My half-sister didn't pick up either. Next came my best friend; again, voice mail. I considered my mother. However, after a series of frontal-lobe strokes, her brain resets and loops back on any conversation every fifteen to twenty seconds, so she could offer little in the form of solace.

At the end of my short list of those I felt comfortable reaching out to, I stepped back inside the main building of the Monroe Institute, knowing exactly who to find: Karen Malik, my workshop leader. I didn't need to explain my desire for a hug and fell into her loving arms. Once wrapped in her warm and nurturing embrace, I felt my tears break free, a reaction that surprised me. Karen didn't interrupt my sobs or offer any trite words after I told her the news. She knew the history my father and I had shared. She had been with me—holding that same space of unwavering compassion—when the father-grandfather-abuse connection first cracked through my consciousness, back in 1992 during my second Monroe workshop.

I had planned to call my father when I got back from the October 2010 visit to Virginia, to confront him about avoiding my calls, as he had been doing since summer. Starting in July, he had taken on the habit of passing information to me through his sister, Aunt Pat, whom I had just met.

Growing up, I knew I had two aunts, my father's older and younger sisters. I met Aunt Franny—once—as a child, on one of those court-enforced father weekends, but I have little memory of her. She's the aunt who died young, of uterine cancer. My other aunt escaped to Alaska, right about the time I was born, and as far as I knew, didn't stay in touch. So the paternal side of my family tree contained a large, gaping hole.

Fast-forward to the twenty-first century. Occasionally, during check-in phone calls, my father would mention his younger sister—that's how I found out she had moved to a small town in Oregon. He even passed along her address and phone number but never offered to initiate contact. So while I was curious to meet her, how to go about doing so remained a mystery.

As the reality of my abusive roots became clear, I'd suspected the aunt-I-didn't-know could offer additional keys, and perhaps even be willing to share her own Hawley secrets. However, any way I imagined it, I couldn't find a way to ask my most insistent question, *Can we talk about incest?* So I was duly surprised when, in June 2010, I received a letter bearing my aunt's return address.

In her neat and legible script, Aunt Pat explained that when my father had taken a spill and ended up in the hospital, ". . . he tried to call you, but your number had been disconnected. He thought I would have it, but I've never had that or your address."

EPILOGUE

My father's confusion didn't surprise me. The last time I'd spoken to him, during that same hospital stay, we'd been exchanging our routine surface banter for several minutes when he asked, "Who am I talking to?" So the point of Aunt Pat's letter—to contact my father—was moot. However, her closing statement, "I really miss being a proper aunt to you . . ." opened a door I excitedly walked through.

The first time we spoke, I found myself relaxed and talkative, downright gregarious, as we crammed more than fifty years of catching up into a two-hour phone call. How bizarre to suddenly have a relative who, unlike my parents, was fully cognizant. I immediately fell in love with her spunky personality. The fact that we shared a similar outlook regarding my father—I love him, but don't like him—added to our instantaneous bond.

Within three weeks of receiving her letter, I sat in the dining room of my one-and-only aunt (my mother has no siblings), looking at old family pictures. Not only did I gain a vibrantly alive relative, her penchant for chronicling the family history opened a world I had never dreamt of seeing.

Spread out before me, page after page of images looked back: Grandma and Grandpa as young adults, the one-by-one addition of Aunt Franny, my father, and Aunt Pat, and eventually, as the years progressed, Pat's multiple generations of offspring. The three-ring binder also contained my aunt's life story interspersed between the photos. She'd created the memento for her children, six of them, not to mention her grandkids and ever-growing number of great-grandkids. I was thrilled when she gave me a copy.

Later that afternoon, satiated with family history, we moved into current day, visiting with a couple of my cousins, Pam and Judy, who came by to meet me. While Aunt Pat prepared dinner—refusing help—the girls and I stayed seated around the dining room table and continued to chat. Before long we realized we had similar interests in books, both authors and topics such as spirituality and healing.

In a bold move—no one had mentioned the topic of sexual abuse—I pulled out a magazine containing an article I'd written: *Musings from a Visit with Dear Ol' Dad*. In it I candidly share my father's—their uncle's—pivotal admission, "I know my father had sex with my sisters, though Pat would never admit it," a statement clearly involving their mother. Suggesting they might want to simply take the magazine and read my contribution at another time, I passed the periodical to Pam, the oldest.

After a satisfying dinner—Aunt Pat is also a great cook—I stepped outside to allow my dog some leg-stretching time. We'd just finished a lap up and down the modular-home-lined street, when Pam joined us.

"I read your article," she shared excitedly. "We've got a lot in common. Though my mother likes to deny it, sexual dysfunction runs wild in this family."

If you've not been abused, it may be hard to understand her enthusiasm, and mine in return. Knowing I'd found another member of "the club" added to our bonding, especially since I believe our wounding traces back to the same individual: Grandpa. Pam and I didn't go into more details that night, though we talk often, continuing to form a lasting connection.

Sensing I would need some space to sort through the myriad of emotions regarding my visit—fortunately, all were positive—I'd made arrangements to stay elsewhere. Promising I would return for lunch before driving home, I said a contented "good night" to my family.

A couple of days later, I returned to Aunt Pat's. While the two of us enjoyed a meal of tuna salad and garlic bread, the family history lesson continued.

Enthralled, I listened to stories about my father: his drunkenness, his fist-fights with Grandpa, and how Franny hated him. Pat also talked about how much he loved their mother, and how Grandma was the primary reason he continued to visit their Hollywood Hills home as an adult.

Caught up in the flow of information, my aunt switched to her own childhood. Not daring to break her momentum with any questions, I sat at the edge of my mental seat, hoping the dam surrounding the topic of sexual abuse would burst.

It did.

With heartbreaking transparency.

EPILOGUE

I'm not comfortable revealing my aunt's story. However, she shared enough with me to validate everything I most feared—and needed to hear.

Still somewhat in shock over my father's death, I settled into my window seat for the flight from Virginia to California and the unpleasant—and unexpected—process of dealing with his "estate." Twelve hours had passed since I'd heard the news, and sleep hadn't come easily.

The pilot's voice partially interrupted my daze as he welcomed us to his vessel and passed along particulars regarding our travel. "Our flight time today is four hours and forty-four minutes."

Nice, I thought, pleased with the repetitive number.

"And we'll be landing at 4:44 p.m."

Taking comfort in the doubly stressed digit, I made a mental note to look up the meaning of multiple fours when I got home. The following afternoon—reminded by the clock and its display of 4:44—I pulled out the book *Healing with the Angels* by Doreen Virtue. Turning to the section titled *Number Sequences from the Angels*, I read its text:

"**444**—The angels are surrounding you now, reassuring you of their love and help. Don't worry, because the angels' help is nearby."

The next day, as I checked into a Sheraton hotel near my father's empty apartment, I smiled broadly when the desk clerk announced, "You'll be staying in room 444."

Of course.

Thankful that the angels were with me, I kept my heart open as my brother—whom I'd picked up at the airport on the way down—and I combined forces to dissect the remains of our father's lifetime. A task made easier by the fact he had been on the verge of moving into an assisted living home, and, as a result, had already made arrangements with his current apartment manager to clear away anything he didn't take with him.

When we pushed open the front door, the stench of old man combined with dirty cat box pushed back—hard. Afraid of letting the feline escape, Jim and I took a quick inhale of "fresh" San Fernando Valley air before stepping inside. Unfortunately, throwing open the windows did little to help.

While my brother picked through the collection of electronics packed into multiple desks and bookshelves in the living room, I focused on finding Chessie. A sweet little kitty, she came out willingly, snuggled up in my arms and purred gratefully—until my brother moved in with the cat carrier. A few frantic seconds—and puncture wounds—later, she was safely contained and ready for transport to her new home with an elderly woman friend of my father's. I considered bringing her back with me, but decided against disturbing my nineteen-year-old male's sole-kitty status.

With the cat taken care of, I moved on to the bedroom. Reminding myself to stay grounded, I offered a prayer of gratitude to my unseen guardians before accessing the situation and opening the first drawer. Between two dressers and two nightstands—which reminded me of the French Provincial furniture my step-father had selected for me—there were a total of sixteen potential hazards. Yes, I could have allowed my brother to sort through the minefield, but I didn't; I stepped into protective-big-sister role. I also felt the need for closure.

I didn't make the connection at the time, but now it becomes evident: by clearing out my father's personal belongings, I hoped to also dispense with any lingering sexual demons. It had been sixteen months since I'd rewritten my life's contract that day in the park with Sage and Christine. And during that time, primarily spent crafting this book, I thrived. Stepping into my father's bedroom consciously, with an open heart, was another step in owning and honoring my power—as well as my healing.

A few of the drawers contained typical items of clothing like socks and underwear, but the bulk of the storage contained X-rated videos. Though I have to commend my father on his organization—he kept the adult content separate from his small collection of family-friendly titles. In a bold move, I packed up all the pornos and loaded them into my car, feeling the need to keep my father's sexual world away from the apartment manager and his cleaning crew. *Besides*, I thought, *maybe I can get some money for them.*

EPILOGUE

I also didn't want strangers going through my father's clothing, so I folded—neatly—all the hanging items. Saying a prayer of blessing and release for each, I piled up shirts, the majority of them plaid; slacks; and an occasional jacket to donate to Goodwill on my way out of town.

What I didn't donate or put into my car were the contents of his nightstand. That drawer-of-fun—at least to my father—went straight to the dumpsters out back, along with the travel case I found in the bathroom cabinet, similarly outfitted for to-go pleasure. Thankfully, I found latex gloves too, so I didn't have to actually touch any of his "toys."

I made a couple of calls about finding a good home for his cherished musical instrument, but wasn't successful, so lacking both room in my house and interest in making any, I left it for the apartment manager.

By midday Saturday—we'd started early Friday morning—my brother and I had reached the end of our olfactory tolerance. We'd also reached our be-nice-to-each-other limit, slipping into well-etched childhood roles.

"Stop telling me what to do!" Jim yelled.

"You can't leave the back gate open like that," I countered with building frustration. "Either move his car or close the gate."

With communications declining rapidly from that point forward, we managed to close up the apartment, pass along the keys, and get on the road—me in my car with my brother following behind in our father's Ford Focus.

Ordinarily the drive from L.A. to my house takes seven efficient hours—gas, pee, tea, go. However, having my little brother in tow added an excruciating number of pit-stops. Thankfully, one of them was the Sacramento airport—my brother's point of departure and a somewhat easy spot for me to retrieve the car. With our fury from earlier in the day spent, we managed a hug before saying good-bye.

Relieved I no longer had to keep my eye on the rear-view mirror, I drove the final hundred miles in record time. Still, it was near midnight when I pulled onto my driveway.

Exhausted from out-of-control emotions, not to mention a whirlwind week of travel that had started nine days earlier with a red-eye flight to Virginia, I questioned my plan to be back in the car early the next morning.

Sleep on it, my inner voice encouraged, *but remember, this date will only happen once.* "This date" being October 10, 2010; the ultimate tribute to another of my favorite numbers—ten.

I'd been excited about celebrating the day for months and had planned an "over-the-mountain" journey to the *Isis Oasis Sanctuary* in Geyserville. I first learned of the relatively local goddess-centric temple in July of 2010, when I returned to Mountain View to attend the Feast of Miriam celebration for a second time.

At 7 a.m. on Sunday morning, rejecting the desire to roll over, I pushed myself to a sitting position. A simple *Go* rang clearly through my still foggy head. Isis Oasis had promised a "most auspicious" Sunday mass for 10/10/10, in combination with their annual gathering of sacred priestesses, priests, and supportive onlookers, and I wasn't going to let my father's death derail my worship. However, before leaving, I lit a seven-day candle to honor his life and placed it on my altar. In front of the candle, I put two of my father's personal effects, both recovered from the county morgue.

The first item, a small, well-worn leather change purse, folds down into a twisted octagonal design. It reminds me of his—and my—love of puzzles. The second item, the only photograph from his wallet, is of him and his beloved mother, taken near the time of her death.

Despite my reluctance to get back in the car, the drive went by quickly, allowing me time to stretch my legs before services began. As I worked my way up and down paths that cut through the rugged hillside, I peeked at the sanctuary's collection of exotic cats and birds. My eyes filled with tears as I felt a tender moment toward my father, who had owned and lovingly cared for both.

Once comfortably seated in the temple—it looked more like an old theater, complete with velvet-covered chairs—I reviewed the program, recognizing the call-and-response-style Eucharist. As the steady beat of a single drum called the congregation to attention, several women dressed in flowing white garments took their places on the stage. After a welcome that included several devotional songs, the goddesses were invoked. There were four total: Sophia, Isis, Mary Magdalen, and Mother Mary.

EPILOGUE

I felt reverence and joy as the beloved Magdalen's presence was requested, then acknowledged. However, with the invocation to Mother Mary, I felt uncomfortable, estranged, a sensation I attributed to lingering guilt regarding my own mothering abilities.

Later in the ceremony—after singing a repetitive chant to the point of being in a light trance—I offered a simple prayer for my father's crossing.

"May you be free. May you be at peace."

That's when I saw them, my father and his mother, arm in arm. Behind them stood Mother Mary, blessing not only them, but me.

Acknowledgments

Birthing this book has been an amazing journey, helped along by many individuals.

First up: Ann Randolph and the Tight Circle. Gathered in Esalen's "Big House," I first wrote and then spoke the secrets that exploded into this book. It was truly a Fourth of July celebration of independence. As my life stories continued to pour forth, Ann listened, gently encouraging with her famous phrase, "I'd like to know more about . . ." Ann, I treasure you and your passion, curiosity, and unwavering acceptance of my life's eccentricities.

Next I'd like to acknowledge Lynda Beth Unkeless, a trusted member of the Tight Circle, who courageously read my first draft, then gently pointed out that I might want to consider a rewrite.

For ongoing support, I wish to thank the members of the Lower Lake Writers Group. This collection of authors as diverse as their genres listened and encouraged—even when I brought "red flag" content. Month after month you offered invaluable literary guidance and, over time, friendship. My writing, along with my world, has benefited greatly from my association with each of you.

In particular I would like to acknowledge Vicki Werkley, leader of the Lower Lake group. Despite limited eyesight, her bigger-vision for my

ACKNOWLEDGMENTS

book came through in countless hours of reading (by me), discussion, and finally, agreed-upon perfection. It is an honor to know you, Vicki.

I also offer a gracious thank-you to my writing sisters: Constance Rock and Sequoia Lyn-James. Sharing my story with you, and in turn listening to each of yours, allowed me to both deepen and expand my heart to the fullness it holds today. I cherish having you in my life.

To Sage Knight, my "literary midwife," I truly appreciate your assistance in helping this baby come to life.

To my early reviewers: Elizabeth Cunningham, Jean Houston, Barbara Sinor, Katherine Woodward Thomas, and Marj Barlow, your feedback and enthusiasm offered the spark I needed to keep going.

I would even like to acknowledge the computer gremlins, those pesky breakdowns that ultimately led me to Pamela Sweda, whose stunning artwork graces this book's cover. Thank you, Pamela, for sharing your amazing talent and gracious self.

Deep gratitude and appreciation to the final-stretch and keen-eye angels: Linda Guebert, Taira St. John, Lourdes Theusen, and Lisa Kaplan.

To Jean Laidig, I can't say a big enough "merci beaucoup." Your dedication to, and knowledge of, the craft is a joy to behold.

I also wish to offer gratitude to my parents. Although our lives together were harsh, and often devoid of kindness, I believe it takes a soul of great substance to step into an agreement such as ours. May you be blessed and know that you are loved.

Lastly, I wish to recognize the myriad characters who wove in and out of my life's tapestry. While I won't say "thank you" to everyone, I will acknowledge the light of your soul—and mine—however hidden from sight it may have been during our interactions.

This book may be an "independent" publication, yet a community of amazing women came together in its formation. And more show up every day. . . .

Permissions

The author gratefully acknowledges the artists, authors, producers, and publishers who gave permission to reprint from the following works:

Excerpt from *Healing with The Angels: How the Angels Can Assist You in Every Area of Your Life* by Doreen Virtue. Published by Hay House, Inc. Carlsbad, California, 1999.

Excerpt from *Money (That's What I Want)* Words and Music by Berry Gordy and Janie Bradford © 1959 (Renewed 1987) JOBETE MUSIC CO., INC. All Rights Controlled and Administered by EMI APRIL MUSIC INC. and EMI BLACKWOOD MUSIC INC. on behalf of JOBETE MUSIC CO., INC. and STONE AGATE MUSIC (A Division of JOBETE MUSIC CO., INC.)
All Rights Reserved. International Copyright Secured. Used by Permission. Reprinted by Permission of Hal Leonard Corporation.

Resources

I have personal experience with each of the following practitioners, businesses, and organizations. All are highly recommended for their integrity, wisdom, and invaluable support. Books listed are some of my favorites.

Arvigo, Rosita
> *Rainforest Home Remedies: The Maya Way to Heal Your Body and Replenish Your Soul.* New York, NY: HarperCollins, 2001.
>
> https://arvigotherapy.com
> Maya Abdominal Therapy™ and spiritual healing inspired by traditional Maya healing techniques. Site includes additional books, Rainforest Remedies, and practitioner/teachers listing.

Austin, Stephanie
> http://ecoastrology.com
> New and full moon updates that offer timely information plus thought-provoking resources. Personal consultations, books, and trainings are also available.

Bergstrom, Betsy
> http://www.betsybergstrom.com
> Heart-Centered Shamanic Healing information and classes. Site includes referrals for compassionate depossession and curse unraveling.

Brown, Brené
> *The Gifts of Imperfection: Let Go of Who You Think You're Supposed to Be and Embrace Who You Are.* Center City, MN: Hazelden, 2010.
>
> http://www.brenebrown.com
> Research professor whose focus is a concept she calls Wholeheartedness. Based on her studies of vulnerability, courage, authenticity, and shame. Additional books are shown on her site.

Brown, Byron
> *Soul Without Shame: A Guide to Liberating Yourself from the Judge Within.* Boston, MA: Shambhala, 1999.
>
> http://soulwithoutshame.com

Bruyere, Rosalyn
> *Wheels of Light: Chakras, Auras, and the Healing Energy of the Body.* New York, NY: Fireside, 1989.
>
> http://www.rosalynlbruyere.org
> A modern mystery school, the Crucible Program trains medical practitioners along with others from varying professions in the tradition of the healing arts.

Castell, Cayelin
> http://cayelincastell.com
> http://shamanicastrology.com
> Offer monthly newsletters, information-packed websites, a core curriculum for becoming a certified Shamanic Astrologer, and personal readings within an archetypal and mythical framework.

CHURCH OF GNOSIS (Ecclesia Gnostica Mysteriorum)
    http://www.gnosticsanctuary.org
    This site offers a wealth of information related to Gnosis—a matter of experience, not belief—and the Holy Order of Mary Magdalen.

Cunningham, Elizabeth
    The Maeve Chronicles. Rhinebeck, NY: Monkfish, various.

    http://www.passionofmarymagdalen.com
    Four volumes recount the fabulously sassy life of the Celtic Mary Magdalen. These novels top my favorites list.

ECLECTIC GENERATOR SERVICES
    http://eclecticgenerator.com
    Jean Laidig's professional publishing services include book design, editing, formatting, page makeup, and proofreading.

FEMININE POWER
    http://femininepower.com
    http://www.womenontheedgeofevolution.com
    Evolutionary women's discussions and teleclasses led by Katherine Woodward Thomas and Claire Zammit.

Fiore, Dr. Edith
    The Unquiet Dead: A Psychologist Treats Spirit Possession. New York, NY: Ballantine Books, 1995.

FLOWER ESSENCE SERVICES
    http://www.fesflowers.com (Products and Practitioners)
    http://flowersociety.org (Research)
    Five-Flower Formula (Dr. Bach's natural stress relief remedy) and *Yarrow Environmental Solution* are "must have" pre-blended flower essence combinations. The FES *Grace Flourish Formula* is also a personal favorite.

Gouvea, Jen
> http://engagedheart.com
> Flower essence and astrological counseling.

HEARTMATH
> http://www.heartmath.com (Products and Programs)
> http://www.heartmath.org (Research)
> Offers leading-edge education on heart/brain communication, stress relief, and overall well-being.

Ingerman, Sandra
> *Soul Retrieval: Mending the Fragmented Self.* New York, NY: Harper San Francisco, 1991.
>
> http://www.sandraingerman.com
> Books, trainings, and ongoing news related to shamanic journeying, healing, and Medicine for the Earth. Site includes a link to the worldwide practitioner listing at www.shamanicteachers.com.

ISIS OASIS
> http://www.isisoasis.org
> A nonprofit retreat center, temple, and animal sanctuary located in the wine country of Northern California.

Judith, Anodea
> *Wheels of Life: A User's Guide to the Chakra System.* St. Paul, MN: Llewellyn, 1987.
>
> http://www.sacredcenters.com
> *The* resource for chakra psychology. The website includes a wide variety of books, CDs, and DVDs, plus workshops.

Levine, Peter
> *Waking the Tiger: Healing Trauma.* Berkeley, CA: North Atlantic Books, 1997.

http://www.traumahealing.com
Home of the Somatic Experiencing Trauma Institute™. Includes books, CDs, practitioner listing, and training information.

Levine, Stephen & Ondrea
http://levinetalks.com
Guided meditations and talks that focus on loving kindness, compassion, conscious living/conscious dying, and more.

Malik, Karen
http://karenmalik.com
Transpersonal therapist. Senior Residential Facilitator, the Monroe Institute.

McLaren, Karla
The Language of Emotions: What Your Feelings Are Trying to Tell You. Boulder, CO: Sounds True, 2010.

http://karlamclaren.com
Empath, social science researcher, teacher, and prolific author.

MONROE INSTITUTE
http://www.monroeinstitute.org
Hemi-Sync™ audio technology, books, and consciousness exploration workshops. See below for Robert Monroe's classic works.

Monroe, Robert
Journeys Out of the Body. New York, NY: Doubleday, 1971.
Far Journeys. New York, NY: Doubleday, 1985.
Ultimate Journey. New York, NY: Doubleday, 1994.

Ortelee, Anne
http://www.anneortelee.com
Weekly Weather astrology blog, podcasts, and consultations.

Randolph, Ann
> http://annrandolph.com
> A brilliant teacher/performer who first encouraged me to tell my story.

Roth, Gabrielle
> http://www.gabrielleroth.com
> The heart of 5Rhythms, this site includes teachers, music, DVDs, and books related to following the beat.

Runningbear, Sage
> http://runswithtwobears.com
> A true medicine woman and teacher.

Sinor, Barbara
> *Gifts From The Child Within.* Ann Arbor, MI: Loving Healing Press, 2008.
>
> http://drsinor.com
> Offers spiritual support and inspiration for recovery, including additional books and a blog.

Virtue, Doreen
> *Healing with the Angels: How the Angels Can Assist You in Every Area of Your Life.* Carlsbad, CA: Hay House, 1999.
>
> http://www.angeltherapy.com
> *The* resource for angel-related topics. Includes a list of practitioners.

Woodward Thomas, Katherine
> See FEMININE POWER

Zammit, Claire
> See FEMININE POWER

www.ingramcontent.com/pod-product-compliance
Lightning Source LLC
Chambersburg PA
CBHW031939080426
42735CB00007B/190